OIL BEACH

Oil Beach

How Toxic Infrastructure

01/09   *CB 19*

THE UNIVERSITY OF CHICAGO PRESS

CHICAGO AND LONDON

The University of Chicago Press, Chicago 60637
The University of Chicago Press, Ltd., London
© 2023 by Christina Dunbar-Hester
Published 2023
Printed in the United States of America

32 31 30 29 28 27 26 25 24 23   1 2 3 4 5

ISBN-13: 978-0-226-81969-3 (cloth)
ISBN-13: 978-0-226-81971-6 (paper)
ISBN-13: 978-0-226-81970-9 (e-book)
DOI: https://doi.org/10.7208/chicago/9780226819709.001
.0001

Library of Congress Cataloging-in-Publication Data

Names: Dunbar-Hester, Christina, 1976–, author.
Title: Oil beach : how toxic infrastructure threatens life in the ports
of Los Angeles and beyond / Christina Dunbar-Hester.
Other titles: How toxic infrastructure threatens life in the ports of
Los Angeles and beyond
Description: Chicago ; Illinois : The University of Chicago Press,
2023. | Includes bibliographical references and index.
Identifiers: LCCN 2022021784 | ISBN 9780226819693 (cloth) |
ISBN 9780226819716 (paperback) | ISBN 9780226819709 (ebook)
Subjects: LCSH: Environmental sciences—California—San
Pedro Bay (Bay) | Ecology—California—San Pedro Bay (Bay) |
Environmentalism—California—San Pedro Bay (Bay) | Container
terminals—Environmental aspects—California—San Pedro Bay
(Bay) | Infrastructure (Economics)—Environmental aspects—
California—San Pedro Bay (Bay) | Capitalism—Environmental
aspects—California—San Pedro Bay (Bay) | San Pedro Bay (Calif. :
Bay)—History. | BISAC: NATURE / Environmental Conservation &
Protection | BUSINESS & ECONOMICS / Infrastructure
Classification: LCC GE155.C2 D86 2023 | DDC 333.91/70979493—dc23/
eng20220723
LC record available at https://lccn.loc.gov/2022021784

♾ This paper meets the requirements of
ANSI/NISO Z39.48-1992 (Permanence of Paper).

The best place to view Los Angeles of the next millennium is
from the ruins of its alternate future.

Trade is our nation's economic lifeblood. You are helping to keep
that lifeblood healthy and running.

Welcome to San Pedro Bay, home to the nation's largest port
complex and millions of plants and animals . . .

Infrastructure is the spine of the Wiindigo, but is also the essential
architecture of transition to a decolonized future.

Contents

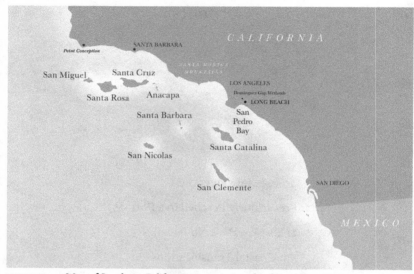

FIGURE 1.   Map of Southern California coast, 1967, edited by author. US Navy Hydrographic Office, public domain.

Preface

Twenty miles south of downtown Los Angeles, on the eastern bank of the LA River, is an unassuming wetlands in the city of Long Beach (fig. 1). I walk on trails here most weekends, and it is an especially pleasant place for winter walks, when the sun is less intense and the wetlands are in use as a stopping point for migratory birds. Waterfowl are particularly easy to spot without binoculars. Over the course of dozens of walks, northern shovelers, widgeons, cinnamon and blue teals put in winter appearances. Coots, pied-billed grebes, and mallards are usually on the water all year round, and blue, green, and black-crowned night herons stalk among the reeds. Red-tailed hawks cruise overhead, riding updrafts. Rarely, in spring, American white pelicans pinwheel very high up in the sky, and sometimes Forster's terns dive-bomb into the water, fishing. Grackles, red-winged blackbirds, bushtits, and house finches are so ubiquitous that my walking companion is wont to say that we "aren't seeing any birds" when in fact these creatures are hopping and chirping in trees and bushes all around us. Also in the spring, coast sunflowers bloom, and a few budding trees reveal last year's oriole nests.

Lest this paragraph conjure an idyllic scene, the reality is more complicated, and more absorbing. The river can be accessed from a few points in the wetlands; but "river" is a misleading term to those unfamiliar, as it is channelized in cement and generally barely trickling past, confined to the deeper center course, maybe five feet wide in drier months (fig. 2). The "riverbed" is a mostly dry cement basin, at least for another mile or so to the south, where it widens and pools, closer to its discharge into San Pedro Bay (fig. 3). Shorebirds such as black-necked stilts and an occasional avocet can be seen wading around and picking at small aquatic animals and insects

FIGURE 2. Looking north along the LA River from the cycling path near the Dominguez Gap, 2020. Note the tire reflected in the shallow water.
Photo by the author.

FIGURE 3. Looking south along the LA River toward San Pedro Bay, 2021. Flecks in the water include some birds but are mostly trash. Shipping cranes in the port are barely visible on the horizon, and the nearer structure that looks like a bridge is a petroleum pipeline. Tents in an informal settlement peek above the west bank (right).
Photo by McKenzie Stribich.

to eat in the muck at the edge of the water. The white pelicans, when they are not circling in the sky at a dizzying height, sit sleepily in a patch of river to the south for a month or two each spring.

Trash in the river channel is ever present: tires, broken pallets, shopping carts, soccer balls, all manner of industrial and household detritus. The Dominguez Gap is likewise full of trash: coots pick at vegetation in the water adjacent to plastic bags, Big Gulp cups, bicycle wheels, and sodden clothing. A mallard paddles past a stand of reeds festooned with a purple latex glove: a litter bloom.

A somewhat forbidding walking and cycling path runs along the river on a higher plane than the wetlands. (Forbidding because there are no guardrails between the path and the steep river embankments, and because it is often strewn with broken glass that menaces bike tires.) From it, one can get the lay of the land. To the north, on a clear day, the San Gabriel Mountains are visible on the far side of Los Angeles. To the south, one can glimpse the filaments of a large new cable-stayed bridge high above the river, and, at a lower altitude, a few orderly rows of metal arms of container cranes jutting skyward. They are in the Port of Long Beach, tucked into San Pedro Bay, where the river empties into the Pacific Ocean. The port complex is not visible other than the bridge and a few cranes. This bridge replaced an older, smaller one, and the harbor can now accommodate "megaships" (very large, as the name implies; they also require specialized equipment on shore, like larger cranes).[1] Just on the far side of the river is Interstate 710, the "commercial spine" of Southern California, a truck route bringing goods from the ports of Los Angeles and Long Beach to inland distribution centers.[2] Bisecting the wetlands overhead is a train bridge, also serving the ports. These infrastructural clues—the train bridge; I-710 (its din audible even from the lower path along the wetlands); the crane arms peering up from the massive port complex—give a hint of the nearby massive force field that is belied by the drama of a duck skirmish or the wonder of nesting swallows one might witness on any given walk, or narrate later in a description of the wetlands.

Wildlife in the Dominguez Gap cohabits with unhoused people, who have made semipermanent settlements under the train bridge, in tents on the eastern bank of the wetlands, and under road overpasses on both sides of the river going both north and south. There were around 66,000 unhoused people in Los Angeles County in 2020, a sharp rise from 2019.[3] In the Gap, people use the train bridge as shelter, the irrigation system as a water source, and a small dam in the reservoir as transportation infrastructure—as a foot and bike path out to the road on the eastern side of the wetlands.

Because it is fairly near my home, when I have weekend visitors, I invariably bring them along for a Gap walk. We look for birds and other species—rabbits hopping across the path; turtles sunning on the embankments; possum remains decomposing on the walking path; once, standing still in the scrubby vegetation on the bank of the wetlands, a coyote. Often walkers share the paths with vacqueros, working-class Mexican cowboys, who have stabled horses on the land near the river for generations: on weekends they ride on an unpaved path on the eastern side of the Gap. Sometimes the background freeway noise is pierced by young men riding small, very loud motorbikes too fast, looping on the bike and wetlands paths, startling people and wildlife.

I tell my visitors they are getting the "real LA" in this tableau. Though my statement is somewhat tongue-in-cheek, multiple species sharing space amid heavily industrialized land use and against a backdrop of stunning lack of social solidarity—the policy choices that have led tens of thousands of people to sleep outdoors—is indeed how I would try to explain twenty-first century LA. It is, in fact, explanatory well beyond the confines of LA.

And yet, this surreal, apocalyptic, and heavily managed space would likely not appear in a tourist guide. Guides that do include the Dominguez Gap as a "nature walk" tend to emphasize only the "nature" here. Its description on Google Maps reads: "Urban escape along the LA River with trails for hiking, biking, bird-watching & horseback riding." Horses and wild birds fit within a pastoral narrative (or, more specifically, they reinforce an urban-idyll binary, confirming this space as a pasture within a city). Unhoused people, their cat and dog companions, and the industrial features of the landscape are not mentioned, let alone foregrounded, but nonetheless this is a site where stunning infrastructural violence is on display, if one chooses to see it.

My own confidence that this is a representative, if also singular, place in LA County is a fairly recent acquisition. When I moved out here for work about seven years ago, I was naive to the ecologies here. By this I do not mean I was entirely unfamiliar with coastal Southern California. Though I had lived elsewhere most of my life, I was well acquainted with estuarial sites and canyons containing many of the same plants and animals as this wetlands, further south in San Diego County. Nor was I unaccustomed to industrial landscapes, having in young adulthood clambered around train bridges, walked railroad tracks, and occasionally trespassed in abandoned industrial sites in midwestern and East Coast cities. But there are features of this setting that are singular, and my learning to see them occurred alongside learning about the area's history and present.

Aspects of the landscape were jarringly unfamiliar: the Gap is an interzone that is fully urban but also in heavy, conspicuous use by wildlife. In Long Beach and parts of LA, I was surrounded by active oil wells—visible on residential blocks, in parks and parking lots, along the river, and even macabrely overlooking cemeteries. (Inactive, plugged wells even dot the Gap itself.) The port complex was also captivating. An East Coast commute I did for several years took me past the Port of New York and New Jersey (Newark Bay) and dingy-looking distribution warehouses; one business that never failed to catch my eye was called Preferred Freezer Services. This sort of water-to-intermodal-shipping-and-distribution landscape was not extraordinary—but the scale of it in the LA harbor was. (The Port of New York–New Jersey is no slouch, but it seems frankly quaint compared to the San Pedro Bay complex: in 2020, New York–New Jersey moved about 7.5 million containers, measured in "20-foot-equivalent units," or TEUs, while Long Beach moved around 8 million TEUs and LA over 9 million.[4]) The port complex here handles a massive volume of North American trade, including petroleum. Docks transition into massive refineries, one space flowing into the other. This gave the ubiquitous pumpjacks further context—and caused features of the landscape like a petroleum pipeline over the LA River just south of the Gap to come into focus (see fig. 3). There are also at times people encamped in oil infrastructure, only a few blocks from the Gap, closer to my home.[5]

I also learned that the wetlands park was created (some might say restored) only recently, in 2008.[6] The purpose of the Dominguez Gap is to capture and filter water, much of it contaminated runoff, aiding in flood control and replenishing an aquifer that sits beneath Long Beach. It also provides habitat to wildlife—this wetlands is located along the Pacific Flyway, a migratory route for multitudes of birds traveling along the Pacific coast throughout the Americas. It struck me that, in some ways, more was being done for the animals and landscape than the people who had the misfortune to live here (courtesy of powerful logics of racialized economic exclusion). Both housed and unhoused people living in the shadow of the port complex and downwind of the refineries and I-710 freeway, which has been described as a "diesel death zone" for its contributions to air pollution, are casualties of a host of social and economic policies: financial investment in logistics systems; casualized and racialized labor in trucking and warehouse work; and rampant real estate speculation driving up housing costs and generating revenue for investor classes.[7] All of these reflect global patterns of capitalism, yet with local effects in Southern California and elsewhere.

As I learned more, these became patterns I was unable to unsee on walks. But the Dominguez Gap is not that large—thirty-seven square acres, including a site on the far side of the river that is less in public use. To more fully understand the tensions between flourishing organismic life on the one hand and industrial uses of landscape on the other, one needs to think with San Pedro Bay and the port complex itself. Indeed, though the Gap is literally upriver, it is formed downstream, its conditions are an *effect*; the port complex is a *cause*. That area possessed even more of the contrast that captivated me: more marine and terrestrial life *and* a more central position in a lethal world system (shipping; oil; and the US empire). That site was, however, not accessible for weekly walking; I had to approach it differently, through trade statistics, wildlife management documents, and newspaper accounts. What emerges is San Pedro Bay's recent history, where, despite California's reputation for environmentalism, multitudinous life is juxtaposed with patterned violence. Life here accumulates but also breaks down, conjoined to circuits of global capital.

INTRODUCTION

On December 9, 2019, Colonel Douglas Burgher of the United States Army Corp of Engineers made a presentation to an eager public, in a large auditorium at the Long Beach Aquarium. In it, he announced that the Army Corps (USACE), which oversees shoreline management, was making a series of unexpected recommendations about the future of the harbor that contains the aquarium as well as the Ports of Los Angeles and Long Beach, major oil facilities, including extraction, refining, and shipping, and US military operations. He said that the US military, one of the biggest consumers of fossil fuel on the planet, was moving to implement swiftly a plan for "greening" itself.[1] This was not mere "greenwashing" or an environmentally-friendly public relations spin; the service would soon cancel orders for weapons systems and reassign its workforce. It would instead turn toward civilian clean energy projects; remediation of toxic waste; building and maintaining domestic infrastructure for not only human but wildlife benefit; auditing goods and infrastructure supply chains for transspecies justice; repairing ecologies along the coast and inland; and it would withdraw from bases across the globe. This ambitious plan would lead to a clean break with fossil fuels and to a rebalanced economic strategy, which was expected to strengthen international relationships and promote global stability without military force.

Locally, these effects would be felt nearly immediately. Colonel Burgher pledged that USACE would dismantle some of the San Pedro Bay breakwaters, long lines of rock which keep wave energy low so that ships in the LA harbor can load and unload mercantile cargo and even ordnance with ease. (Breakwater removal excited local surfers especially.) This was possible because the port complex was anticipated to scale down operations.

Commercial shipping traffic would decline substantially, so more of the area could be used for other things, like ecology-tending apprenticeships and nonmotorized recreation. He announced that local stewardship of San Pedro Bay would be turned over to a civilian task force comprised of local residents whose mandate was to prioritize ecological justice; it would include schoolteachers, abalone divers, dockworkers, amateur seahorse enthusiasts, and researchers.[2] A separate council with equal say in governance matters, and veto power, would be appointed immediately by Indigenous Gabrielino (Tongva, Kizh) residents.

One of the first tasks would be to cap, seal, decontaminate, and dismantle or recommission all the leftover petroleum infrastructure that the oil industry had hastily abandoned following this commodity's sudden plunge into the red.[3] Fortunately the industry had been compelled to leave behind a large fund for these measures, and the State of California was standing by to oversee the transfer of payments, with enforcement power if needed.[4] After Colonel Burgher's presentation, people spilled excitedly out into the evening, chattering about the harbor plans; the faint singing of red and white abalone could also be heard on the evening breeze.[5] The harbor, whose shifting shores had over the last century contained a Coney Island–style amusement park and sea bath, an air strip along the beach, man-made "islands" whose palm trees and garish lighting disguised oil extraction activities, and a navy shipyard as well as the ports, would be transformed once again. And not a moment too soon, as sea level rise threatened the coast, the US empire inflamed geopolitical tensions and promoted domestic inequities, and poor air quality, heat waves, and myriad social vulnerabilities plagued the region.[6]

No. That didn't happen. And it is the only part of this book that is fiction.[7] The thing about fiction is, it has to be believable.

The description of the harbor is accurate. But what actually happened in the December 2019 USACE presentation at the Aquarium of the Pacific was a much more modest recommendation, to restore eelgrass and kelp in open water and build some "rocky reef" habitat for fish and other aquatic animals. USACE proposed wildlife habitat restoration in only the eastern (Long Beach) side of San Pedro Bay, having declared the western side (port complex) off limits, because of crucial maritime operations. USACE's entire analysis of the area, and thus the plan it set forth, began from the premise that commercial and military maritime activity as well as oil operations were *not* to be interrupted in any way. Very few members of the public attended the presentation, on a dark Monday evening, and the ones who did seemed disappointed, surfers included.

Would it be more believable to claim that the US Navy once trained a dolphin to deliver mail to men living on the seabed, in an experimental aquatic habitat mirroring fantasies of colonizing space? Or that after a failed forced relocation of sea otters to a remote island, wildlife managers concerned about the prospect of otters being annihilated by spilled oil began a program in which orphaned pups were raised in captivity by adoptive parents? These stories, however implausible, are true. I present a series of multispecies stories (including these two) about San Pedro Bay that juxtapose, on the one hand, a site of multitudinous life with, on the other, hyperindustrial, toxic shipping, oil, and military operations. San Pedro Bay is paradoxically home to all of this, and thus to apprehend the significance of its operations, we must consider how ecologies and infrastructure relate to one another. In the twentieth century, the environmental sciences "were and are essentially infrastructural sciences," that is, they played a major role in planning, maintaining, and combating large infrastructural systems.[8] To simultaneously plan and combat infrastructural projects may appear paradoxical, but essentially identical expertise is brought to bear in both, and whether this constitutes a harmonious or conflictual undertaking is not straightforward, especially in locations designed to mediate between global and local scales like this port complex.[9]

The setting of this book is San Pedro Bay, a natural bay twenty-odd miles straight south from downtown Los Angeles. It contains the present-day Los Angeles River mouth, into which the ports of Long Beach and Los Angeles have been built. Invisible from much of metro Los Angeles, the ports are administered separately but are physically contiguous. The Los Angeles harbor is massively important in US trade, as something like 40 percent of the goods that enter North America do so there (other ports like New Orleans, Savannah, Oakland, Tacoma, and New York–New Jersey are also significant, but smaller in relative terms).[10] In fact, the Port of LA's trademarked slogan is "America's Port." The shallow river is not navigable by ship. Nearly a century ago it was channelized in cement; confining the river to a channel transformed acres and acres of estuarial wetlands into dry land that could be used in other ways. A prominent use is freight infrastructure: lines of rail and trucking connect the ports to distribution warehouses and ultimately to retail and consumers across the continent.

San Pedro Bay sits roughly the middle of the Southern California Bight, a gentle curvature of the coastline that runs from just north of Santa Barbara (Point Conception) to Punta Colonet in Baja California, Mexico. The bight, containing the Channel Islands archipelago, is an ecotone where warm and cold Pacific waters meet and mix, so quite a variety of aquatic plants and animals live in it or transit through it along migratory routes. The area is of global significance for wildlife. But because of its history, in

San Pedro Bay, shipping and industrial uses of the land- and waterscape are in tension with wildlife habitat. According to the US Army Corps of Engineers, "the bight's location makes it one of the most threatened biodiversity hot spots in the world."[11]

Across four chapters, I present stories of life-forms as they live in or transit through San Pedro Bay. Each centers on a charismatic life-form: birds; bananas; sea otters; cetaceans. The "natural" inhabitants of the bay have emerged as objects of environmental knowledge and concern around whom mobilization has occurred. Bananas, meanwhile, may seem like a peculiar choice in a natural history of the area, but they too are a form of biological life that has occupied an ecological niche in the harbor's recent history. I approach each of these subjects as enmeshed within ecologies: webs of relations within lively systems, including capital and petroleum. I am concerned with wildlife management within a major industrial infrastructure project; and the history of oil in one specific locale, informed by a multispecies perspective; within the time period since the modern environmental movement in the US, which has seen both domestic environmental regulation and a steep climb in global trade and emissions.[12] Both oil and shipping are local to San Pedro Bay but situated within vast global infrastructures, so this book is also an attempt to localize those very large topics and understand them in one specific location, albeit one which is a part of a global system. The whole of each (and certainly the whole of the whole) is constituted by a network of relations which is difficult to characterize, as it is present in many places and many levels at once.[13] Oil, for instance, is not only the slick you see reflected back up at you in a puddle after a rain, or the daily background smell and slight sore throat you might have as a resident of Long Beach, or your sister's cancer diagnosis, or an acutely toxic event for an otter or an osprey, but a hardened material infrastructure of pipelines and refineries and a highly complex international governance project.[14] Here I excavate relatively small stories, unnatural histories, all sited within San Pedro Bay, which take on additional significance because of how they relate to global infrastructures of shipping, fossil fuels, and earth (sediment) moving.

In spite of enormous economic and environmental impacts, San Pedro Bay's lively and deadly history (and present) remains largely hidden from most North Americans. Even some lifelong Angelenos may be relatively oblivious to this facet of their region, as ports and container cargo occupy "the forgotten space" in globalized modernity.[15] In 2021, as a global supply-chain crisis unfurled, media spotlighted the forgotten space: a cargo ship traffic jam in the Los Angeles harbor; bottlenecks in the flows of shipping containers; lags in goods reaching consumers. In October of that year, a Southern California seabed oil pipeline burst, and burst into the news. Investigators of the leak suggested that its likely cause was a cargo ship's anchor striking and dragging the pipeline, which connected an Orange County offshore drilling platform to the Port of Long Beach.[16] Nonetheless, supply chains are generally shadowy and mystified to consumers and citizens.

FROM VITAL INFRASTRUCTURE TO INFRASTRUCTURAL VITALISM

This port complex, harbor, and bay require ecological thinking, in the sense of ecologies (plural) as "inextricable lines of relationality."[17] "All living, human or not, takes place within a relational matrix," writes anthropologist Arturo Escobar.[18] Ecological lines of relation occur between and among living entities and nonliving infrastructural ones. The key term is relationality: to rupture a link will produce other effects, including new linkages and new ruptures. In highlighting "living entities," I do not make an uncomplicated appeal to an essentialized "nature" or even "life."[19] I do however mean to draw some distinction between ecological relations favorable to flourishing biological life-forms and the relations that are constituted in what I am calling *infrastructural vitalism*: heavily managed, industrial infrastructure which, I argue, is structured by violent logics and *possesses a "life force" of its own.*[20] I do not mean this infrastructure literally *is* alive, but an animistic belief in infrastructure's life force motivates its creators and maintainers. This belief does real work in the world—and, ironically, is often deadly for biological life.

Infrastructures are "built networks that facilitate flows of people and materials necessary for sustaining society."[21] More conceptually, infrastructures are sets of standards codified into the built environment; sites of struggle; also an often-invisible nested or stacked set of relationships, substrate upon substrate, upon which other systems are placed and fixed in increments; always relational (for example, "municipal water" is one person's working infrastructure, at the ready for making dinner or doing wash, but another person's maintenance job and, to the latter, not invisible).[22] Infrastructures exist at large scales: their time frame is historical (bigger than human lifespans; smaller than geophysical time); and they are built on large economic and social organizational scales, requiring complex organizational efforts involving entities like large firms and governments (though they are also experienced in more micro ways, and are amenable to micro, meso, and macro analysis).[23] The port complex in San Pedro Bay is nested within multiple infrastructures including those of freight movement and distribution; petroleum extraction, refining, and movement; manufacture of goods; informatics and logistics related to inventory management; maritime conventions; air quality monitoring and regulation; and national security apparatus. (This is a nonexhaustive list.) It is a complex and heterogeneous node where each of those systems "fixes" itself but also mutably renews itself.

In invoking *vitalism*, I refer (loosely) to debates in history and philosophy of science over whether there is a "life force" that is not reducible to mechanistic forces or chemical reactions.[24] Philosophers Sebastian Normandin and Charles T. Wolfe, in examining vitalism from the late Enlightenment to the present, write that vitalism is "a moving target, an explanatory and/or metaphysical construct which appears, depending on the context, as a form of overt supernaturalism or as a useful heuristic for biomedical research and theorizing."[25] Conceptually, vitalism is generative, regenerative, mutable, and emergent; not fixed. My use of it here is, on the one hand, metaphorical, and certainly not (fully) literal. But it conveys something, well, vital: infrastructure gets "fixed" through a set of epistemic and material commitments, whereupon it begins to demand something like care and feeding, exhibiting the stirrings of a self-organizing system that reproduces itself, monstrously, excessively, and even cannibalistically.[26] Of course, it is not *literally* autonomous. On the other hand, because of how managers in essence *treat ports, pipelines, and freeways as alive* and are committed to their vitality, these animistic beliefs do work in the world. Infrastructure has momentum, even "spiritual force," and is mutable, adaptive, lively; it is unclear who or what is in control.[27]

What is at stake in suggesting that infrastructure is possessed by vitalism? And why is this both metaphorical and, potentially, not? Take the reference (in the preface) to a freeway as the "spine" of the region. Or the common assumption that the "health" of the nation depends on the flow of commercial goods,[28] and even that such a flow is a "lifeblood."[29] "Lifeblood" and "spine" are somatic metaphors, but they are not only metaphors. They serve to *naturalize* the "life" of circulation. In an exploration of how deeply the notions of blood flow, blood loss, circulation, liquidity, and the like are embedded and naturalized in the conceptual vocabulary of economic relations, anthropologist Kath Weston urges going "beyond metaphorical readings of economic discourse."[30] In seventeenth-century England, physician William Harvey's novel contributions to understanding the physiology of blood circulation were elaborated into economic language and concepts that "appeared to be ordered by systemic and cyclical properties . . . sometimes like water, but more often like blood."[31] This ascendant biological understanding of finance as circulatory coincided with

European colonization of the Americas and expansion of trade, and the linkage has endured.

Later, around the turn of the twentieth century, planners and policy-makers began to explicitly elevate infrastructure as a critical concern, characterizing flows of oil, water, or electricity as *vital* systems.[32] Such terms do work to build (both conceptually and literally) a set of relations imbued with a liveness, a biological imperative, central to the reproduction of capitalism and empire.[33] Here, I aim to *denaturalize* the infrastructural and economic "vitality" of a set of *systems in which the port complex is a node.* I demonstrate how infrastructural vitalism is often in violent tension with biological life (even if the latter cannot be pointed to as an essential "nature").[34] As Normandin and Wolfe write, vitalism plays a role in imagining "between . . . the dead and living."[35]

USELESS TIDAL FLATS? A BRIEF HISTORY

In 1971, port managers reflected on their stunning achievement: "Since its beginning with the dedication of the first municipal wharf in Long Beach in 1911, Port of Long Beach has, in its brief 60 year history, progressed from *useless tidal flats* into a major West Coast harbor."[36] This turn of phrase hailed the Port of Long Beach on the occasion of its sixtieth anniversary. Historian James Tejani describes the tidal flats in and around the harbor differently: "land and sea acted upon each other to construct a third space that was neither fully continent nor ocean."[37] But his statement supports the notion that to become a productive locale for trade, transmutation of land and sea was required. Regional managers were "dredging the future" when they sited the ports of Long Beach and Los Angeles in San Pedro Bay as part of a project to "make" Los Angeles, establishing its presence within the American West, the Pacific, and the world.[38]

Though this transformation was massive and thorough, it took just over a century; key features such as the breakwaters, lines of rock that soften wave energy near the shore, are not even a century old (a blink in geologic time, but mature in historical time).[39] Though the ports are composed of massive and seemingly durable structures, there has also been flux in the area as it has been built up, then rebuilt and tweaked. Inestimable tons of concrete have been poured into the port complex, most recently in erecting a new and massive bridge over the Port of Long Beach; completed in late 2020, it will accompany deeper harbor dredging to allow even bigger ships to dock (even as sea level rises), and is engineered at a higher seismic (earthquake) standard. Environmental concerns have been part of this picture especially since the 1970s, in keeping with national and state regulations, including measuring water pollution and, more recently, air pollution in the port complex as well as rail and trucking corridors to which it connects.[40]

Prior to 1825, the Los Angeles River dispersed laterally over an "extensive wetland matrix" and downward into aquifers. During the winter rainy seasons, its runoff flowed into the Pacific Ocean at a number of places, according to memoirs and histories.[41] A massive flood rerouted it south to San Pedro Bay in 1825, cutting a new channel through wetlands. In the early twentieth century, the harbor was developed to house the ports. After a major flood in 1938, USACE oversaw construction to channelize the river (contain it within a fifty-one-mile cement channel), begun in 1938 and completed in 1960; this dried up wetlands and spared growing urban settlements from future flooding, but the river was never navigable by ship, even after it was contained.[42] (This is part of a global story: over the twentieth century, wetlands areas totaling the size of Canada were drained and dried worldwide.[43]) Before the river was channelized, the area was indeed tidal flats, useless[44] or no: "Each estuary contained on its shoreward margin areas of sand bars and thinly vegetated dunes. Low tide left the flats and marshes as dry and contiguous land, only interrupted by narrow channels of sub-tidal water. High tide, however, inundated and fractured the interior into a collection of islands, shoals, and open water."[45] On the western side of the bay toward the Palos Verdes peninsula were two islands, Dead Man's Island (since removed in dredging the harbor) and Rattlesnake Island (now Terminal Island, and utterly transformed by infill). Rattlesnake Island was more a spit of sand protecting the wetlands from the open water than an island in the sense of rock formations.[46] Dead Man's Island bore its name because some casualties from an 1846 military engagement at Rancho San Pedro, part of the Mexican-American War, were buried there.[47]

Around the turn of the twentieth century, Northern California had an active marine research station run by Stanford University, and some in Southern California considered siting an equivalent station in the LA River mouth. Southern California was an ideal site for marine research; in addition to the diversity of life supported by the estuarial land, deep ocean could be reached only a few miles offshore. Headed by biologist and University of California professor William Ritter, a marine research station was established on Terminal Island and operated between 1901 and 1903.[48] The islands' other occupants included fisherfolk and squatters: a contemporary source wrote that "the squatter community is made up of hard-working people, mechanics, longshoremen, boat builders, shop keepers, machinists, artists, clam diggers, fishermen, and a stray scientist or two."[49] Some of them collected fossil specimens to sell to scientists and amateur collectors;

the island areas were rich with fossil specimens, as the same geologic processes that had produced oil in this location also resulted in fossils. But in 1912, the squatters were evicted so the port could be built up.

Whether the massive ports would be sited in San Pedro Bay was a matter of controversy. According to Tejani, "while the Los Angeles region held many natural resources to support settlement, it lacked environmental conditions to support modern maritime transportation and to provide a hub for commercial and industrial growth." In particular, the greater Los Angeles coastline did not naturally support a deep-water port (unlike San Diego, San Francisco, and Puget Sound), and the lack of navigable riverways meant it was nearly as beholden to railroad power as a landlocked town. As noted above, some envisioned the bay and rich estuarial environs as a site for marine research; historical ecologists estimate that the combined estuaries of the Los Angeles coastline once totaled between fifteen thousand and eighteen thousand acres.[50] Railroad interests jockeyed for favorable positions in rail-port linkages; for example, railroad baron Collis Huntington sought to site the port in Santa Monica, on the western edge of Los Angeles, around the other side of the Palos Verdes peninsula, in hopes of maintaining monopoly control of rail lines in San Pedro. Nearby Redondo Beach was also in the running, as it could accommodate large ships in deep water, but high mountain passes to the east restricted rail connections during the winter, and it was also more exposed to storms, facing the open ocean. San Pedro had rail connecting to routes that could ship cargo east more of the year.[51] After back and forth between Huntington and his allies, and those promoting San Pedro, San Pedro was selected as the site for LA's main port (fig. 4).[52]

That there would be a massive port *somewhere* in Southern California was not, however, a matter of debate. Business leaders agreed that an expanded port was necessary to participate in growing trade enabled by and exemplified in the Panama Canal, the construction of which the United States oversaw beginning in 1904 (and under US administration for the entire twentieth century before being returned to Panama in 1999).[53] Los Angeles would need a deep-water port to connect its business center and its harbor to expanded international shipping.[54] Leaders of the US armed forces, fresh off armed conflict in the Philippines, also saw in Los Angeles's waterfront a means of American expansion into the Pacific realm.[55] The only issue was where to locate a major port. Though Ritter had at one time declared his certainty that Rattlesnake (Terminal) Island would be the place for a permanent marine laboratory, he later pursued San Diego sources of funding, in part because he feared the Los Angeles harbor would grow in commercial importance, impinging on the site's ability to support

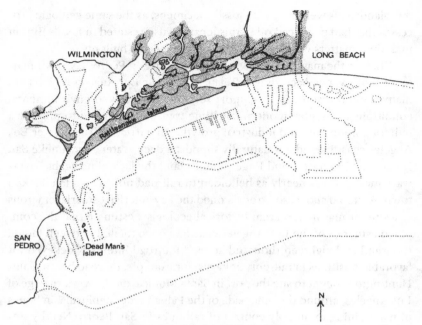

FIGURE 4. Diagram showing manipulated, infilled coastline and breakwaters overlaid onto 1872 map. From Reish and Soule 1980.
© Biologische Anstalt Helgoland/ BioMed Central Ltd; used with permission.

marine research. Founded as the San Diego Marine Biological Association in 1903, the present-day internationally renowned Scripps Institution for Oceanography in La Jolla is testament to his successful fundraising outside of LA.[56] Decisions made in this period cemented the San Pedro harbor as a major industrial site in greater Los Angeles and, indeed, in North America (fig. 5).

San Pedro Bay was the site of the ports of Long Beach and Los Angeles before the "discovery" of oil slightly inland (the Long Beach Oil Field) and adjacent and underneath (the Wilmington Oil Field), but only just barely. California had been an oil-producing state prior to the industrial development of the harbor. But the discovery of one of the most productive oil fields in the world in 1921, in Signal Hill (an unincorporated patch of land surrounded by Long Beach, a few miles inland from the ports), happened at a time when oil was becoming more valuable nationally, as easterners in the United States were turning to oil for heating and railroads were turning to it for fuel; in addition, automobiles were becoming more plentiful and elevating demand for fuel.[57] Signal Hill was the richest oil deposit in the world in terms of barrels per acre.[58] Southern California's oil boom appears in novelized form in Upton Sinclair's *Oil!*, published in 1926 and also the inspiration for the 2007 film *There Will Be Blood* (fig. 6).

In 1932, the petroleum industry first tapped the Wilmington Oil Field, in the harbor's immediate vicinity. Soon, oil companies, city officials, and the Los Angeles Harbor Department recognized that the harbor itself contained oil, under the land under the water (but note that what is water and what is land are, definitionally, somewhat fluid here, as both human and natural forces have made and remade the harbor). This led to conflict with the State of California, which claimed that Long Beach had been given permission to develop the harbor as a port but not as an oil field; the original "tidelands grant" did not permit land use for oil extraction.[59] Nonetheless,

FIGURE 5. Present-day aerial shot of the Port of LA and coastline.
Courtesy Port of Los Angeles.

FIGURE 6. Oil derricks in coastal Huntington Beach, 1920s. Slightly south of San Pedro Bay, this is near where an undersea oil pipeline burst in October 2021.
Used with permission from Orange County Archives.

paralleling the development of the ports, the conflicts that ensued were not over whether oil would be extracted in this site but who would oversee and reap profit from it.

Though it is now off its high-water (high-oil?) mark of midcentury drilling, it is nearly impossible to overstate the presence of petroleum in San Pedro Bay. In addition to the inland and tidal basin drilling, offshore oil extraction commenced in the 1950s. At this time, man-made "oil islands" were built in the Long Beach side of the bay. The islands, built of rock from nearby Santa Catalina Island, are drilling platforms that have been modified aesthetically to disguise the industrial activity; a casual visitor to the Long Beach waterfront would not necessarily realize the islands contain oil wells, let alone that this is why the islands are there in the first place. The port facilities are connected to massive oil refining operations, barely inland: infrastructure including ship-to-shore pipelines allowing crude oil to be moved directly on or off ships and into storage and refining facilities. Though diminished since its twentieth-century heyday, some extraction still occurs within and around the edges of the port complex as well. Sun-faded pumpjacks languorously sip oil up from underground while others stand completely idle, bleak metal skeletons. According to Port of Long Beach spokesperson Mario Gonzalez, if the port were to shut down, Southern California would run out of oil in about five days.[60] Petroleum has been the Port of Long Beach's biggest import and export for decades, according to annual reports. And Southern California is not an outlier here: crude oil, transported in tankers, constitutes around 30 percent of all maritime cargo globally (fig. 7).[61]

Increasingly, as coastal reserves have been tapped and regulations and public opposition have made it harder to site new wells coastally, California fossil fuel production has moved inland, less in view for coastal residents and recreationists. (Major spills in Santa Barbara and San Francisco around 1970 led to public opposition to new coastal drilling.) Nonetheless, the refining and transport functions of the port complex are significant, even if extraction is sited further away. The Los Angeles harbor was, by the early 1930s, a "petroleumscape": "Port cities are the quintessential petroleumscapes, where the physical presence of oil infrastructure—storage tanks, pipelines, shipping facilities—overlaps with oil-related administrative and cultural functions," writes architecture and planning scholar Carola Hein.[62] Invisible though it may be from other vantage points in greater LA, the Los Angeles harbor made a long-term, fixed investment in petroleum decades ago, and that commitment remains to this day.[63]

Oil literally fueled trade, another major harbor operation. It both powered ships and drove the generation of wealth. By midcentury, port

FIGURE 7. Oil tanker, Long Beach Harbor, 2012.
Photo by McKenzie Stribich.

managers and other officials moved to reinvest oil wealth in further building up shipping infrastructure.[64] In Los Angeles's harbor, this was a local and regional decision, but it was simultaneously notched into a national economy and a global system. Trade ramped up in the economic boom after World War II; managers in this harbor and others decided to invest in the technological innovations of containerized shipping and expanded dredging capacity.[65] The Los Angeles–Long Beach port complex is an infrastructural node within a system of global trade. As scholar of international politics Laleh Khalili writes, maritime trade, logistics, and hydrocarbon transport "are the clearest distillation of how global capitalism operates today."[66]

As noted above, US imperial expansion into the Pacific had happened by the turn of the nineteenth century, including occupation of the Philippines and annexation of Hawai'i. After World War I, American naval power became concentrated in the Pacific rather than the Atlantic. A fort had already been sited on the Palos Verdes peninsula by the early twentieth century. Unsurprisingly, World War II saw the further buildup of US military power in the harbor. The navy undertook infrastructure projects in the harbor, building a naval station and a shipyard, and expanding breakwaters to allow for miles of protected shoreline (reaching nearly to Orange County, all across San Pedro Bay and the Long Beach shoreline).[67] After the Japanese attack on Pearl Harbor in December 1941, Los Angeles blacked out its harbor to remove it as a target, and the harbor was considered a defensive stronghold through World War II. For a brief moment after the war, it looked as though the navy might draw down its personnel and equipment, but when the United States entered the Korean War, it opted to maintain a navy presence in the harbor, and many naval vessels "homeported" there through the Korean and Vietnam Wars. In the 1990s, the navy did finally relinquish some of its space in the harbor, shuttering a base and naval hospital; its space was then converted to commercial shipping use. However, the US military is still very much present: it uses Seal Beach on the far side of San Pedro Bay for fueling and for a weapons station, and the navy consolidated its Southern California presence further south in San Diego County. Finally, oil and the military are intimately linked in myriad ways, especially through ideologies of national security through energy independence and through the US military's heavy reliance on fossil fuel.

Of course, the history of this land and marine area does not begin with USACE's and Los Angeles business magnates' decision to build massive industrial infrastructure. The prehistory of the tidal flats includes the 1825 flood rerouting the LA River, Mexican rule, Spanish colonial settlement, and indigenous settlement by humans, animals, and plants prior to that. But the transmutation that the siting of the port complex accomplished is significant, as it locked in a series of commitments, which inarguably changed the area massively in a very short time.

ECOLOGY, VIOLENCE, AND FLUX IN SAN PEDRO BAY

It is not my aim to tell the entire history of the port complex and surrounding estuarial/ecotone zone over the last half-century or so, nor is this necessarily even possible. Rather, the stories here prioritize a handful of themes that help to reveal meaningful developments in San Pedro Bay. They help to make sense of a local story and how it fits into much bigger global patterns. The Los Angeles harbor is itself a truly massive site, taking into account not only the square footage of its land and water, and tons of concrete and steel, but also the complex technopolitical systems and knowledge that run through it. In other words, the port complex is not just a collection of objects or systems but a large assemblage in an even more vast, heterogeneous, and intricate sociotechnical system that is both deadly and lively. I do not mean to suggest the ports of Los Angeles and Long Beach are especially singular or unique in this context; they merely constitute a node in a global system. At the same time, this book insists on approaching this vast assemblage as a local site, through resolutely partial and even provincial stories.

Shocking 2018 reports indicated that 60 percent of vertebrate species have been lost worldwide since 1970, mainly through decimation of bio-diverse rain forest.[68] With each subsequent tally, the global "outlook [for biodiversity] gets worse."[69] We are experiencing a major extinction event and multiple ecocides.[70] This book insists, perhaps counterintuitively, on: thinking about multitudinous life within a hyperindustrialized, highly man-aged site. The port complex is sited in an area that is home or way station to a multitude of life-forms. Some of these creatures were nearly extermi-nated in earlier eras and are seeing their populations rebound somewhat due to legal protections and conservation efforts. Yet their fragile gains are happening against a backdrop of rapid and dramatic climate crisis, which is deeply stressing planetary systems and throwing heretofore taken-for-granted conditions for life into question. Meanwhile extraction, trade, and consumption march (drill, dredge, pave) along, imbued with a logic of ex-pansion and resilience. I call the latter infrastructural vitalism and juxta-pose it with organismic ecologies.

Infrastructural vitalism is the premise for a global system that drives violence and lethality. In October 2021, when a seabed oil pipeline off the coast of Orange County burst, it fouled water and coastline during the autumnal Pacific Flyway migration. The pipeline connected drilling in the seabed to the port of Long Beach. Amid global supply-chain chaos and while dozens of ships crowded the coastline near the harbor, waiting their turns to dock in the ports, a cargo ship's anchor had likely struck and dragged the pipeline. Tar showed up on beaches as far south as San Diego County. Some in the region revisited commitments made in the 1970s; a journalist noted that, even at that time, "selling offshore leases for oil drill-ing in the middle of shipping lanes seemed reckless."[71] It is overwhelmingly clear which priorities this infrastructure supports: petroleum and goods movements at scale. In spite of local conservation efforts, because of how the port complex connects commodity chains and labor across the globe, it can arguably even be said to participate in habitat loss and even ecocide well outside the borders of San Pedro Bay.[72] The endless growth that in-frastructural vitalism demands is both practically and morally hazardous. Birds make charismatic victims, but they are not the only ones.

The port complex in San Pedro Bay is implicated in capitalist, colonial relations. Even as it creates wealth, capitalist expansion is destructive. In fact, destruction is a precondition of expansion; it is built into the cycle. As geographer David Harvey writes, a central contradiction of capital is that it "has to build a fixed space or landscape necessary to its own functioning at a certain point in history only to have to destroy that space (and devalue much of the capital therein) at a later point in order to have to make way for a new spatial fix (openings for fresh accumulations and territories) at a later point in its history."[73] In the port complex, a fixed-capital commitment to petroleum was cemented by the 1930s. This was necessary to accumulate wealth through oil extraction and trade on a continuous basis. Such activities perpetuate ecological damage at extraction sites, of course. But the kind of destruction Harvey draws attention to here is different: in an eventual crash of the value of petroleum, the value of the commodity itself will be destroyed, and moreover the value of the investment sunk into petroleum *infrastructure* (the refineries, the pipelines, etc.) will also be destroyed, if and when an energy transition occurs. This will leave the port complex, built up to process and transport petroleum, as a ruin: a toxic ghost of capitalist expansion and subsequent abandonment. Capitalism, if unchecked, will meanwhile merrily and wantonly go on to fresh accumulations, territories, and acts of destruction: lithium (a key ingredient in batteries for electric vehicles) is in the upswing part of this cycle at present.[74]

Capitalism is a dominant economic system, but its tendency toward expansion is enhanced by the seizure of land and natural resources, often in lockstep with colonialism. Capitalism allows for the enclosure of natural resources to promote wealth accumulation, but the colonial project also claims space to pollute, to discard waste (a by-product of capitalist commodification processes).[75] In San Pedro Bay, the lives I survey in this book are all characterized by having relationships to commodification *and* by being implicated in processes of territorialization, that is, colonialist projects. I take as axiomatic that the land claim processes of settler colonialism structure relations in San Pedro Bay. In this site, it is especially important to note that in the context of goods movement, meaningful distinctions between "civilian" and "military" collapse. Movement of goods and management of space and lives (of people, of wildlife, of stuff, and certainly of oil) is an imperial project as well as a capitalist one. "Protecting trade networks from disruption creates new spaces of security and in doing so problematizes the political and legal status of subjects," writes geographer Deborah Cowen.[76] Finally, though it is particularly easy to see how the conjoinment of capitalism and colonialism produces degraded organismic ecologies (often hideously so), other political and economic systems can as well. Infrastructural vitalism is potentially flexible enough to accompany multiple systems of extraction and expansion.[77]

Capitalist expansion is *violent*, in a literal sense. This book introduces the reader to life-forms that live within and transit through the port complex that have been harmed, directly and indirectly, through industrial commodification processes. California sea otters were hunted to near extinction for their pelts centuries ago. Gray whales were hunted for blubber: the eastern Pacific population off the coast of North America is relatively stable, but their Atlantic cousins are gone, and their western Pacific siblings are quite imperiled. Least terns were hunted for decorative feathers. Seabirds, cetaceans, and otters, meanwhile, can also be maimed and killed by spilled oil and other forms of industrial violence, from fishing nets to agricultural runoff.[78] In these instances, they are merely collateral damage in the commodification of another substance (petroleum, which used to be lives) or other lives (agricultural crops; commercial fishing). Banana importation consumes petroleum fairly intensively and leaves in its wake a plume of chemicals (and political relations) harmful to laborers and to wildlife.[79] And ship strikes constitute a prominent risk to whales; their bodies can be in the wrong place at the wrong time with regard to goods movement. Though spilled oil can be a media event, more often violence is not especially spectacular or cataclysmic but the slow accumulation of injury and multiplication of harm.[80]

But life has tendencies of its own: it multiplies itself. Life can regenerate, and mutate. The point is, life inherently contains the ability to create more of itself (and sometimes plays a supporting role in the multiplicative efforts of other life-forms through mutualisms). For lives recently placed in the shadow of the port complex, there has been a tendency to accumulate more life, over eons.[81] Capitalism is set to accumulation as well, and this explains its harm to life at scale: capitalism tends to claim for commodification the capacity of life to generate more of itself, or it seeks accumulation of resources in landscapes where life dwells rapidly and often very destructively. For collectivities of organisms suffering under the burden of cumulative industrial injury, life's tendency to accumulate can serve as a counterweight, but only to a point. Given the destructive power we are witnessing, we might wonder, what if global systems could be set to accumulate not wealth, but life?[82]

Organisms have generative and dynamic tendencies, and so do ecological systems more broadly. Even in spite of the (recent) constancy of the port complex and the obduracy of its construction, the harbor is in a state of *flux*. After San Pedro Bay became the mouth of the Los Angeles River, the "useless tidal flats" were constantly made and remade with tides and storms. Upon identifying the area for a project of infrastructural fixity, managers built breakwaters and docks and then petroleum infrastructure.

Silt might be the most obvious example of flux. To create a harbor suitable for ship traffic, the coastline needed to be dredged. Indeed, in the period when officials decided to site a major port in Los Angeles, LA lacked "what observers universally considered the essential component of a commercial metropolis: a natural deep-water harbor and anchorage."

Overcoming this obstacle to building a large port required using then-new hydraulic dredges to remake the coastline.[83] Dredging is absolutely key to thinking about global trade at scale. Anthropologist Ashley Carse suggests that much globalization of commerce has actually happened "below the waterline": the environment itself becomes infrastructure.[84] But of course silt replenishes itself. For working port infrastructure, it has to be continually dredged away, not only to allow bigger ships needing deeper channels but simply to maintain open shipping channels at all.

Land above water is also in flux. (More accurately, what is "land" and what is "underwater" is variable and contingent.) By the 1940s, oil extraction here had produced wealth and an unintended consequence: significant land subsidence.[85] In fact, Long Beach was called the "Sinking City," because oil and gas extraction caused land subsidence, up to twenty-nine feet deep at the center of the "subsidence bowl," afflicting the port area and coastal strand going south and east toward Seal Beach.[86] There was also a severe earthquake in Long Beach in 1933, which is now assumed to have been triggered by extraction. By the late 1950s, under threat from federal lawsuits, port engineers implemented a water injection program to repressurize the area, flooding the emptied underground oil field with seawater. This worked to stabilize the land, and regulators were pleased enough with the result that they dropped their suit.[87]

In an "envirotechnical" space like a harbor, even fixed commitments require maintenance and upkeep to respond to flux.[88] Definitionally, there are human-made and natural forces exerting pressures of various sorts on the infrastructure at all times. In the present day, port managers the world over are eyeing climate change, including more intense storms and sea level rise. Sea level rise is, of course, caused by warming. Polar ice is melting even faster than anticipated due to runaway carbon emissions. Planetary systems are veering off course, and meanwhile we are living through a confusing moment with regard to energy. Experts agree that fossil fuel consumption needs to be halted immediately (especially by rich countries) in order to stave off the worst effects of the climate crisis, which are becoming more evident and more severe with each passing year. Due to interruptions to global trade during the initial stage of the coronavirus pandemic, the price of oil futures fell in 2020, reaching negative levels that April before recovering.[89] And yet, even as many predict the demise of fossil fuels and seek to hasten a major energy transition, in many territories across the globe, energy companies and states are falling over themselves to drill. US energy companies in particular are currently doubling down on their commitments to extraction, even as some other fossil fuel firms invest significant resources in alternative energy research and development.[90] As of 2020, as the Trump administration was ending, the United States was a net exporter of petroleum (though most regions, including California, were net importers). This was in part a result of expanded hydraulic fracturing ("fracking") authorized under the Obama administration. According to the US Energy Information Administration, this was the first time the United States had been a net petroleum exporter since recordkeeping began in 1973.[91] Petroleum remains a significant priority for the Biden administration. Of course, energy is important in trade, but it is also held to be a major concern for national security, so energy transitions will have multiple complex implications at geopolitical levels.[92] If and when fossil fuel as an energy regime falls, the port complex and San Pedro Bay will be ripe for transformation, but the future is murky and still extremely oily for the time being, by bipartisan consensus.

All of this is to say that flux, both controlled and otherwise, is endemic. A lingering question about the Los Angeles harbor is who or what is in control. Regional officials and port managers have sought to capitalize on trade opportunities as an economic strategy, with significant booms in growth in the 1960s, 1990s, and 2020s.[93] Yet local control can be elusive, in a sense, as officials respond to capital's complex currents, which take cues from forces well out of the control of economic advisers in Los Angeles County.[94] The life-forms in this book all live (or attempt to) in the spaces opened up for them within control—of wildlife, of landscape, of supply chains, of trade patterns. Their ability to do so is in uneasy tension with an infrastructural vitalism that drives extraction and circulation regimes, pushing planetary boundaries to their limits.

THE MULTISPECIES, THE HUMAN, AND THE NONHUMAN

Recently it has become common for scholarship in critical humanistic fields to address the nonhuman (commonly called the more-than-human) and to orient toward multispecies accounts.[95] I am heavily indebted to research in those modes but, at the same time, the acknowledgment that nonhuman life-forms matter and participate in the world does not necessarily resolve epistemic, analytical, and political problems. Researchers still need to account for specific historical and contemporary formations and how power shapes them. To exalt the nonhuman or more-than-human through "turning" toward it may do a disservice to analysis because the categories are simply not stable enough, and much is at stake. There are common instances of humans and other life-forms being different as a matter of legal status, of course, but this boundary always is a situated historical accomplishment, not an a priori difference.[96]

This matters in at least two ways. First, throughout the history of the West and specifically in the settler colonial legal regime of the United States, not all humans have been equally or universally human, that is, in racial capitalism and projects of colonial domination, "humans" have been sorted into "full humans; not-quite-humans; and nonhumans."[97] The processes of "splitting" humans from "others" have "engender[ed] a lot of violence."[98] As this book is centrally concerned with showing how the stewardship of San Pedro Bay aligns in many ways with capitalistic and US imperial (including settler colonial) pursuits, it needs to acknowledge how complex both anthropocentrism and systems of oppression are, and how attempts to contest both together do not always neatly align.[99] A human-nonhuman binary masks that history and present, conflating and universalizing humans *and* consolidating a "generic animal." A more nuanced approach, in the words of literary and Black studies scholar Zakiyyah Jackson, might interrogate both categories and identify "shared being with the nonhuman without suggesting that some members of humanity bear the burden of 'the animal.'"[100] Second, not all humans have been equally responsible for imposing conditions of violent domination on "others" (other people, other life-forms, and terrestrial formations from rivers to veins of coal and cobalt), so blaming "humans" for ecological degradation, for example, obscures power relations and responsibilities.[101] Furthermore, politicizing "animality" does not *necessarily* unseat structuring relations that perpetuate ecological violence.[102] In this text, when I refer to humans, I place them on continuum with other life-forms—all of whom shape, co-create, and respond to conditions of mutualism and domination, by turn. In this site, specific epistemic, political, and economic commitments have been given disproportionate power to shape the lives (and deaths) of a host of creatures, and one in particular—a commitment to infrastructural vitalism—is the structuring force that I draw out in this multispecies analysis.

Ultimately, of course, infrastructural vitalism was conjured by *agents of capitalism and colonialism*, and landscape management is racialized on the coast and elsewhere. Writing of Northern California in the nineteenth century, geographer Lindsay Dillon shows that inland swamp reclamation transformed "waste" land into "productive" space subject to fixed property regimes (not dissimilarly from the Port of Long Beach managers' boast in 1971). "Civilizing" the swampland secured it for whites' health and economic gain; and swamp-clearing utilized racialized labor.[103] Following on the heels of Indigenous dispossession, landscape transformation produced settler ecologies that articulated with emerging racial formations, which persist into the present.[104] Racialized coastal management can be seen in myriad ways in present-day San Pedro Bay: in the ports' economic and labor logics; in whites' claims to the coast for recreation, including yachting, surfing, and restored coastal wetlands like the Dominguez Gap; and on Terminal Island, which houses a federal prison, itself infrastructure for racialized securitization and enclosure.[105] Infrastructural vitalism subjects biological life-forms spanning humans and nonhumans to violence, but as much as possible I refer to living creatures by labels at the level of species groups and social groups.

Speaking of species, one trade-off in this account is that I treat quite a few terms and concepts in this book as though they are static, even though they are in fact lively and often contested. A different analysis would get *inside* some of the controversies that attend concepts from natural sciences like biodiversity; species; endangerment; conservation, a "self-declared 'crisis discipline'"; and, last but not least, "biological life" itself.[106] Using these terms and especially treating them as fairly settled concepts draws me into engagement with findings from scientific research, but it is not my intent to uncritically center or reproduce the authority of scientific knowledge.[107] I certainly do not mean to imply that the Western natural sciences offer the only, let alone the best, account of biological life. At the same time, work in these disciplines has effects in the world, informing landscape and wildlife management. This work shapes both my own knowledge and popular representations of the lives and spaces of multispecies dwelling, which needs to be acknowledged, especially as it is a goal of this book to cultivate recognition of some "intimate particularities" of multispecies lives as they dwell and die.[108]

Finally, my focus on "charismatic species" is both an asset and liability.[109] On the one hand, this can reproduce some of the problems with the species concept in conservation: it can lead to "typological essentialism," treating the differences between individuals as insignificant in order to render them as equivalent in terms of species-identity; it can draw attention away from ecologies, mutualisms, and patterns of relationality; and it can underrepresent the needs and significance of noncharismatic species, leading toward heroic measures to save individual creatures or species at the cost of overlooking habitats and dynamic ecologies.[110] A more *natural* natural history might choose, for example, to center algae, gnats, and snails. On the other hand, my approach capitalizes (as it were) on the familiarity of life-forms like birds, whales, and otters. Readers' assumed acquaintance with and affection for these creatures can serve different ends here, locating their presences in the port complex especially as they relate to capital and petroleum, in order to draw out infrastructural vitalism. It also has a methodological advantage, allowing engagement with media representations in addition to scientific papers, trade, and gray literature.

The chapters that follow all chronicle biological life in and out of commodity chains, while attending to ecological lines of relation, violence, and flux. Biological life in the harbor comes into focus, and species become managed objects of conservation, as a direct result of encounters with industrial practices that also harm them. The production of scientific knowledge in this context supports biological life but also enlivens freight and petroleum infrastructure. Cowen's work on supply chains as constitutively violent and deadly, even as they are also "lively systems," is mainly concerned with transnational networks where workers' lives and bodies are disciplined. But she gestures toward nonhuman migration in logistics and suggests that nonhuman border crossings (of both goods and animals) speak, in some fashion, to the possibility of circulation of oppositional and alternative logics.

My project here picks up some of these threads, taking Cowen's work as a prompt to think with *liveness, life,* and *liveliness* (as well as death) in relation to the circulation of goods and capital in logistics spaces. In these pages, I surface the persistent (if embattled) lines of biological relationality that circulate in the heavily managed logistics space that is San Pedro Bay. San Pedro Bay is teeming with life-forms, but its harbor is also a site of environmental injury, and a node within a violent world system. The port complex is always in a state of flux, and energy regimes in particular are poised for transformation, but there is little reason to believe that new "clean" energy sources alone will remake local worlds in a fairer image.[111] If we understand the port complex as a chokepoint, circulating not only goods but a world system, we might be able to reconceptualize it as a node for "unfixing" the lethal world system of infrastructural vitalism in which it has been implicated for over a century.[112] Logistics space is "a tool of imperial dispossession and capitalist power, [but] it also produces new sites of vulnerability and *potential emancipation*," write geographers Charmaine Chua and coauthors.[113] What if the port complex could be imagined as an *audit point for transspecies supply-chain justice, including labor practices, environmental harm, and resource use*?[114]

A multispecies analysis of San Pedro Bay can attune us to some of the destructive patterns produced by the movement of capital; and multispecies lives here can even point us to somewhat hopeful stories of life pulled back from the brink. But the annihilative forces of capital expansion mean that the stories cannot be too hopeful; multispecies hope under ascendant infrastructural vitalism is fragile and contingent. Biological life in San Pedro Bay can prompt us to ask: how might we reimagine and retool infrastructures to promote not commodity "chains" but intricate loops, interconnections, and renewed lines of ecological relation?[115]

FIGURE 8. Nazca booby as it appeared on social media, September 5, 2020.
Photo by Angie Trumbo; used with permission from International Bird Rescue.

1

PRECARIOUSLY PERCHED IN A PORT

In September 2020, a striking white-and-black Nazca booby peered at a social media audience from high above San Pedro Bay (fig. 8). The booby's charismatic visage beamed out to viewers from a drab cinderblock building at the southern edge of Los Angeles. Block letters proclaim the facility, twenty-odd miles south of downtown, to be the "Los Angeles Oiled Bird Care and Education Center" (fig. 9). Though it was designed to support care for up to a thousand birds during an oil discharge event, the facility also treats many other avian injuries and ailments during nonspill periods.[1] Another social media post that day showed the booby again and listed 175 birds in care across two California facilities. For the next couple of weeks, the booby, who had been discovered injured and near starvation on a pier in the port of Long Beach, was under expert veterinary care.[2]

The land abutting San Pedro Bay would be acres upon acres of marshland if not for the managed and industrialized nature of the ports. In fact, only through shoreline management is land consistently surfaced *as land*. Otherwise, tidal patterns would reveal, rearrange, and submerge land under water twice daily; recall that for eons before recent coastal management, "low tide left the flats and marshes as dry and contiguous land, only interrupted by narrow channels of subtidal water. High tide, however, inundated and fractured the interior into a collection of islands, shoals, and open water," according to historian James Tejani."[3] These features make land, water, and land-water marshes attractive to a wide range of resident and migratory species, including fish, mollusks, insects, marine and land mammals, birds, and more. For birds, the estuarial Southern California coast is important as a stop along the Pacific Flyway migratory route, which spans over 4000 miles from Alaska to Patagonia. According to the

FIGURE 9. Oiled Bird Care facility, San Pedro, Los Angeles, 2019.
Photo by the author.

Audubon Society, over a billion birds per year use the Pacific Flyway (and
this is just a fraction of the number that would have a century ago).[4] The
Dominguez Gap, a restored wetlands slightly inland along the LA River,
may host as many as 180 avian species over the course of a year, including migrants and year-round residents.[5] The Colorado Lagoon, a more recently restored coastal wetlands in Long Beach on San Pedro Bay, boasts
habitat that can accommodate seventy-five species of birds.[6] There is no
reason to think that either of these areas is exceptional in terms of capacity
for supporting multitudinous life.

The Los Angeles harbor is a space of flux; it has been built and rebuilt
since the early twentieth century to accommodate different uses, with substantial commitments to commercial shipping; petroleum extraction, refin-

ing, and movement; and militarism. Since the introduction of regulations to protect wildlife and coastal areas a half-century ago, growing sophistication of managerial care for wildlife has emerged here, amid the ascendance of techniques and apparatus for the movement of goods in San Pedro Bay.[7] The wayward and ailing Nazca booby which had turned up in the port of Long Beach was far from its home base in the Galápagos Islands. What the booby's experience shows is that the systems and facilities established in the wake of oil accidents end up with broader mandates, providing significant support. Both in acute events and with more mundane injuries, wildlife adjacent to and in the midst of hyperindustrial activities, manages to live *in spite of capitalism* (exemplifying what anthropologist Anna Tsing has called "third nature").[8] Perversely, at the same time, wildlife here manages to live *because of capitalism* (or, more precisely, the effectuation of wildlife management within a regime of infrastructural vitalism). But it is a fragile and precarious existence.

The economic vitality of the systems in which the port complex is a node implicates biological life, often violently. This chapter presents vignettes of support for the booby and other avian wildlife within the hyperindustrial LA harbor. Life-forms' tendencies to create more of themselves lead to complex (and evolving, literally) mutualistic relations. One life-form is another species' prey; a third lives commensally on the leavings of the predator; while still another springs up to populate an environment that has undergone some change, like new growth after fire. San Pedro Bay contains multiple lines of ecological relation in its tidal flats, its ecotone (the Southern California Bight's mixing waters), in the Channel Islands archipelago, within and among shipping lanes, petroleum pipelines, and military vessels (the latter of which are all bound to one another). Several decades on from the introduction of regulations intended to respond to a regime of infrastructure building that had rapidly altered ecologies in San Pedro Bay and elsewhere, such regulations and their institutional instantiations support and constrain biological life at the same time. Attempts to manage and support wildlife coexist with regional managers' unquestioning commitment to infrastructural vitalism. My aim across this book is to *denaturalize* the infrastructural and economic vitality of the systems that are ascendant in San Pedro Bay. In the background is a question: what are the potentials if the area were to "reorient accumulation *away from wealth* and *towards life*"?[9]

"OIL MENACE"

Oil—which was once, of course, biological life—beads up in the seams between San Pedro Bay's biological life and its economic vitality. The

FIGURE 10. Petroleum storage in Port of Long Beach, left, with dry bulk handling for cement components on right, 2021.
Photo by McKenzie Stribich.

presence of petroleum here is hard to overstate. The harbor became a "petroleumscape" by the 1930s, embodying a fixed commitment to extraction, refinement, and especially circulation of fossil fuel as well as the circulation of other goods (fig. 10). Regional managers' pledge to build a deep-water harbor (achieved through dredging) in San Pedro Bay at the turn of the twentieth century attracted oil companies' interest. Acting in concert, private oil companies and the municipal Board of Harbor Commissioners developed the harbor for transportation, storage, and refining of petroleum. The "transshipment" function, that is, the ability to move petroleum to and from intermediate destinations between point of origin and final destination, and often from one mode of transit to another, meant that this harbor had a built-in advantage with the discovery of oil fields in greater Los Angeles. Without the ability to transport and transform petroleum, the supply would have overwhelmed the local market, but with this infrastructure in place, the local surplus could easily enter export markets.[10] These commitments, cemented a century ago, created inarguable path dependency for the port complex and the regional economy.

In the present day, California has the fifth-largest share of US crude oil reserves and is the seventh-largest producer of crude oil in the nation; California ranks third in the nation in petroleum refining capacity, after Texas and Louisiana; and California is the second-largest consumer of petroleum in the nation, and the largest consumer of motor gasoline and jet fuel. Fully 85 percent of California's petroleum consumption is in the transportation sector (another 12 percent is other industrial uses). While California's coastal oil production has declined during the past thirty years, inland extraction helps the state retain its status as a top producer.[11] As California moved somewhat away from oil production locally (compared to high-water marks in the twentieth century), it became more dependent on foreign oil, implicating it in global petropolitics.[12] Recall that crude oil constitutes around 30 percent of all maritime cargo globally.[13]

Offshore drilling in California began in the late nineteenth century, off the coast of Santa Barbara, but not in the harbor off Long Beach until the 1950s. Because they were so visible from shore, to disguise the industrial activity, Long Beach's oil platforms were built to resemble islands, replete with palm trees and building facades intended to enhance the harbor aesthetically (fig. 11). The oil islands and other offshore drilling rigs connect via pipelines to storage and refining facilities on shore; it was one of these pipelines that burst in October 2021 and fouled the coast during birds' critical fall migration.[14] "The Port of Long Beach is probably unique in all the world for combining commercial shipping operations, the development of a major oil field[,] and recreational facilities into one integrated unit,"

FIGURE 11. A Long Beach oil island, with the shoreline in the far background, 2018. Built in the 1960s, the four oil islands were designed with visual aesthetics that would disguise industrial activity, but they are massive oil drilling platforms. Photo by Ian E. Abbott, CC-BY-NC-SA 2.0 license.

crowed a 1966 annual report.[15] Aesthetics were paramount, but environmental concerns received less attention. This is not to say that the risks to wildlife from extraction activities were unknown. Marine wildlife can be subjected to industrial oiling in the context of offshore drilling, spills from ships, or leaks from ship-to-land pipeline infrastructure. (Wildlife can also be subjected to natural oiling from seeps, but this is of a different scale than industrial oiling.) A 1926 international conference was convened in Washington, DC, to discuss oil pollution, indicating that the "oil menace" was already acknowledged as a global problem by this time.[16] Oiling of seabirds in the United States was recorded sporadically as early as the 1920s but not systematically tracked prior to the 1970s.[17]

In 1969, a substantial leak in an offshore rig in Santa Barbara caused oiling of beaches, harming many birds and other marine life. Perhaps more significantly, it unspooled as a dramatic event in a narrative of growing environmental consciousness for the mainstream US public, especially Californians.[18] Another spill after a tanker collision near San Francisco in 1971 again attracted public attention to oil spills, and the 1970s saw federal and state regulations introduced to reduce oil pollution.[19] Systematic attempts to monitor and catalog bird-oiling emerged in this context, in keeping with a broader movement of environmental concern and regulation beginning in the 1960s and 1970s.

Oil can injure birds who inhale, swallow, or become coated with it, potentially leading to illness or death.[20] An organization dedicated to caring for oiled birds was founded in 1971 after volunteers leaped into action in response to the San Francisco oil discharge, trying to aid more than 7000 birds. Alice Berkner, the founder of the International Bird Rescue Research Center (colloquially shortened to "Bird Rescue," according to Berkner), was a registered nurse who had been solicited by a friend to volunteer on the occasion of the January 1971 spill.[21]

The organization was on call to respond to spills, and its operations expanded over time. Berkner published a field manual to rehabilitating oiled birds in 1985. Her organization gratefully accepted donations of Dawn dish soap from Procter & Gamble, which still sponsors Bird Rescue, and often features the product's use for cleaning wildlife in ad campaigns and product packaging (fig. 12). In 1989, the large *Exxon Valdez* spill off the shore of Alaska renewed the urgency of oiled wildlife care. This led to the passage of national legislation, the Oil Pollution Act of 1990, which dictates that spillers of oil are financially liable for the cost of cleanup. Southern California saw its own spill at Huntington Beach in 1990, and state legislation established the Oiled Wildlife Care Network (OWCN, headquartered at University of California, Davis); the state taxed oil processed and transported

FIGURE 12. Dawn bottle featuring ducklings, 2021.
Photo by the author.

in California to generate revenue to prevent discharges, clean them up, and
rehabilitate and care for oiled wildlife.[22] The Los Angeles Oiled Bird Care
facility, where the booby found itself in care, came into being in 2001 as
part of the OWCN, thirty years after the founding of Bird Rescue in the Bay
Area.[23] Researchers wrote in 1999, "Today, in almost every community in
California some form of wildlife care and rehabilitation is available (over
100 organizations or individuals)."[24]

In spite of evident public enthusiasm over care for oiled wildlife, researchers were not wholly certain of its efficacy. Though Dawn was hailed
for its cleaning powers, at least when compared to other substances, in
practice, oiled seabirds often tend to fare poorly.[25] Writing in 2003, one researcher stated that "return of more than a few rehabilitated oiled birds to
breeding populations has yet to be demonstrated in California," but other

researchers pointed to more variable results.[26] And the realities of different spill conditions and different species (American coots versus little penguins versus Western gulls, to say nothing of sea otters) made systematic comparison of efficacy extremely difficult.[27] Researchers have even asked, "Why do we respond at all (rather than just leaving oiled wildlife to fend for themselves)?"[28] Answers varied, but often combined some measure of public pressure ("the answer to the question 'why rehabilitate oiled wildlife?' is that we have to, not to enhance populations but to meet a public demand") with an ethical injunction.[29] The ethical obligation ranged from the notion that "individual animals . . . have intrinsic value" to the idea that "consumers of petroleum products . . . have an obligation to reduce suffering and mitigate injuries associated with such accidents."[30] And yet, as researchers acknowledged, the mandate to clean and release individual animals was not necessarily in line with conservation efforts at population, species, or ecosystem levels; some also acknowledged the critique that these cleanings could amount to "greenwashing," that is, public relations for polluters without meaningful benefits for wildlife.[31]

Oiled and injured wildlife undoubtedly provides a subject both charismatic and tragic. Located next door to the Oiled Bird Care facility in San Pedro is the Marine Mammal Care Center, which is open to the public every day of the year.[32] Visitors can view a few cement pools outdoors that house seals and sea lions in care (and attract opportunistic herons, hoping to snatch fish while seals are being fed). There is a small one-room visitor center, and an even smaller gift shop. Sea lions can wind up in care for a host of reasons: malnutrition; injuries from fishing lines or boats; parasitic, bacterial, or viral infections; poisoning; cancer; ingestion of plastics; and even gunshot wounds.[33] Though it is free to visit, the facility solicits donations to fund its activities; one evocative yet grim banner hanging in the parking lot reads, "Injured sea lions don't have health insurance" (fig. 13). Needless to say, many injuries are brought about by violent encounters with industrial activities; though any individual sea lion's injury may be acute, the wider pattern is attritional, accumulative harm.

The Oiled Bird facility, by contrast, is less welcoming of the public, at least in person. Though a 2001 press release from when the center was newly open says the public may get in touch about scheduling a tour, there is nothing about visiting hours posted in person or online.[34] Marine Mammal Care Center staff told me that the Oiled Bird facility's patients would likely be more stressed by visitors. Perhaps to make up for the lack of public invitation on site, the OWCN maintains an active online presence. Some reports from the San Pedro facility can be found on the OWCN's social media and blog, which is how I encountered the Nazca booby. This booby

FIGURE 13. Marine Mammal Care Center, San Pedro, 2019.
Photo by the author.

hailed from the Galápagos Islands, where it had been banded as a nestling in the 2017–18 breeding season.[35] Most chicks leave the colony for several years and scientists know little about their travels and migration patterns during that time, so sightings like this one in San Pedro Bay are especially important for study, according to researchers.[36]

The San Pedro center also operates a live webcam. While I was watching one day shortly after the above social media post, two workers entered the outdoor aviary, and one scooped up a distinctive, largish, mostly white bird in a towel. I assumed it was being taken out of the aviary for a test or exam, but to my surprise, the worker gave it a gentle toss lengthwise in the enclosure. I realized she was checking its flight or urging it to use its wings, and, after watching the cam a while longer, I surmised it might be the booby from social media because of its distinctive black-on-white plumage. A brown pelican and what appeared to be a juvenile Western gull, both sporting small leg bands, looked on from a perch above the water (fig. 14).[37]

Upon subsequent viewings, the booby was not visible in the enclosure, but this was not especially meaningful given that it might be out of the frame at any particular moment, or in another enclosure not on the bird cam.[38] The social media feed did not provide updates until a few weeks later, when International Bird Rescue announced that the booby had died:

FIGURE 14. Gull and pelican, enclosure-mates of the Nazca booby, and caregivers. Screenshot from International Bird Rescue "PeliCam," San Pedro, September 9, 2020. Photo by the author.

"We had hoped our staff veterinarian . . . might be able to pin the damaged wing area, but the bone was already set in the wrong position. While we were unsure whether the bird was going to be able to fly, our team provided expert care and the booby rallied for more than a week. Into the second week, she took a turn for the worse and died suddenly, despite our best efforts."[39] Though rescue staff (and this viewer) were disappointed, given that the bird had arrived injured and in a weakened state, hungry, and suffering kidney problems, this outcome was hardly surprising. The organization planned to donate the bird's remains to the Los Angeles Museum of Natural History's avian collection.

ENDANGERED SPECIES CARE: LEAST TERN HABITAT (NON)RESTORATION

Both the ports' industrial operations and the bay's wildlife habitats are, like everywhere else, increasingly subject to intensifying climate change. The US Army Corps of Engineers (USACE) has a long history of building and manipulating shorelines, including this one, and its current remit includes responding to ocean rise and emerging climate conditions through massive engineering projects. In a report released in 2019, USACE scored potential scenarios for proposed habitat restoration in the Long Beach (eastern) portion of San Pedro Bay (fig. 15). As the report notes, marine ecologies globally are under significant and persistent threat from climate change.[40] USACE acknowledged that inaction in San Pedro Bay was undesirable.[41] The massive review process that fed into this report and recommendation took several years, using biological survey data collected in two surveys since 2000. Public consultation began in 2016, and Army Corps representatives reported findings to the public in a meeting at the Aquarium of the Pacific in Long Beach in December 2019.

The report detailed several possible alternatives for restoration of habitat: "Restoration objectives include restoring aquatic ecosystems in a marine environment, to increase abundance and biodiversity. . . . Restoration measures considered include establishing additional rock habitat structure that would support kelp, eelgrass and other sensitive species or habitat types, and expanding sandy shorebird habitat and coastal wetlands."[42] The study focused on the restoration of habitats with "broad ecosystem value" and did not privilege restoration for the benefit of individual species. A USACE representative told me, "We are not trying to target a specific marine animal species or a specific [type of] habitat. We're wanting to let the planning process unfold, not letting the sea otter dictate, or steelhead salmon [for example]."[43] The report presented several possible alternatives and scored them to enable comparison, using a quantitative metric called the "average annual habitat unit," designed to gauge "usefulness" of habitat to a range of species that might use it for dwelling, breeding, migratory

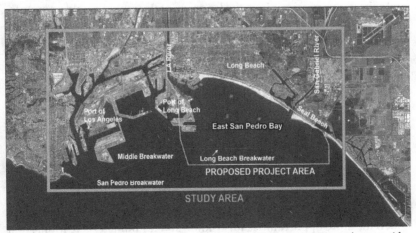

FIGURE 15. San Pedro Bay, showing the proposed habitat restoration area (eastern side, in lighter industrial use, excepting the oil islands), 2019. The California least terns that nest in San Pedro Bay already use the western side (a pier in the Port of LA).
US Army Corps of Engineers, public domain.

stops, and so on.[44] USACE also evaluated possible plans as to whether they would have an impact on factors such as coastal and shoreline hydrology, noise, recreation, air and water quality, essential fish habitats, and others.

USACE's report compared the plans in terms of cost to administer and the gain in terms of average annual habitat units, producing a cost-benefit analysis: "Average Annual Costs range from $3.2 million to $38 million. Average Annual Habitat Units range from 125.4 to 330.6."[45] From eleven possible "best buy" alternatives, USACE selected one as being the most desirable in terms of the aggregated evaluations. The report describes the plan:

> National Ecosystem Restoration (NER) Plan [is] identified as the Tentatively Selected Plan (TSP) after evaluation of the three action alternatives based on Completeness, Effectiveness, Efficiency and Acceptability. The NER Plan reasonably maximizes ecosystem restoration benefits compared to costs. It is Complete in that it accounts for all necessary investments and actions to realize the planning objectives. It is Effective in that it directly restores over 200 acres of aquatic habitat and generates 161 AAHUs. It provides connectivity for productive habitats including open water rocky reef, intertidal zone rocky reef, eelgrass and open water kelp. The NER Plan provides habitat for key life stages of a diverse population of fish and other aquatic species, primarily by providing foraging, sheltering and critical nursery functions that support population health and growth.[46]

As the above passage hints, the language of the report would be stultifying to anyone who is not a truly committed bureaucrat. It runs to nearly 500 pages and is accompanied by fourteen additional appendixes.

In the public presentation in December 2019, USACE strongly advised adoption of this plan, intimating that federal funding for any restoration would be contingent on going along with USACE's recommendations. (A USACE representative later clarified that the local sponsor is free to choose another plan, but the federal funding will only rise to the level of the commitment in the USACE-endorsed plan.[47]) Many members of the public who attended the presentation were disheartened, as there was, it seemed, an expectation of a more ambitious plan. As noted above, it is nearly impossible to overstate the presence of industrial activity in the harbor, including oil operations and commercial shipping, and some residents hoped for more opportunities for wildlife and for human recreation. After the USACE presentation, the floor opened for public comment. One Long Beach resident, a white-presenting woman perhaps in her forties, opined,

"The quality of life of the people of Long Beach is suppressed by the Port, military, and oil industry. I'm disappointed that the Breakwater options aren't being moved forward. Can we consider human aspects? What's good for our kids is good for the kelp, clean water."[48] This matter of the breakwater she raised has to do with how the Long Beach shoreline (and recreational beach) is sheltered by a man-made breakwater, a line of rock infill that curtails wave energy, resulting in much calmer water at the shoreline than would be the case without the breakwater. Many residents believe that this modification causes more concentrated pollution in the water at the shoreline, as this water is not mingling as freely with the open ocean. The breakwater is also particularly despised by local surfers, who must travel to adjacent beaches to find waves. Some of the options that USACE considered, but dismissed, would have involved "notching" or even removing some breakwater to allow more water and wave energy to pass in and out, and this dismissal is what dismayed the resident. However, USACE was heavily resistant to affecting military or shipping operations that rely on the calming effect of breakwaters: docked ships loading and unloading cargo benefit from subdued waves, and even more so when the cargo is ordnance, which the Navy insists be loaded on and off ships in controlled conditions.

Despite the residents' and surfers' disappointment with the tentatively selected NER plan, I draw attention here to the NER's effects on another constituent, who was not present at the public meeting. Least terns, a species of migratory seabird, were on the verge of extinction in the 1970s. Their populations had been affected in the nineteenth century by egg collecting and feather collecting for ladies' hats, practices that were restricted by the Migratory Bird Act of 1918. Killing birds for decorative feathers was less of a factor in later eras, but in the middle of the twentieth century, habitat was affected by landscape management practices (dams, channelization, and the like), and breeding was harmed by pesticides such as DDT, which weakened eggshells.[49] In the early 1970s, so few breeding pairs of the California least tern subspecies remained that scientists feared they might die out entirely.[50] California least terns winter in South and Central America and breed in marshlands in North America, including Southern California. They have been observed in the area that is now the ports since the 1800s, and have been observed, especially in the outer harbor, "almost every year" since biological surveys began in 1973.[51] (The federal legislation that allows for the designation of an endangered species is the Endangered Species Act of 1973, which triggered the extensive monitoring practiced today.[52]) Conservation efforts since then have combined with the terns' own multiplicative potentials (life's propensity to create more of itself) to bring them back from that brink.[53] Though they are still regarded as endangered, the "edge of extinction [was] deliberately flattened and drawn out," as environmental philosopher Thom van Dooren writes.[54]

The California least tern features prominently in a 2013 brochure produced with participation by both ports, entitled "Harbor Habitat: Our Biological Treasures." Unlike the biological surveys and the 2019 USACE report, this document was produced for a general audience. The tern was featured in a half-page display and mentioned several times. The brochure reads: "Certain species of seabirds, including the endangered California least tern, a small seabird that nests in Los Angeles Harbor and elsewhere along the coast of Southern California, are drawn to the shallows because the small fish they feed on are abundant there and easy to see and catch." It claims that the Port of Los Angeles "has taken extraordinary steps to provide the birds with the best possible chance to succeed. [It] monitors and maintains the nesting site on Terminal Island each year. The Cabrillo Shallow-Water Habitat and the shallow-water areas next to Pier 400 and the Navy Mole [all in western San Pedro Bay] provide rich foraging grounds for this sensitive species."[55] The tern is also featured in port press photography (fig. 16).

According to both state and federal law, USACE had to give special consideration to how its plans might affect endangered species. The two endangered bird species determined to be possibly affected by habitat restoration in San Pedro Bay are the California least tern and the snowy plover, both of whom use "sandy island habitat" and coastal sand dunes

FIGURE 16. Press photo, nesting California least tern in the Port of LA, 2013. Courtesy Port of Los Angeles.

for nesting. The report acknowledged that the Southern California Bight, the broader ecosystem in which San Pedro Bay is located, has lost sandy island habitat.[56] A 2008 biological survey actually reported that the least terns' numbers were down, speculating that the "decrease in nest numbers is believed to be related to increases both in vegetation and predation at the Pier 400 [in the Port of LA] nesting site"; it counted 521 nests. (The number of terns nesting had fluctuated in the years prior; a high point was 1,332 nests in 2005, but only around 500 in 2001.[57]) However, the 2014 survey showed drastic-seeming decline: only 126 nests and 64 fledglings.[58]

In the present day, "the most critical threat to least terns is habitat loss from coastal development."[59] And yet, the National Ecosystem Restoration plan that USACE recommended contained no expansion of the sandy island or dune habitat that snowy plovers or least terns might nest in, writing, "The Corps has determined that the project NER Plan would have no effect on the California least tern, western snowy plover, white or black abalone, or any of the Federally listed [endangered] marine mammals that may occur in the area."[60] This decision reflected a series of judgment calls. First, the biological surveys included all of San Pedro Bay, but the habitat restoration USACE proposed was for the eastern portion only (the municipal Long Beach side); the western (ports) side was excluded because, as report authors state, "Western San Pedro Bay does not offer large scale habitat restoration opportunities due to existing Port of Long Beach and Port of Los Angeles infrastructure and heavy vessel traffic."[61] In other words, industrial activities were deemed too important to interrupt, which limited consideration of conservation efforts in that area (see fig. 15). California least terns do already nest in an area in the western side of the bay, on Pier 400 in the Port of LA.[62] Snowy plovers are apparently scarce in both areas, though "a few individuals also have been observed at Point Fermin and Cabrillo Beach outside the breakwater" (even farther to the northwest of the harbor).[63]

In recommending against expanding sandy dune or island habitat, it could be argued that USACE exercised something of a circular logic: "No critical habitat for these species is found in or adjacent to the project area, therefore, no impacts to critical habitat would occur."[64] Of course, strictly speaking this is true. But this framing brackets out the possibility that *expanding* habitat might *increase* the presence of a given species in the area; the decision to not expand habitat for the most critically endangered species seems like a potentially missed opportunity to promote the accumulation of life. The USACE representative characterized this as mainly having to do with economic cost: "Habitat that [the tern] uses, sandy island, is pricey, [so we're] not adding it. It's hard to justify a super expensive plan, even though I'm sure the [natural] resource agencies would have loved it. . . . I [too] would have loved to include all the wetlands and sandy habitat [that the feasibility study explored], but we can't justify it from a cost [perspective]."[65]

The intervention that USACE recommended, the National Ecosystem Restoration (NER) plan, recommends adding habitat that might *indirectly* support the California least tern, through the cultivation of eelgrass. Eelgrass is an underwater plant that grows completely submerged in shallow water, of which the harbor has lost a lot because of dredging to accommodate large ships. Eelgrass beds provide a nursery environment for fish, which are in turn attractive to "aerial fish forager" species like the terns, who dive into the water to catch very small fish to feed to chicks. It is possible that the NER would benefit terns, who might, with abundant food nearby, either take to Pier 400 in greater numbers or utilize sandy habitat elsewhere for nesting. (One asset of Pier 400 is that, while it is entirely surrounded by industrial activity, it is secured from disturbance by recreational users of the shoreline. Designating beach areas for recreation deters terns who might otherwise nest there.)

RESITING A HERON ROOKERY: THE LOGISTICS OF DWELLING IN LOGISTICS

San Pedro Bay is a locale, one of many, where the global apparatus of US military power "touches the ground" (and water).[66] While the United States has staged military engagement here since the nineteenth century, its presence increased after World War I, when American naval power shifted from the Atlantic to the Pacific.[67] Oil drew the strategic military interest closer: from the earliest days of local oil extraction, conflict developed over mineral rights to the tidelands upon which the ports were built. The State of California challenged Long Beach's rights to oil in the tidelands, and so did the federal government, with an eye to including it in the naval oil reserve. The navy first established itself with a submarine base on land deeded by Los Angeles in 1917, and it had a landing in San Pedro (the village, now incorporated as a neighborhood of Los Angeles, facing the harbor on the Palos Verdes peninsula) from 1928 onward.[68] As World War II approached, the navy sought more land and water access on Terminal Island[69] and began renting a patch of land for use as an airfield from the Port of Los Angeles in the 1930s.[70] Throughout the 1930s, Japanese tankers were regular callers at both ports, buying California oil for homeland use; Japan was the Port of LA's largest trading partner.[71] The navy built a dry dock for ship repairs, and it expanded the breakwaters to allow for miles of protected shoreline

FIGURE 17. Statue of Japanese fisherman, with shipping cranes in the background, 2021. Photo by the author.

(reaching nearly to Orange County, all across Long Beach's shoreline).[72] As tensions with Japan heated up, officials worried about the harbor; Terminal Island was home to a fishing village populated by Japanese and Japanese Americans, and the mayor of Los Angeles, Fletcher Bowron, fretted about Japanese fishing boats having contact with submarines.[73] After the attack on Pearl Harbor in December 1941, Los Angeles blacked out its harbor to remove it as a target. Soon after, the US government acted on what the mayor called "common sense," destroying the Japanese American community on Terminal Island and forcing fishing village residents into internment camps.[74] Today, Terminal Island houses a federal corrections facility, commercial shipping facilities, a small area of bird sanctuary, and a monument to the displaced residents of the fishing village (fig. 17).

Several large tuna canneries operated on Terminal Island for much of the twentieth century. Even as the inner harbor was heavily polluted, tuna processing provided a food source for birds and other fish, who took advantage of dumped fish waste until the cannery discharge was rerouted into sewage treatment facilities in the 1970s.[75] Although San Diego also had a sizable tuna industry, as a whole production in Southern California languished by the 1980s. Some commercial fishing operators blamed federal regulation for its demise, in particular the Marine Mammal Protection Act, which passed in 1972 and regulated the harm that cetaceans could incur from fishing operations.[76] But warming waters played a significant role as well: in the early 1980s, skipjack and yellowfin tuna migrated from the Eastern Tropical Pacific marine region (off South and Central America) to the cooler, deeper waters of the Western Tropical Pacific.[77] This affected the California-based fishing industry. Some fisherfolk did follow the fish, and,

FIGURE 18. Intersection of Cannery and Tuna Streets, Terminal Island, 2021. Photo by the author.

FIGURE 19. Long Beach Naval Shipyard with Kilauea-class ammunition ship anchored in foreground and *Queen Mary* and *Spruce Goose* dome in upper right, 1984. U.S. National Archives (public domain).

from the Western Pacific, it was less expensive to process the fish overseas than return to use the existing labor and infrastructure in California.[78] The Starkist Tuna factory on Terminal Island, which had been the largest cannery in the world in the 1950s, shuttered in 1984.[79] Today, formerly bustling cannery sites contain empty streets and boarded-up buildings (fig. 18).

Like the tuna industry, the navy departed from San Pedro Bay by the 1990s. After the Soviet Union's dissolution, the US shifted the stance it had built up and maintained during the Cold War. The navy pulled up stakes on its shipyard and naval station, which had occupied several berths in the Long Beach portion of Terminal Island (fig. 19).[80] (It lingers to the present day with ordnance movement and fueling, but its presence is much diminished.) The Port of Long Beach opted to reallocate much of the navy's space to commercial shipping, but in the course of this shift, port personnel noted that black-crowned night herons used a portion of the "Navy mole" for nesting. Their rookery was located in a stand of trees on the mole, a 100-acre, hook-shaped man-made peninsula jutting off from the main land mass of the island (itself also man-made), which served as an additional breakwater for docked ships.[81] The planned conversion of the area was set to cause the "loss of a significant biological resource," specifically the heron rookery.[82] The navy's biologists estimated that at least fifty mating pairs used the site for nesting, and the US Fish and Wildlife Service confirmed that the herons were protected, per the Migratory Bird Treaty Act.[83]

Because they were required to accommodate the herons, Port personnel proposed the unusual step of relocating the rookery. Writing after the fact in 2002, researchers stated that "trees and other plants are commonly relocated successfully, but projects involving relocations of bird colonies are rare and largely undocumented." Port-contracted personnel studied the herons and their use of the trees carefully in 1996 and determined that the herons' nests were concentrated in seventy-one trees with as many as fifteen nests per tree (the herons favored the *ficus microcarpa* trees, an introduced species from Asia). They determined that the colony was likely the largest in all of Southern California; only a colony in San Diego was comparable.[84]

Monitoring continued in subsequent nesting seasons, and by 1999 Port personnel determined they had enough information to proceed. The Port employed an arborist to supervise relocating fifty trees, which were unearthed and transported a little over a mile to a former recreation spot (called Gull Park) at the end of the mole, where personnel remediated the soil to accommodate the trees' arrival. Personnel also utilized heron decoys and rigged up a sound system to play recorded vocalizations twice daily, dawn and dusk, to attract herons to the newly sited trees. Last, they trapped and removed predators such as feral cats. As researchers reported in 2002, this effort to support accumulating life was successful: the herons took to the new roost. The 2000 breeding season produced more chicks than any other season since monitoring began in 1996, and the herons utilized both the transplanted trees and the ones that had already been present in Gull Park.[85] American crows and great-tailed grackles used the trees for nesting as well.

The heron relocation also featured in Port of Long Beach public relations: two annual reports from 1999 and 2000 make reference to the herons. In the 1999 report, they featured in a short write-up that mentioned the trees, decoys, and sound system: "Redeveloping the naval complex displaced a colony of black-crowned night herons. So the port lured them to a new home on the former Navy Mole by relocating trees, deploying decoys and broadcasting mating calls. More than 150 chicks were found at the bird sanctuary in 1999, four times as many as the previous year at the naval complex."[86] Twenty years later, on a boat tour run by the Port in 2019, the operator, a Port employee, mentioned a small patch of "undeveloped" land for migrating birds (though not visible from the boat, he took care to point it out in vague terms).[87]

One might take exception with the term "undeveloped" here: the herons' roost sits atop infilled land, on remediated soil, in trees native to Asia, individual specimens of which were transported from over a mile away using trucks and cranes. Nonetheless, this episode shows that support for herons, motivated by a desire to increase commercial shipping, could arise from the conjoined interests of the navy and the Port. The regulatory apparatus provided by the Migratory Bird Treaty Act and the US Fisheries and Wildlife Service guided the Port's and navy's intervention chronicled here. Black-crowned night herons are currently listed as of "least concern" status, but with "population decreasing."[88]

CARE IN CONTEXT: EVERYDAY VIOLENCE

Birds like the Nazca booby routinely turn up in the port complex because they become inadvertent stowaways on cargo ships. Sometimes the outcomes are happier than that of this booby: a staff veterinarian told me that in 2011, a red-billed tropicbird that came in on a ship was deemed releasable after care and subsequently flown (on an airplane) all the way to Midway Island.[89] This island is an atoll in the North Pacific, an unincorporated US territory in the Hawai'ian archipelago with a history as a US military airfield and designation as important seabird habitat. Though the booby's arrival in the Port of Long Beach was not necessarily as a stowaway (its caregivers said this was possible, but unknown), the bird's appearance in an area designated for cargo handling is what ultimately delivered it into expert care. The circuits of global commerce and US empire that pull the birds off course can paradoxically rehome them too, at least sometimes.

But this is not to suggest a symmetrical relationship between the circuits of biological life and those of goods. Indeed, the expert knowledge that is brought to bear here—biological surveys; cost-benefit analysis to restore habitat; veterinary care for oiled or injured animals; novel techniques to resite a roost—all sits within a context of industrial violence. This does *not* mean that the people staffing these facilities do not "care" in meaningful ways; plainly, they do. Speaking of the booby several months later, a staff veterinarian said, "I remember the bird pretty well and was bummed that the bird's orthopedic problem couldn't be fixed."[90] This indicates sincere, affective care for the life of an individual bird; as does the veterinarian's joy at the rehoming of the red-billed tropicbird. And a USACE representative represented her work on the habitat restoration project as driven by care for the LA River and San Pedro Bay ecosystem, with historical awareness of the role played by USACE in past harms. She told me, "Part of why we [USACE] want this project is the role we played 100 years ago. We played a major role in the destruction of San Pedro Bay, parts that we buried or dredged up or blew up . . . *I wouldn't have come to the Corps if I didn't have the opportunity to work on this.*"[91]

FIGURE 20. Three-eyed fish painted on drainage infrastructure near a municipal park, 2021. This fish is an unofficial mascot of the San Pedro neighborhood, wryly invoking the toxicity faced by biological life here.
Photo by the author.

Nonetheless, port managers' support for infrastructural vitalism here remains intact. The movement of petroleum and the movement of goods and matériel cause harm to wildlife. Not all of this harm is spectacular like spilled oil; much more of it is "slow violence," "calamities that are slow and long lasting," like breathing air pollution, epigenetic harm due to toxic exposure, and other accumulative injuries that may accrue over living a lifetime in a built environment erected to accommodate petroleum, commercial shipping, and military activities (fig. 20).[92] In this, wildlife is not so different from poor and racialized people in California, who were for decades without legal protection from living near active oil and gas wells, and who choke on toxic emissions from freight movement—by bipartisan consensus.[93]

In all three vignettes, the care efforts are circumscribed. USACE would not countenance habitat restoration that would unseat or disturb the industrial activities in the western portion of San Pedro Bay. Indeed, the USACE planner offered an almost tautological explanation: "We can't restore in the western part, conditions are too poor, water quality is poor, traffic is too great."[94] The herons were heavily monitored and managed through field surveys—observing the nests from hydraulic lift vehicles, counting eggs and chicks visually, and observing droppings and eggshells on the ground.[95] But the space allotted the herons and the least terns was minimal in the spatial context of the port infrastructure, and monitoring of these birds is arguably as much *to meet legal requirements that will allow industrial activity to persist* as it is to allow the birds, fish, eelgrass, and kelp to flourish.[96] Port personnel were eager to accommodate the herons because, with the 1990s departure of the navy, they faced economic pressures which they chose to meet by significantly expanding commercial shipping operations. The context for care and support is always *conditioned not only by available resources but even by countervailing interests*.[97]

International Bird Rescue's mission is also restricted. From early days, Bird Rescue received significant funding from oil companies including Chevron; and the organization even had a member of the petroleum industry serve as president of its board of directors.[98] In an undated recollection, Berkner admitted that her embrace of the oil industry in Bird Rescue's operations was perhaps unorthodox. She said, "I made it plain that it was our wish to work with Chevron and not against them. My attitude was not that of the stereotypical 'environmentalist' of that time but that of a consumer who accepted responsibility for what could result from petroleum consumption on an individual and even species level."[99] Berkner is not alone in this framing of the phenomenon of oiled birds: contemporary (2018) researchers in the *Journal of Fish and Wildlife Management* echo this language when they write, "We, as consumers of petroleum products, have an obligation to reduce suffering and mitigate injuries associated with such accidents. . . . We believe it is the ethical responsibility of humans to minimize suffering to wildlife when that suffering is caused by humans and human-related activities."[100] This framing addresses spectacular, discrete events like spills, but not slow violence; and it elides which "humans" bear most responsibility, as well. To further muddy (or oil) the waters, funding for rehabilitation of oiled birds and environmental cleanup is perversely reliant on the transport and processing of petroleum known to cause harm, as legislation provisions industry revenues for spills and prevention.

This being said, Bird Rescue's position is eminently more sympathetic than that of Procter & Gamble, makers of Dawn dish soap. For decades it has provided care for errant boobies and all manner of other avian patients, even in the absence of spills; and its workers have inarguably saved lives and otherwise benefited quite a few. (Even if the Nazca booby's story lacked a happy ending, it received excellent care.) Ironically, Dawn is a petroleum-based soap, sold in disposable plastic bottles made from petroleum. Its public relations campaigns using oiled wildlife appear more cynical in this context, as critics have pointed out: "[Some] are concerned that the bird rescue groups are fighting oil with oil. Ben Busby-Collins, the founder and chief executive of Ballard Organics Soap Co., says, 'If we're trying to reduce our demand for oil and you're using a petroleum-based product, it's creating more demand.'"[101] Surely the demand for other petroleum products is much greater than that for dish soap, so it is unclear whether switching to vegetable-based de-oiling cleansers (as Busby-Collins suggested) would make much difference in shifting fossil fuel demand. But the wider point stands: at present, even *de-oiling* birds sits within a frame that takes for granted their constant exposure to toxicity, created by petroleum extraction, refining, and consumption, including both oil and plastics. (Neither oil nor plastic is "all bad," of course; the problem is how petroleum is implicated in systemic injury and violence, when it is a "poorly tended relation."[102])

San Pedro Bay is a significant node in operational and organizational violence wrought through logistics, both within and extrinsic to the organization of states.[103] The US military is a significant polluter globally and thus must be included in a tally of violence. Radioactive waste from its imperial pursuits is strewn across many corners of the earth, including the Marshall Islands and the American Southwest.[104] As for petroleum, the US military is the single biggest consumer of oil on the planet; over time it has consumed more fuel and emitted more carbon dioxide than most countries.[105] As people and nations struggle to adapt to accelerating climate crisis caused by runaway emissions, the military has expressed concern. In 2019, the Department of Defense produced a sweeping report for Congress, stating that "effects of a changing climate are a national security issue with potential impacts to Department of Defense (DoD) missions, operational plans, and installations."[106] Of course, those overseeing the armed services have embraced climate issues in order to argue for a "greener" military, reliant on renewable energy (and no doubt requiring large procurement orders of new equipment), not to engage with concerns about American imperialism or draw down the size of the US armed forces.[107] We might thus consider oiling as a form of violence experienced by wildlife that is in many ways functionally inseparable from militarism.[108] But it is an "everyday militarism," bounded differently in space and time than punctuated warfare.[109] Everyday militarisms are gradual and unspectacular.[110]

It is also worth remembering that before oil was industrial fuel, it was a black, gooey, naturally occurring substance that Indigenous people in the LA Basin used to seal canoes, and that, eons ago, oil was plants and animals.[111] Oiled seabirds can occur naturally as well as due to human activities; oil seeps from the seabed are a regular occurrence, though their proportionate damage is less than that caused by human industrial activities.[112]

Critical Indigenous studies scholar Zoe Todd offers an incredibly generative assessment of oil, which she has challenged herself to understand as
"weaponized fossil kin." Todd writes of seeing oil from extraction activities invade rivers and harm fish, but, realizing that this harmful, polluting
substance was constituted by "bones of dinosaurs and the traces of flora
and fauna from millions of years ago," reframing (and reclaiming) them as
kin. It took deliberate (capitalist, colonialist) human activities of claims to
property and ownership, extraction, refining, and burning to transform
them into the weaponized, harmful forms they now assume. She characterizes this weaponization as having occurred because the "dominant human
ideological paradigm of our day forgot to tend with care to the oil, the gas
and all of the beings of this place."[113] For Todd, these "paradoxical" fossil
kin have been *converted into* threats to life and ways of life. Weaponized
fossils' threats to life take the form of pollution, which is now permanent,
and act by "rapidly" erasing prior knowledge systems and capacities to cultivate landscapes and adjust to environmental change.[114] But this is due to
the ascendance of a deadly regime, that of infrastructural vitalism, rather
than to an inherent property of petroleum.[115]

What we see in these vignettes is a post-1970 apparatus that is arguably
geared toward providing reactive care after harm has been done, including
aiding protected birds with their processes of accumulation of life when
numbers are dipping too low. There is little expectation that industrial violence will be preempted, let alone that flourishing will be prioritized. Note
that in the happiest scenario above, the relocated herons, species numbers
are still declining. The wider context for vertebrate life is its shocking decline over the last fifty years. This heron colony was relocated in order to
accommodate a greater volume of commercial shipping, which surely is
not good news for abundant biological life in thriving ecological relation.
The sea lions will be injured. If lucky, they may be found in a condition
where they can still be cared for and mended enough to be released. (But
they don't even have health insurance![116]) "Natural" ecologies are violent
too—the food chain, starvation, disease—but there are meaningful distinctions, not least of which is scale, between the systematized, industrial violence of capital accumulation tied to settler colonialism, and the myriad
relations among biological life-forms.

A vivid, poignant illustration of these patterns was on display in summer 2021, when a small protected area of coastline a short distance to the
south of San Pedro Bay that was hosting nesting elegant terns saw its colony disrupted. The cause was a drone crash on the sand where birds were
nesting (in the Bolsa Chica Ecological Reserve, a restored wetlands still in
use for oil operations).[117] This upset caused around 3000 adults to aban-

don their nests and take up residence on nearby barges, where they again commenced nesting. However, upon hatching on the barges, many chicks tumbled from the decks into the water, where many drowned as they were too young to fly and unable to scramble from the water up onto the barge decks. When dead chicks began to wash ashore, rescue personnel sprang into action, scooping up fallen chicks from the water and rearing them at the San Pedro bird care facility until they could be released.

The barges were en route to the Naval Weapons Station at Seal Beach, where they were to be reconfigured as navy boats. The unfortunate lack of guardrails notwithstanding, they made for attractive nesting because they were covered with rocks, reminiscent of sandy coast. Once the birds took up (temporary) residence, barge operators had to leave them be, due to laws protecting birds along a migratory path. According to wildlife managers, similar incidents had also occurred in 2006 and in 2007: nesting terns had taken up residence on barges in the Long Beach harbor, and many chicks had drowned in 2006 when harbor operations spooked the birds. This had prompted discussion over building an artificial sandy island for the terns to nest in, but steps had not been taken toward this; in fact, USACE rejected such a measure in its 2019 habitat restoration planning, saying it was "too pricey." A Bolsa Chica Reserve manager said, "The reason we want to do that is *these terns keep wanting to nest in the port.*"[118]

What this episode plainly shows is deep strain between the ascendance of infrastructural vitalism in the harbor and the biological life-forms there seeking to eke out space to gather themselves to create more life. The elegant terns proved resilient and adaptable up to a point, but the combined toll on the terns' 2021 nesting season was quite high: "That's a full generation of birds not established," said a California Department of Fish and Wildlife officer of the terns' abandonment of their Bolsa Chica nests.[119] Debates over whether to add sandy island habitat occurred within a context where *scaling back industrial operations was unthinkable*; for USACE and many other managers of this coastal space, ameliorative measures for terns or herons would only be considered to the degree that they could be slotted in between or among industrial operations. Media accounts, meanwhile, often celebrate the heroic efforts of humans to save individual animals, like a plucky elegant tern chick named "Little Mike," whose 2021 "resuscitation from near death" was described in the *Los Angeles Times*.[120] In foregrounding heroic rescues, stories tend to gloss over the larger context for terns' use of these spaces along the Southern California coast: severe habitat loss, climate stress, population loss, and the industrial commitments of regional managers. Nonetheless there is something very revealing in the statement that the terns "keep wanting to nest in the port." One assumes that the lines of ecological relation that draw the terns to the port are both the exceptionally rich support for tern lives that San Pedro Bay could potentially provide *and* the dearth of nesting options elsewhere along the coast. (Bolsa Chica is one, but it still contains oil extraction, in spite of concerns over that threat to habitat.[121])

To insist on orienting around the accumulation of life could provide a different context for "care" here. Naming "accumulation of life" as an aim does not in itself answer the thorny questions about *whose* lives, but it can potentially begin to denaturalize cargo shipping, petroleum, and military operations as the unnamed de facto beneficiaries of the vast majority of infrastructural support here.[122] The "lifeblood of the nation"—goods movement—is not the only life force with a claim to San Pedro Bay.[123] Yet the industrial scale in the port complex has been dramatically increasing over the past half-century, and, in this context, expert attempts to provide care and to palliate or ameliorate violence exist within *unstated requirements for violence.*

2

YES, WE HAVE NO BANANAS

A 1966 article in a Vancouver paper, *The Province*, described Long Beach's port with envy. Its author wrote that "a glance at the financial report reveals why Long Beach['s port] has grown so rapidly in the past 25 years."[1] The reason was oil profits. The journalist noted that, even after oil operating expenses and paying royalties to the State of California and City of Long Beach (owed for tideland and interior oil operations), the port had revenue remaining to develop state-of-the-art facilities. Two projects that he highlighted were a new banana terminal, built for $3 million, and oil terminals that "can handle the largest ships afloat," with fifty-two deep-sea berths. Other terminals could accommodate dry bulk such as iron ore, petroleum coke, and potash; Long Beach imported far more than it exported. The Vancouver journalist also archly noted that the Port of Long Beach annual report, upon which his article was based, was "a model of what such reports should be. Printed on glossy paper with full color illustrations, it is a far cry from the drab and uninformative annual report of the [Canadian] National Harbors Board." The Port of Long Beach's decision to spare no expense on its shiny annual report could be said to have paid off.

Like many other seaports, the Port of Long Beach embraced the new wave of containerization in the early 1960s.[2] As the Vancouver journalist indicated, it was well positioned to undertake capital improvements, in large part due to oil revenue.[3] The harbor in San Pedro Bay, which contains the Port of Long Beach and its sister port, that of Los Angeles, is a node in a global system. Two commodities, petroleum and bananas, locate the ports of Long Beach and Los Angeles as a crucial and revealing passage point within a global system of international shipping and trade, from 1960 to the present. I trace these commodities to advance the book's project of thinking with San Pedro Bay to further understand infrastructural vitalism.[4] The normal functioning of the port (which has over the past half-century included an unceasing commitment to scaling up its operations) sets up conditions for disquieting and even violent circulation in San Pedro Bay and elsewhere.

The ebb and flow of the tidal area are mirrored in patterns of building and remaking the harbor for different purposes over time. Petroleum and bananas bring into focus a particular pattern of ebb and flow: petroleum profits led to the import of bananas at an increased scale, but the subsequent imperative of growth then drove them out of the LA harbor and into other ports. Energy demands increased as trade volumes increased, even if "efficiencies" were created in labor and by containerization. Thus the movement of a perishable biological commodity out and greater volume of nonperishable commodities in and through the harbor tells one small story in this period of globalized capitalism, exemplified by these commodities transiting through this space. What the port has been producing since at least the 1960s is *scale*, accompanied by pollution and violence, locally and remotely.

The violence of this circulatory system is *attritional*, "delayed destruction that is dispersed across time and space . . . typically not viewed as violence at all."[5] While its violence is out of sight from many vantage points, it is not truly invisible, locally in Southern California or across supply chains and their supporting infrastructures.[6] Infrastructural vitalism begets violence toward biological life. Oil is not inherently an alien substance or a poison, but a relation that has been poorly tended, "weaponized fossil kin."[7] Fossil fuel has often been referred to as "zombie energy"—kept alive past its time by subsidies that promote its production beyond what markets would dictate.[8] We might think of petroleum here as "zombified" in another sense, too—biological matter that is involuntarily reanimated after death. Its grave has been desecrated, and it labors untiringly without dignity or right of refusal, in turn causing violence to living beings. How might undead biological matter that is currently lethal become nonlethal, if not inert? If material drawn from deep in the earth is *not violent in itself*, what needs to be done to interrupt the processes by which it is made to become violent and destructive?

The history of how this port complex came to produce scale invites questions about how things might be otherwise. Analysts of ports and related infrastructures suggest they can be seen as *chokepoints* as well as "spaces of flow."[9] This is why Indigenous and other activists in North America have recently been targeting pipeline and rail infrastructure, hoping to inhibit the flow of petroleum through it.[10] It is (remotely, speculatively) possible to imagine this port complex retrofitted as a space to audit just resource use and labor practices, if logistics techniques could be applied "otherwise": "Even as logistics is taken up as a tool of imperial dispossession and capitalist power, it also produces new sites of vulnerability and *potential emancipation*," to reprise geographers Charmaine Chua and co-authors.[11] If the port complex here currently enables the circulation of scale and violence, how can it inform thinking about transspecies supply-chain justice? The entwined tales of petroleum and bananas draw attention to scale, and to ebb-flow, push-pull dynamics both within local sites and vis-à-vis their relation to complex world systems which are ripe for remaking.

The Ports of LA and Long Beach are administered separately and compete for clients. They also coordinate on some matters, especially infrastructure, and environmental compliance. They are differentiated by the fact that Long Beach is a much smaller city than LA, and it built and controls its port. Meanwhile Wilmington and San Pedro, abutting the Port of LA, opted to be annexed by Los Angeles in 1909, so these former towns are now neighborhoods and parts of a much bigger administrative apparatus (whereas Long Beach is really a "port town").[12] The Port of Long Beach is the more central focus in this chapter mainly because its tight interlocking with its controlling municipality offers a story of a city proactively approaching and responding to the regulatory environment and global forces that shape it; it also produces voluminous public-facing records, reflecting its status as a point of pride for Long Beach. Because the ports are competitors, it is unsurprising that they have some different features and tenants—but they are also colocated and interlocked in local, regional, national, and global economies and in local, regional, national, and global infrastructure. In the story below, the Port of LA offers a couple of meaningful contrasts, but the ports are far more similar than different. As geographer Juan De Lara writes, to survey commodities, labor, and logistics in Southern California is to provide more than just a case study: "they provide a way to examine how a particular iteration of modern capitalism was shaped by and helped to transform a specific place" that is significant on the world stage of logistics and goods movement.[13] To repeat, the two ports combined strain to bring in about 40 percent of inbound containers for the entire United States.[14] Change over time in the ports is complex: on the one hand, there is uniform directionality (increased movement of goods); but on the other hand, ebb and flow better captures the dynamics of the way the landscape and entities using it build up, shift, and fade away over time. In fact, the port area required investment in new infrastructure in the 1960s in part to capitalize on containerization but also because it needed to manage land subsidence brought about by oil extraction in earlier decades.

BANANA TIME

Unlike terns, herons, gray whales, and sea otters, bananas are not a native species in San Pedro Bay, and they are not even cultivated locally.[15] But my aim is not to produce a natural history in a traditional sense. The harbor's significance as a hub for circulation and distribution widens the frame to include nonobvious species, such as bananas, petroleum, and capital.

The Port of Long Beach boasted in 1966 that its new banana terminal was the "world's largest and most modern banana processing plant."[16] Whether or not this claim is factually true, it was undeniably aiming to handle a larger quantity of bananas and process them in a different way than banana handling of yore. Its claim to innovation was that it was able to take shipments of the fruit directly from freighters into a refrigerated processing plant, reflecting dominant trends toward modularity and mechanization in shipping and freight handling. The processing facility and terminal together cost the Port over $4 million, an expenditure shared jointly with Standard Fruit, the lessee of the facility.[17] This new facility aimed to distribute 160,000 tons of bananas per year to the western third of the United States and parts of Canada. In 1964, when construction for the terminal began, the Port reported zero banana imports, and in 1967, the first year when bananas appeared in the annual report, they were listed as the eighth-biggest import for the Port of Long Beach, worthy of their own category in the report.[18] A 1970 report listed bananas as the sixth-biggest import (fig. 21).[19]

To understand the significance of the Port of Long Beach's new banana terminal requires looking both backward and forward in time. The widespread popularity and importation of bananas in North America was certainly not a new trend; far from it. Refrigerated transoceanic shipping of perishable foodstuffs began in the latter half of the nineteenth century; refrigeration machines were patented as early as the 1850s, and notable early voyages brought frozen meat between Australia, South America, and Europe in ice- and ammonia-compression-cooled chambers on ships in the 1870s.[20] Bananas were introduced as a tropical treat in the United States in the late nineteenth century; a 1954 account recalled that they "appeared at the Philadelphia Centennial Exposition in 1876 wrapped in tin foil to sell at 10 cents apiece to a free-spending crowd," and imports had reached 10 million stems annually by the 1880s.[21] Fast-moving steamships contain-

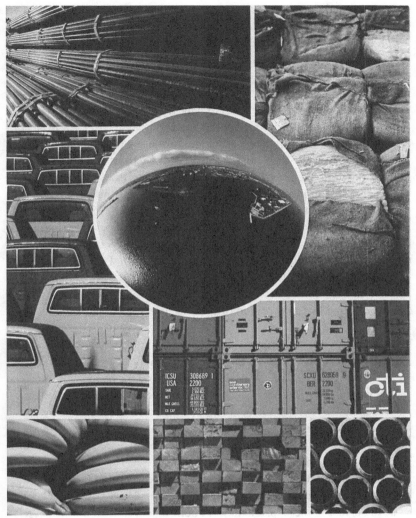

FIGURE 21. Bananas (lower left) among top ten imports. Also pictured: containers, lumber, automobiles, and metal pipes, portrayed as if zoomed in from an aerial view, 1980. Courtesy Port of Long Beach.

ing refrigerated chambers (cooled to 56–57 degrees Fahrenheit; bananas will be damaged if stored closer to freezing) transported bananas regularly to the Gulf coast and the Eastern Seaboard of the United States. Bananas consumed in the western United States typically would have arrived by ship in the Gulf Coast (New Orleans, Galveston) and been transported by rail.[22] Bananas were mainly exported from the Caribbean and Latin American countries on the Atlantic coast, though during the 1930s, Honduras increased shipments out of its Pacific ports, and Ecuador stepped up banana export.[23]

On the West Coast, United Fruit began importing bananas into the Port of Los Angeles in 1927. In 1935, the Port of LA redesigned the facility for receiving bananas, implementing a new system whereby the fruit could be unloaded directly into refrigerated rail cars: "It sported vertical conveyors that moved the bananas from ship to wharf, and from there, the fruit was transferred directly into four horizontal conveyor belt systems. These conveyors delivered the fruit at box car height to waiting refrigerated Southern Pacific railcars."[24] According to the Port of LA, New Orleans and New York had the only two facilities larger than LA's in the prewar period.[25] During World War II, shipping patterns were interrupted, as the US government required United Fruit and the far smaller Standard Fruit to lend their ships to the war effort, among other factors.[26] Some bananas were imported from Mexico, transported by truck, but interruptions continued into the early postwar period. By the mid-1960s, patterns had shifted again, and ocean shipping accounted for around 99 percent of banana importation to the United States.[27]

In 2007, one Los Angeles longshoreman recalled,

> My first day on the waterfront was in Wilmington. . . . I was 5 foot 8½. . . . I went to walk up the gangway, the boss says hey you're too small to work on the ship. . . . You go back on the dock, you work on the boxcar. . . . There's a guy lined up by the conveyor belt with the banana stalks. The banana stalks, they're five and a half, six feet, taller than I am, weighs over 150 pounds. I see these guys, guy loads it on his shoulder, walks it in [to the boxcar], he stands it up. They put the first one on my shoulder, I go down on my knees, I drag it in, I stand it up there, everybody looks at me, who is this kid. I make it through the day, I'm frustrated as hell. In the middle of the day, when the sun comes out, these banana stalks, you know, are kept at 56 degrees in the ship, and now it's hot. All of a sudden you see these tarantulas come walking out of the stalks, and these little green snakes run up your arm. And I went home and told my dad, I don't wanna be a longshoreman.[28]

Though he does not state the exact year of his experience unloading bananas, his vivid description of the setup places it in the period of the United Fruit facility after 1937, and given his age and the interruption to banana importation during the war, likely not earlier than 1960. It contains details that provide insight into the changes over time in the material practices of banana shipping. The system had cooled ships, cooled railcars, and labor-saving technology in the form of a conveyor belt between ship and rail. The bananas were transported in stalks, requiring human labor to load and unload each conveyance in the transfer from ship to rail. According to the Port of LA, because the work was arduous, the longshoremen working to haul bananas from ship to conveyor belt and belt to railcar were given a twenty-minute break per hour. It took two days to unload a ship even after the creation of the conveyor belt system, handling about 2000 banana bunches per hour.[29] And the banana stalks were accompanied by hitchhikers, other organisms whose presence reminds us that though the bananas are commodities, they were recently alive plants, growing in banana plantations, heavily managed yet less industrial environments than the port. It was essential to process the banana shipments expeditiously because the fruit is perishable.

I sketch a few key details here. As noted above, United Fruit (later, Chiquita) was the force behind the Port of Los Angeles's banana importation. United Fruit (nicknamed "El Pulpo," the octopus) is perhaps best known today for its notorious practices in pursuit of monopolistic control of the banana market, which included bloody campaigns of worker suppression (most notoriously a massacre of striking workers in Colombia in 1928) and partnering with the United States government to interfere with the sovereign affairs of Latin American countries where the company operated.[30] United Fruit's agents were not the first growers of bananas for export but their impact in the period 1880–1945 cannot be overstated. In extremely broad strokes, United Fruit's consolidation of power that had begun in the late nineteenth century unraveled in the postwar period, as the US government investigated it for antitrust behavior and the company was forced to share the market with competitors. In direct relation, United Fruit lost control over labor and politics in Latin America;[31] in Guatemala, Costa Rica, and Honduras, workers, landowners, and governments challenged its hold.[32] The era of United Fruit's control over between one-third and two-thirds of the entire banana market had ended by 1970.[33]

These developments bring us up to the moment when the Port of Long Beach planned and built a new banana terminal. As noted earlier, this terminal was a joint venture between the Port of Long Beach and Standard Fruit, a smaller competitor to United Fruit, founded in 1899 in New Orleans but acquired in the mid-1960s by Castle & Cooke of Hawai'i (which later became the Dole brand).[34] Standard Fruit had initially established banana trade in Honduras, and it moved into Ecuador during the 1940s when importers sought to trade with the Pacific coast. By the time of its partnership with Long Beach, Standard Fruit's relationship with Ecuador represented a de-emphasis on Central America in the banana trade, and

also the beginnings of a shift away from the direct control of farms by companies.[35] Long Beach unloaded its first cartons of bananas from Ecuador in
December 1964.[36]

Long Beach's banana terminal reflected a couple of significant changes
in the banana industry since the Port of LA longshoreman's recollection.
The Port of Long Beach described the new facility: "New technical and
engineering features within the 331,000 square-foot terminal are designed
to unload a box of bananas in one minute from a ship's hold to truck, rail
car, or refrigerated processing plant."[37] While it might at first glance seem
a very similar setup, and in certain ways it was, the fact that the new facility was built to transport *boxes* of bananas reflected some major developments (fig. 22). The first was a shift in banana cultivar. The banana that was
popularized from a tropical treat into a ubiquitous mass market food in the
period 1910–40 was a variety known as the Gros Michel, indigenous to the
Caribbean. It was grown in monoculture plantations by United Fruit and

FIGURE 22. Boxed bananas being unloaded from a ship by conveyor belt in the Port of
Long Beach, 1967.
Courtesy Port of Long Beach.

other growers, but it was vulnerable to two fungal diseases, Sigatoka and Panama disease, the latter of which decimated crops and set a precedent for widespread deployment of fungicides in tropical agriculture, according to historian John Soluri.[38]

Currently bananas are the most traded and consumed agricultural commodity worldwide, and therefore one of the most significant seaborne products.[39] Anthropologist Ashley Carse writes that the banana is an "infrastructural species," well adapted to "edge environments where transportation networks and lowland ecology meet."[40] The banana North Americans eat today is the Cavendish, Chinese in origin, and introduced to mass market by Standard Fruit, which started cultivating it in reaction to the decimation of Gros Michels by disease. The Cavendish is resistant to Panama disease (though it is also a "monoculture," a standardized and homogenous crop cultivated in great quantity in a farm, region, or country, and as such, also vulnerable to other pathogens, discussed below). Standard Fruit began shipping Cavendish bananas that had been processed in the country of origin: fruit was cut from the main stalk into "hands" (a cluster of bananas attached to a bit of stem, with single bananas resembling fingers), washed, sorted for ripeness and quality, and packed into boxes. Soluri argues that this was both to protect the more delicate Cavendish fruit and to meet changing consumer needs: with the rise of self-serve supermarkets, processing the bananas into customer-ready bunches was attractive.[41] The boxing of bananas also created efficiency; transforming the fruit from its natural formation on large stems into modular units meant that it could be stacked tightly and moved around by machines, requiring less human labor. These practices reduced overall handling costs.[42] Within ten years of Standard Fruit initiating the boxing of bananas, all the bananas bound for the United States were boxed.[43] The Port of Long Beach's new facility reflected these changes as well as an intention to import an ambitious scale of bananas.

And import bananas it did, for a time. The Port of Long Beach's new facility was built to unload 3,000 boxes of bananas per hour from the ship.[44] The modular, efficiently packed boxed bananas were easier to handle with a combination of human and mechanized effort, enabling movement of greater volume with less effort than that required to move whole stems of fruit. As noted above, bananas were listed as the sixth-biggest import in 1970. Data from the Port of Long Beach shows that it kept up a steady pace of banana importation: a 1979 report showed bananas as the seventh-biggest import, and bananas were consistently in the top ten imports for many years.[45] But by the late 1980s, a new trend was visible: the port reported around the same tonnage of banana importation, but the relative position of this commodity had dropped: bananas were in fifteenth place in 1987.[46] In the 1990s, "foods, misc." were in the top ten, but this included both processed and fresh/perishable foods and did not break out fruit or bananas separately anymore.[47] In 2005, the Port of Long Beach reported that it and the Port of LA combined had tripled the volume of cargo they handled in the past decade, but in 2006, no produce was reported among the top commodities.[48] Though around one-third of inbound commodities were listed as "other," and produce was doubtless some portion of that, it did not merit a listing of its own; by contrast, "foods" were listed among the top exports.[49]

SHIFTING SILT, SHIFTING PRIORITIES

What happened to bananas in the Ports of LA and Long Beach? The answer reflects an outgrowth of decisions made about priorities for the ports, tied to both regional and global patterns. Once again, to understand what happened requires looking forward and back.

Southern California experienced a boom in the postwar period. Though LA is better known for images of palm trees against a blue sky as well as Hollywood, the region is also home to a "vast grid familiar to the casual visitor mainly from the air, Southern California's industrial underbelly, the thousand square miles of aerospace and oil that powered the place's apparently endless expansion," in the 1993 words of essayist Joan Didion.[50] Military spending drove growth, and manufacturing jobs for defense contractors were plentiful in fields such as aviation. Housing was built for workers attracted to the region's economy; many of these well-paying blue-collar jobs went to white workers who capitalized not only on job opportunities but racial housing covenants that ensured enhanced property values for white homeowners and largely kept workers of color out.[51] But by the 1990s, with the Cold War drawing down, the economy stagnated. Military contracts ebbed, the navy reduced its presence in Long Beach (largely consolidating its West Coast operations in San Diego), and jobs in aerospace and shipbuilding dried up. As De Lara recounts, local political leaders seized on the ports' potential to stave off the downturn caused by the loss of manufacturing. He writes, "they convinced themselves and tried to convince everyone else that goods movement represented economic salvation for a region suffering through the job losses of deindustrialization."[52] Of course, the currents of global capital were sufficiently powerful that it was not solely up to them.

The Port of Long Beach welcomed a Sea-Land container terminal in 1962. Containerization of cargo, as opposed to the "breakbulk" technique of loading all manner of irregularly shaped and packaged material, had far-reaching effects.[53] The Port of Long Beach celebrated a few in 1962; in trumpeting its new terminal, it announced that "loading and unloading time are reduced substantially, damage to cargo is minimized[,] and handling costs are cut down" (while glossing over what critics have noted might be the largest effect of containerization, substantial erosion of worker power).[54] In the 1960s, the Port of Long Beach not only built the banana terminal, it upgraded its facilities with deeper channels to accommodate bigger ships carrying more cargo: "the Long Beach Channel . . . is 2.2 miles in length, 400 feet wide, and has a minimum depth of 52 feet at mean lower low water [low tide]," proclaimed a 1964 report, which also boasted the depth of the inner harbor channels. All were deep for the era. The channels were dredged using what the Port of Long Beach claimed was the largest dredge tool in the world.[55] (For the purposes of this analysis, it is irrelevant whether this is hyperbole, but it is possibly true: Southern California in the postwar period was fairly uniquely positioned to pursue capital-intensive modernist world-building.) "Localized dredging is bound up with global political-economic processes and associated forms of uneven development. For a port, accommodating larger ships may mean increasing competitiveness by making goods movement more efficient and cheaper," write Ashley Carse and urban ecologist Joshua Lewis.[56] But as they note, decisions to accommodate economies of scale in ports accrue uneven benefits: supply-chain capitalism relies upon displacement, exploitation, and exclusion of some groups and creatures for the benefit of others.

Though scholars rightly locate the explosion of shipping activity in the Los Angeles harbor in the 1980s and after, the die was arguably cast earlier. By the early 1960s, Long Beach anticipated decline in oil extraction profits and chose to parlay available revenue into *scale*. In the latter half of the twentieth century, the interstate highway system reduced the cost to move freight while increasing speed. The port complex's embrace of containerization and multimodal shipping makes sense in the context of this infrastructural imbrication. The Port of Long Beach observed in its 1969 annual report, "Long Beach is blessed both physically and economically to become one of the world's few central container ports in that it has a market area capable of sustaining the volume of cargo required for large-scale container operations, the space for the terminals[,] and the inland transportation network to gather and distribute containers."[57] In 1964, it illustrated the freeway system that was becoming increasingly important in distributing containerized cargo, supplementing rail—to the eventual dismay of poorer and racialized residents adjacent to trucking corridors, who were beset by freeway noise and toxic particulates (fig. 23).

TO THE PORT OF LONG BEACH VIA SOUTHERN CALIFORNIA'S FREEWAY SYSTEM

VENTURA FRWY.

HOLLYWOOD FRWY.

GOLDEN STATE FRWY.

PASADENA FRWY.

SAN BERNARDINO FRWY.

LOS ANGELES

SANTA MONICA FRWY.

HARBOR FRWY.

SANTA ANA FRWY.

SAN DIEGO FRWY.

LONG BEACH FRWY.

SAN GABRIEL FRWY.

GARDEN GROVE FRWY.

CITY OF LONG BEACH

PORT OF LONG BEACH

FIGURE 23. The Port of Long Beach boasted of its connections to the Southern California freeway system and the nation, 1964.
Courtesy Port of Long Beach.

"Scale was the holy grail of the maritime industry by the late 1970s," according to economist and historian Marc Levinson, author of *The Box*, a comprehensive account of the shipping container. Shipping companies moved toward bigger vessels. Fuel consumption did not increase proportionately with size, and, indeed, bigger vessels could move through the water more slowly while carrying more cargo, still increasing efficiency overall if the metric was movement of goods rather than port-to-port journey duration. More investments in automation on newer vessels meant that labor costs also did not increase proportionately with size, and especially so compared to breakbulk.[58] Economies of scale became extremely distorted relative to the precontainer system: in 1988, shipping companies began investing in ships too big to fit through the Panama Canal ("post-Panamax" ships, "Panamax" being the largest-dimensioned ships for that route). This made sense only for huge vessels dedicated solely to moving a massive amount of goods between two major harbors like Hong Kong and Los Angeles or Singapore and Rotterdam.[59] Shipping companies rightly predicted that ports would build infrastructure—longer piers, stronger wharves, bigger cranes, and deeper channels—to accommodate their ever-growing ships.

Long Beach and Los Angeles were uniquely poised to turn toward port development. Their ports were well located to handle import volume from Asia, not just for California but for the entire United States.[60] As China opened up to trade with the West, it became an investment target. De Lara points out that "the infusion of investment and state-backed capital enabled Chinese producers to quickly overtake both Mexico and Canada as the biggest importer of goods into the U.S.": Chinese goods shot from 6.5 percent of US imports in 1996 to 16.1 percent in 2006.[61] According to the Port of Long Beach, China was already producing one-third of the toys imported by the United States by the early 1980s, and Long Beach eagerly facilitated trade of all manner of goods.[62]

WHITHER BANANAS?

Los Angeles is notorious for its traffic. What is less appreciated is that congestion is not only a feature of the roads: maritime traffic is also a problem. Increased trade volumes with the Pacific Rim and China in particular meant that the ports of LA and Long Beach, occupying the same harbor, needed to accommodate growing inbound and outbound sea traffic while being responsible for coordinating the movement on land of goods from ship to rail or truck and vice versa.

In essence, containerization drove volume, but it also drove specialization within and across ports. Cargo that was not containerized, like dry bulk, liquid bulk, and automobiles, required its own infrastructure, including specialized terminals, storage facilities, and even ships.[63] Bananas fell into this category and had the extra complication of being perishable. The largest ports in California—Los Angeles, Long Beach, and Oakland—all had incentive to pursue container ships with the economies of scale detailed above, which by definition tended to be laden with containerized goods, ideally nonperishable ones.

Thus bananas, which initially arrived in Southern California as break-bulk with a large footprint in the Port of Los Angeles, needed to relocate away from LA and Long Beach in the era of containerized scale.[64] Del Monte left the Port of LA for Port Hueneme (to the north, near Santa Barbara) early on, in 1979. Dole (previously Standard Fruit) and Chiquita (previously United Fruit) remained in their respective ports (Long Beach and LA) longer, but both largely transitioned out around the turn of the millennium. Chiquita joined Del Monte in Port Hueneme, while Dole moved south, to San Diego. Dole's decision to leave Long Beach was detailed in business press in 2003: "Last year, Dole vessels were delayed 38 percent of the time at the Port of Los Angeles–Long Beach. . . . Dole ultimately decided to relocate to San Diego after completing a study that showed the company's efficiency on the West Coast was slipping because its vessels were being passed over for unloading at the port in favor of bigger ships with more cargo. . . . [The] company needed a port where it could unload cargo on a consistent basis."[65] The article added that Dole's experience in Long Beach was not an outlier; the company had departed several major ports for smaller ones as bigger ports ushered in containerization and volume. This is a national trend, with smaller ports handling a greater proportion of perishable and specialized cargo.

It is worth examining in detail the trajectory of banana handling, because bananas are a rather unique commodity. As recounted by the longshoreman, bananas were initially shipped on the stem in refrigerated ships (reefers). Early automation involved building conveyor belts between ships and ground transport, and, in addition, a system whereby gantry cranes onshore ran a loop of fabric pouches that could extend into the hold of the ship, into which stems could be placed, to be hoisted out by the cranes.[66] Bananas were later coaxed into modular format, transitioning from being shipped on stems to being cut into hands and placed in boxes in their country of origin. Those boxes were then stacked on pallets and moved around by workers operating forklifts. They were not containerized during the decades when so many other goods were. Describing the banana handling in Port Hueneme in 1991, the *LA Times* wrote, "The four forklifts nudged the pallets of bananas into a tight cube in the cage and withdrew. As soon as the steel forks were clear, the crane operator swung the cage up, out of the hatch and down to the dock, where two double-width forklifts shifted the pallets in pairs from the cage to the loading dock. There, the Teamsters Union took over, shuttling the pallets onto waiting refrigerated semitrailers—960 boxes per trailer—for shipment to supermarkets and wholesalers." The journalist described the scene as "a mechanized ballet" and quoted Del Monte's port manager, who said, "We like being here [Port Hueneme] because of the quality of the labor. The L.A./Long Beach/San

Pedro complex has become so dependent on shipping containers. But the labor here is extremely well-conditioned to palletized cargo."[67]

It is interesting to review the ways in which bananas did and did not conform to some of the other patterns we might expect with the explosion of cargo. The business model of United Fruit was vertical integration: the company owned or controlled directly land, rail, docks, telecommunications (telegraph and radio), ships, agricultural research stations; and its operations encompassed all production, distribution, and marketing efforts. The company even offered passenger cruise services on the banana boats; called the Great White Fleet, they were painted white to reflect the tropical sun and to help keep the cargo cooled.[68] The trend since the heyday of United Fruit has been toward "vertical disintegration," in the banana industry and more generally: companies tend to occupy a niche where they deal with suppliers and vendors adjacent to their operations but, as supply chains become longer, they become disintermediated, partitioned, increasingly separated across space and realm of operation.[69] For this reason, it is perhaps truly impossible to know all the "tributaries made up of sub-suppliers trickling into larger rivers of assembly, production, and distribution" that constitute supply chains, which are "staggeringly complex" even in the case of low-tech goods, according to media scholar Miriam Posner.[70]

But bananas are a relatively unprocessed commodity, requiring few transformations after harvest, and of course once they are harvested the clock is ticking. Because bananas are such a specialized item, Dole, the largest banana purveyor, still owned and operated its own ships as of 2015. (Chiquita sold its fleet about a decade earlier, but still operated the vessels; they were just not held by the company as property.) This is due to several factors: unlike seasonal fruits, bananas are grown year-round in the same region, so there is no downtime for the ships or need to coordinate different routes seasonally. The shipping lanes Dole uses are not highly trafficked, thus not competitive; there is far less demand for the route between Ecuador and San Diego than between Rotterdam and Shenzhen.[71] (This reflects an older pattern in shipping; breakbulk companies had often been content to serve a single route.[72]) Dole's ships also had specialized cranes on board, which allowed the company to operate in smaller and less well-resourced ports without optimal shore equipment (fig. 24).[73]

By around 1990, refrigerated containers were an option, but they were not universally or quickly adopted for bananas. Given the year-round production and demand for bananas, specialized boats could be in continuous use along the same routes, and refrigerated containers did not offer

FIGURE 24. Containerized Dole ship *Honduras* unloading in Port of San Diego, 2008. Courtesy Dale Frost/Port of San Diego.

an immediate and major advantage over more specialized box and pallet handling, especially because they were very expensive. A trade publication quoted the director of the port in Corpus Christi, Texas, who said in 2000, "We did our own analysis of the reefer [ship] market and saw that it is definitely expanding." The percentage of shipments handled as breakbulk was declining, but total volume had increased; the volume of fruit traffic from South America was so large that it was more economical to use specialized breakbulk reefer ships than refrigerated containers.[74] That said, reefer containers for bananas, like containers for other goods, offered significant labor savings—and more intact fruit, since it was subject to less handling. Dole, as a large, well-capitalized company was keen to pursue containers. Writing in 1989, the *Los Angeles Times* described the change:

> Under the automated system, plantation workers in Ecuador load nearly 1,000 40-pound boxes of bananas into refrigerated container trucks set at a constant 57.5 degrees. "It's never handled again until it's in the customer's warehouse," said David D. DeLorenzo, president of Dole Fresh Fruit.
>
> The trucks then head for port, where the containers are loaded on ships and embark on a six-day ocean voyage to Los Angeles. Once they arrive, they are again hoisted on trucks, and the bananas are hauled away to buyers as far as Denver and Western Canada in cool comfort.[75]

The article predicted more than 200,000 tons of bananas coming through LA and Long Beach each year, failing to anticipate the departure of bananas from those ports for San Diego (which did handle Dole's containers) and Port Hueneme (which still worked with breakbulk, at least for a time). A big loser in the move to containers was labor: "What once took 200 longshoremen three days to unload now takes about a dozen men less than 10 hours. Even the ship's crew has shrunk to 23 from 35," according to the *Los Angeles Times*.[76]

Further efficiencies were found elsewhere in the distribution system. According to Levinson, as containerization became ascendant, port size mattered, but location mattered less and less.[77] Shippers would plan to dock wherever they could get favorable treatment and rates, and ports competed on service and price. This led to patterns that might seem perverse from the outside. For instance, fruit from Peru and Ecuador, on the Pacific coast of South America, bound for the northwestern United States, might logically seem bound for a West Coast port in the United States. But economies of scale for handling refrigerated cargo (which became increasingly differentiated from nonperishable goods) meant that, for example, it made economic sense to ship fruit through the Panama Canal to the Gulf Coast and then load it onto trucks for distribution, at least in 2000 when the Corpus Christi reefer facility expansion was planned.[78] (Reefer ships were able to fit through the Panama Canal with ease, unlike the most massive cargo ships. The canal was expanded in the 2010s to accommodate bigger vessels.[79]) Reefer ships made more journeys back and forth (and traveled faster) because of the nature of their cargo, which was unlike other kinds of goods. In other words, there were economies of scale for perishable goods, but they were different from the considerations for containerized nonperishable cargo. In both cases, overland shipping (especially trucking) was an absolutely crucial link (fig. 25).

Returning to California, Dole's banana deliveries into the Port of San Diego were, ironically, mostly bound for Los Angeles. When Dole initially moved to San Diego, trade press wrote that this was of mixed benefit: located further south on the Pacific coast, San Diego was about 100 miles closer to the source of the bananas. But "about half of the bananas [Dole] brings into Southern California are destined for the Los Angeles market, so the product will have to be trucked there at a higher cost."[80] And while some bananas were bound for the LA market, many were merely stopping in LA distribution centers before being shipped via truck to groceries throughout the west. As of this writing, Dole's 2012 lease with the Port of San Diego runs through 2036. Port officials have expressed some concern

FIGURE 25. 1973 illustration of intermodal container shipping, from dockside to truck. Courtesy Port of Long Beach.

that Dole's long-term lease might not be in the port's best interest, if the port or the city might wish to court better deals in the nearer term: one former port commissioner wrote, "A lot can happen in 24 years—a lot did happen in the last 24—and everything indicates things are speeding up, not slowing down." Others noted that if San Diego did not accommodate Dole, it could easily decamp to Port Hueneme.[81]

The trajectory of banana importation to the West Coast of the United States over the past century or so neatly illustrates how the ports shifted from handling specialized cargo (breakbulk) to containers at scale. Though this commodity moved into the Ports of LA and Long Beach during the early and mid-twentieth century, it later moved out to smaller ports as Los Angeles's harbor pursued movement of containerized goods at a greater scale. Port managers, guided by their prioritization of infrastructural vitalism, oversaw "a mechanized ballet" (in the LA Times's evocative phrase) as they coordinated and scaled up banana movement from Southern Hemisphere plantations to shifting ports to intermodal overland shipping. Infrastructural vitalism also guided their handling of petroleum, a fundament beneath the docks laden with bananas.

PETROLAND

The story of petroleum in the ports is, in broad strokes, simpler, shorter, and less dynamic than that of bananas. In the fewest words, petroleum has been the main import and the main export for the Port of Long Beach from the early twentieth century onward. On the Los Angeles side, until the beginning of World War II, petroleum accounted for fully 75 percent of the yearly tonnage of cargo moved through the Port of Los Angeles.[82] The

Port of LA has moved toward container cargo as a greater share of revenue, but petroleum is still significant. The petroleum products and derivatives have shifted somewhat, as have their points of origin and destination, but recall again that "Los Angeles Harbor needs to be understood as a long-term, fixed-capital investment into oil-based energy as fuel for industry and transportation," in the words of geographer Jason Cooke.[83] At least five active refineries ring the harbor today, not counting a refinery-turned-distribution terminal, and at least three active refineries lie just a bit further inland, connected to the ports by pipelines (fig. 26).[84]

FIGURE 26. Refining activities near the water's edge, Port of Long Beach, 2012. Photo by McKenzie Stribich.

California had been an oil-producing state prior to the industrial development of the harbor, and the decision to site a major port in San Pedro Bay did not center around petroleum. But the port complex became inextricably associated with oil by the 1920s, and the presence of oil in the harbor had major implications for the trajectory of the harbor's infrastructural development. LA's harbor exemplifies "the historical and geographical *inertia* of oil-based capitalism."[85] This inertia is of major consequence.

By the 1950s, extraction activities in the harbor caused land subsidence to such a degree that the ports had to rebuild infrastructure and shore up the (highly manipulated) land upon which the port complex was built. The gush of oil that had flowed from the rich oilfields tapped in the 1920s and 1930s slowed its pace. "After decades of extraction, pumping California's increasingly tarry reserves became tougher. Much of it was locked underground in diatomites—tightly packed layers of ancient, tiny sea skeletons whose algal innards compressed over millenni[a] into gooey crude."[86] This sent oil producers in search of new sources and new techniques, including steam fracking and related extraction practices. Locally, extraction expanded into the seabed right off Long Beach; managers built four oil platforms disguised as islands in the eastern side of San Pedro Bay in the 1960s, which remain to this day. But even as California's own coastal petroleum production slowed, the harbor's extensive infrastructure for petroleum transport and refining remained in heavy use as a hub for import, processing, and export, that is, *transshipment.*

The Port of Long Beach was and is resolutely committed to petroleum. In reviewing annual reports from 1962 through the first decade of the 2000s, petroleum was consistently the top import and export, exhibiting strong continuity across decades.[87] A harbor tour in 2019 confirmed this trend had not abated: recall a Port spokesperson's claim that a shutdown would cause all of Southern California to run out of oil in about five days.[88] This would affect not only passenger vehicles but fueling for industrial purposes such as trucking, aviation, and the ports' maritime operations, at a minimum. A 2009 annual report listed crude oil imports as about 29 million MRTs (metric revenue tons) and export petroleum products as about 9 million MRTs (slightly over half were petroleum coke).[89] The Port of Los Angeles's data are not presented in the same way or with the same level of detail, but a couple of snapshots are revealing for comparison. In 2011, the Port of LA listed liquid bulk as 10.5 million MRTs and "general cargo" as 146 million MRTs. Dry bulk was listed as 1.2 million MRTs.[90] Scanning across the data from adjacent years, the proportion looks to be about the same: liquid bulk (much of which can be assumed to be petroleum) was around 5–10 percent of the total. What this shows is that LA handles a much larger volume and proportion of containerized cargo than Long Beach does, whereas Long Beach specializes in petroleum. This should not be taken as an indication that petroleum in the Port of LA is insignificant: in 2013 it listed Shell, Exxon-Mobil, Kaneb (later acquired by Valero), Ultramar, and Vopak among its "major tenants."[91] As recently as the mid-1980s, the proportion of containerized goods and liquid bulk in the Port of LA was about equal. Since then, liquid bulk has declined by about 40 percent, whereas general cargo has increased tenfold.[92] This shows that while the Port of LA's petroleum handling is in slow decline, the more significant change over time is its dramatic increase in goods handling overall (fig. 27).

As the share of California's "low-hanging fruit," lighter crude, has declined, it has shifted to extracting heavier (dirtier) oil from other energy reservoirs, usually inland.[93] The coast retains highly visible remnants of the oil boom, including not only Long Beach's oil islands in San Pedro Bay but countless wells, many of which appear idle or all but idle. It is impossible to overstate their ambient presence in Long Beach and around the harbor area (fig. 28). As of 2020, there were 1,046 active wells, 637 idle wells, and 2,731 abandoned wells across unincorporated parts of LA County.[94] Notably, well under half are active, though for an observer it is not always easy to tell which are pumping, albeit slowly, versus stalled entirely (nor is it possible to discern which are idle but accounted for versus abandoned).

By the mid-1980s, Koch Carbon began appearing in the Long Beach reports, as the company sought permits to convert a grain terminal (dry bulk) to one for petroleum coke (also dry bulk) (fig. 29). (This is the Koch

FIGURE 27. Press photo of cargo ships bearing containers, circa 2020. Courtesy Port of Los Angeles.

FIGURE 28. A pumpjack in front of a home in Signal Hill, a part of unincorporated LA County surrounded by the City of Long Beach, 2004.
Photo by Ira Brown, CC-BY-NC-SA 2.0 license.

FIGURE 29. Petcoke handling facilities, which today must be covered so toxic dust will not blow onto residents. Port of Long Beach, 2021.
Photo by McKenzie Stribich.

brothers, who spin their considerable petrofortunes into antidemocratic influence.) Petcoke is a "bottom of the barrel" residue produced from refining heavy oils.[95] The significance of this move was establishing export to China, which used this material to literally fuel its economic boom; a 1998 Port of Long Beach report noted, "Despite the economic slowdown in Asia [caused by the 1997 Asian financial crisis], the Metropolitan Stevedore Co. and Koch Carbon terminals exported 5 million metric tons of petroleum coke and coal."[96] It appears that Koch shipped heavy oil produced in domestic extraction to the harbor for refining and exported the petcoke, which was too dirty for domestic use, to China.[97] A report that does not name Koch notes that the United States is the world's top petcoke producer, and the dominant exporter of high-sulfur petcoke to China, accounting for nearly 75 percent of China's total imports in 2013. China is the world's biggest consumer of petcoke. As of 2015, the United States and China had the world's biggest and second-biggest petroleum refining capacities, though the Middle East was expanding its capacity.[98] The activity in the Los Angeles harbor thus remains important in a global system for refining and distributing petroleum, even if local production is reduced.

Finally, another petroleum residue in the harbor is the fact that the US military has maintained fueling capacity in the Port of Los Angeles even after shuttering other operations. As of 2015, the Defense Logistics Agency provided more than $2.1 billion worth of bulk petroleum annually to support 130 bases, stations, and federal agency sites in eleven western states.[99] The San Pedro facilities have "led the way in expanding DoD's access and innovation into the continental U.S. West Coast commercial terminals, fuel ports and distribution systems."[100] (They also provide habitat to the endangered Palos Verdes blue butterfly and to coyotes.[101]) Recall that the military had built up a heavy presence in the harbor around World War II, but the 1990s saw the departure of the navy from the Port of Long Beach. Even so, the fueling operations in the harbor are significant and, according to military personnel, strategic: "We are ready to repeat the history of the historic fuel logistics successes of our World War II predecessors by ensuring we have the options to push regional and global fuel logistics to the warfighter," said an army colonel in 2015.[102] To preserve an explicit orientation to "warfighting" in some portion of the harbor's operations underscores the manifold deadly potentials of petroleum here.

THE COLD, DIRTY CHAIN

Where the banana meets the pumpjack is in shipping and refrigeration. The well-orchestrated mechanized ballet is reliant on optimized thermoregulation and on speed of shipping and distribution. The successful mass importation and distribution of bananas, like many other foodstuffs (and medical supplies), depends on a cold chain, which can keep items at the optimal temperature for a long journey. The United States prioritized building a nationwide cold chain, becoming the "first refrigerated society," meaning not that Americans invented this technology but that they took to it readily, linking vast distances for food production and distribution.[103] In turn, the successful execution of cold-chain distribution has exerted pressure to intensify and expand associated consumption practices that depend on it. In other words, cold-chain infrastructure has in turn led to consumer expectation of fresh and frozen food from faraway locales, regardless of the local growing conditions and seasonal production of many crops.

In order to be a global commodity, as opposed to a local food, bananas must be harvested and transported while completely unripe. Bananas are unique in that they self-ripen; the ripening fruit gives off gas and heat that spurs the fruit to ripen further. Keeping them cool is important, but it is also essential to not let them cool too much; the optimal temperature is around 56–57 degrees Fahrenheit. Without successful controls, bananas shipped to another continent will arrive overly ripe, if not spoiled. Food geographer Nicola Twilley quotes the manager of a banana-ripening facility who says that "the energy coming off a box of ripening bananas could heat a small apartment," which underscores the need for substantial air conditioning power, calibrated to the right temperature.[104] Ventilation is also critical. When bananas arrive at a US distribution center, they are (ideally) still quite underripe. Their ripening is then managed through controlling a combination of temperature, pressure, and exposure to ethylene gas, a plant hormone.

The Port of Long Beach described its 1966 setup:

> Complementing the new terminal is a $1.5 million refrigerated processing plant, built by the Harbor Banana Distributors Company, which is the only facility of its kind in the United States able to take shipments of the fruit directly from freighters into the plant. The Pier A facility can hold 80,000 boxes of bananas, equal to three and a half million pounds or 200 carloads. It is expected to handle 40,000 boxes weekly at 40 pounds per box. The new straight line feed system will send 3,000 boxes of bananas an hour from ship to cold storage or ripening in the plant. Eighteen of the 56 ripening rooms are arranged in double-story fashion in order to accommodate pallets and boxes, or, if need be, stem fruit.[105]

As this quote indicates, some bananas would be kept cool and unripe and put straight on transport; those destined for fairly local distribution would be moved to ripening rooms. The reason for multiple ripening rooms is that banana distributors strive for always having bananas of differing ripeness on hand; retailers can purchase the ripeness they want based on the volume they expect to sell and their customers' preferences.

Onshore, processing and refrigeration plants run off the electrical grid. But on ships, trains, and trucks, the cooling as well as the movement of the conveyance are powered by diesel or heavy fuel oil (until recently).[106] As discussed above, bananas on ships did not immediately get the reefer container treatment, even when it was available as an option. Banana-handling infrastructure was already in place and it would have required investment to build in a new direction. Refrigerated containers were also initially expensive, so while they were a requirement for certain kinds of goods, they were not immediately adopted for all refrigerated goods. Even during the growth of containerized goods and increasing movement of goods overall, reefer ships, not reefer containers, were still favored for some fresh produce. By 2015, the container share of maritime reefer trade rose to approximately 65 percent—meaning 35 percent was still reefer ships. Meat, fish, dairy, and pharmaceutical commodities are very likely to be containerized, but "most of fruit shipments (typically high-volume, homogenous and/or highly seasonal such as bananas, citrus and deciduous fruits) are still conditioned on pallet transported by specialised reefer fleet." Reefer container fleet capacity was not sufficient to cover global demand for bananas in particular, especially during production peaks. The authors of 2015 research comparing containers to reefer ships in the banana cold chain concluded that there was not a huge economic advantage in bulk reefer transport of bananas over reefer container transport at that time, and they predicted that containerization would continue to rise. At the same time, for the multinationals that control the vast majority of banana shipping, there is no urgency to move fully away from breakbulk reefer vessels for bananas in particular. Shipping companies enjoy the flexibility of having both reefer containers and reefer ships moving perishables around via sea to meet needs in mature markets (Western Europe, North America) and emerging markets (India, China, Eastern Europe, and Russia), which are importing greater quantities of reefer commodities in recent years.[107]

Ground transport is a different story. Once bananas leave the reefer ship or the dockside ripening room, modularity is ascendant. Refrigerated containers (reefers) have been a crucial technology for shipping fresh food, especially when combined with microprocessors that help maintain consistent temperatures for highly perishable foods. They can also control ratios of oxygen, carbon dioxide, and nitrogen, which, if calibrated properly, can inhibit the respiration of fresh produce and slow ripening.[108] The computers in the containers can send updates to a ship's telecommunications bridge or directly to satellites, enabling the cold chain to be managed by logistics techniques similar to those that are used to manage inventories and movement of all manner of other goods, not only perishable ones.

Reefer containers are a key component of the cold chain, and they are responsible for considerable emissions. In addition to transport itself, dis-

tribution centers and grocery stores even wind up using reefer containers to store overflow goods—stationary trucks "waiting for warehouse
access or keeping turkeys frozen behind grocery stores"—which is wildly
inefficient and a source of concentrated emissions.[109] The largely invisible
reefer container (at a casual glance, it appears no different from an ordinary container being hauled by a truck) did step into public view in May
2020, when in Queens, New York, reefers served as mobile morgue facilities for hospitals discharging COVID-19 casualties. Reefer containers can
be plugged into electrical power on ships or in shipyards, or directly into
diesel generators—but this versatility is to satisfy the imperative that while
laden with perishable goods, they must not be allowed to warm up, which
would lead to spoilage.[110] A 2010 analysis of the carbon footprint of bananas
traveling from Central America to Europe found the transport and refrigeration components to be the largest sources of emissions, with farming
emissions related to the use of nitrogen fertilizers coming in third.[111]

Reefer containers thermally controlled by microprocessors can drive efficiencies in importation and transport, reducing loss of bananas to spoilage. At the same time, the efficiencies that the logistics industry pursues
are *those most conducive to scale.*[112] Intermodalism and deregulation of the
transport sector (occurring from the late 1970s through the 1990s) combined with transnational trade agreements that both signified the growth in
cargo flows and amplified them.[113] As described above, what drove banana
importation down in the Ports of LA and Long Beach was an increase in
containerized cargo, that is, adjustments of scale in trade. The same factors
that led to dwindling banana importation in San Pedro Bay saw *intensified
goods movement overall*, with concomitant increases of airborne pollutants
in the harbor and the shipping corridors to and from the port complex.

In fact, by the turn of the twenty-first century, the port complex was
at the center of controversy for its contribution to air pollution. Southern
California is well known for smog, but its industrial sources are perhaps
less visible than rush-hour car traffic. In 2005, it was reported that the ports
accounted for 94 percent of ambient carcinogenic risk in the LA area.[114]
Collectively, sources at the port are responsible for more than 100 tons
per day of smog- and particulate-forming nitrogen oxides—more than the
daily emissions from all 6 million cars in the region, as of late 2020.[115] And
diesel emissions from goods movement account for about half of California's air pollution overall.[116] Both ships and ground transport (trucks and
trains, both running on diesel) are sources of emissions. Despite the state's
reputation for progressive politics and environmental policies, California's
oil consumption has continued to climb, as its dependence on regular and

FIGURE 30. "Green port" public relations graphic showing sea lion and kelp thriving in the water beneath a stacked cargo ship, circa 2020.
Courtesy Port of Long Beach.

diesel gasoline had increased year over year as of 2019.[117] The main culprit for rising petroleum consumption was more vehicles traveling more miles, and freight was implicated in addition to passenger cars. The arc of the past thirty or so years was falling emissions with better regulation, but in the couple of years prior to the abrupt shift in patterns caused by the COVID-19 pandemic, California was actually seeing *increasing* smog.[118]

The ports have launched massive initiatives claiming to be "green"—to clean up their energy sources. The Port of Long Beach's proclamation of a "Green Port Era" dates to approximately 2004 (fig. 30). De Lara has recounted how this "green growth strategy" effectively cemented racial, environmental, and class precarity in the region: the pursuit of "environmentalism" within the context of capitalist accumulation predictably circumscribed the choices policymakers were willing to seriously countenance.[119] Goals of job creation and economic growth were literally at odds with curtailing diesel emissions (with detrimental effects on communities living downwind from the ports and adjacent to freeways and rail, including the expanded Alameda Corridor that in the early 2000s bolstered the connection between the ports and transcontinental rail nearer to downtown LA). These decisions have shaped "L.A.'s socioeconomic geography of air, in which nonwhite poor Angelenos live in the most industrial areas and breathe the most toxic air," sharply limiting the "quality and equality of life" here, according to environmental historian Jenny Price.[120]

Adding insult to injury, policymakers and companies did create jobs "powering the machines of just-in-time production and distribution"—but requiring casualized labor from immigrant truck drivers.[121] This is not to imply that immigrants' provision of casualized labor is a "natural" state of affairs; it reflects policy and economic choices.[122] De Lara concludes that without programmatic attention to matters of social and economic justice, "cleaner trucks [promised by the green port initiative] will only provide a nicer ride into the precarious world of social and economic insecurity."[123]

De Lara is undoubtedly correct in his conclusion, especially with regard to labor and racial justice, but there is reason to question the technocrats' promises of the green port even on their own terms. Though efforts to improve the air in the harbor itself have made some inroads, the increase in movement of goods has brought an increase in emissions along freeways and railways and near distribution centers—and diesel is very dirty and toxic, containing carcinogens and airway irritants.[124] The so-called clean energy alternatives for shipping and transport are a ways off from widespread adoption. Batteries are well suited for delivery vehicles and short hauls, but long-haul trucking is far less amenable. Though the ports are increasingly reliant on battery-powered machines *on site*, trucking and shipping as they are currently configured may struggle to transition to battery power.[125] Speed and range (distance) are undercut by the weight of batteries, the weight of cargo/rig, and the need to pause movement to charge; with perishable cargo, these considerations are even more pressing. "People who are operating trucks as their business are very, very sensitive to time, and very, very sensitive to total cost of ownership," said Craig Scott, general manager for Toyota's Electrified Vehicles Technologies division; this almost euphemistic statement indicates that reluctance to adopt electric vehicles may be high and that incentives or other pressures could be needed.[126]

There are also not-small matters of the energy source in the first place—battery power is "clean" at the tailpipe but not necessarily at its origin in the grid—and heavily polluting and extractive relations are required to source the minerals used in electric vehicles, including lithium and copper.[127] Companies with stakes in freight trucking are looking to hydrogen fueling. This presents an advantage over batteries because fueling stops would be quick, like gasoline; pausing goods movement to charge a battery would not be an issue. In 2018, Toyota was running two modified hydrogen-powered semitrucks as prototypes; partners in this venture were

Shell (oil) and Kenworth (trucking).[128] In 2021, Toyota announced that it would start manufacturing some modular hydrogen fuel cells for market by 2023, for use in long-haul semis. Meanwhile, Hyundai aimed to have a fleet of thirty long-haul hydrogen semis on the road in California by 2023; and Daimler aspires to bring some hydrogen-powered trucks to market by 2027.[129] The details here are relatively unimportant, but the main point is that it is an uncertain moment. A transition away from diesel is possible, and perhaps likely. Nonetheless, no working alternative has fully emerged, and regulatory pressure to lower truck emissions is often accompanied by pushing back enforcement deadlines or creating loopholes in order to promote goods movement, frustrating advocates for cleaner air in California.[130]

Like diesel, heavy shipping fuel emits greenhouse gases and toxic particulate matter; these heavy fuels also emit significant sulfur. Shipping is so dirty that "if shipping was a country, it would be the sixth-largest polluter in the world," according to Nerijus Poskus of the shipping and logistics company Flexport.[131] A 2015 study showed that 99 percent of the vessels that traversed the Pacific, one of the busiest routes, could have been powered using hydrogen fuel cells. Ships on longer journeys would need to either devote some portion of cargo space to fuel or stop to take on new fuel. As of 2020, no large container ships had been fueled with hydrogen, but Japan had developed a liquefied hydrogen fuel carrier vessel.[132] Unsurprisingly, the energy demands of reefer containers are under consideration as well. Sandia National Laboratories (operated by Sandia Corporation, a subsidiary of military contractor Lockheed Martin) described a hydrogen fuel cell generator prototype under development as a portable power supply for reefer containers, for deployment at sea or on land, in 2016.[133] Movement toward hydrogen fuel cells to replace some of the diesel and heavy oil currently used in shipping, refrigeration, and transport is significant. Solar is also under consideration for reefer containers: a container can be mounted with a solar panel and battery.[134]

And yet daunting questions remain. One option that Shell is exploring as an alternative to heavy fuel is liquefied methane gas (so-called natural gas is mostly methane), which, while supposedly able to reduce shipping emissions 15–20 percent, is still a fossil fuel.[135] Hydrogen fuel cells are reliant on pricey platinum and on an infrastructure that does not yet exist at scale (stored hydrogen for fueling, which can itself be sourced from either fossil fuel or "cleaner" sources).[136] At present, a significant source material for hydrogen fuel is fossil gas (producing so-called blue hydrogen). This may be more efficient and burn more cleanly than heavy oil, but some argue that hydrogen fuel is dirtier than burning methane gas directly.[137] And it is still ultimately a fossil fuel (though it is possible to produce hydrogen through a process using renewables; this is called green hydrogen). Need-less to say, the production of methane gas through fracking is highly toxic, controversial, and contributes to carbon and methane emissions; critics might rightly ask whether hydrogen fuel is shaping up to be a shell game (Shell game?). Finally, no matter whether the hydrogen source is fossil gas or something actually renewable, hydrogen fuel technology is very expen-sive for the time being and it is not clear when or if this will tip, spurring (and driven by) mass adoption.[138]

California has declared it will move 100 percent away from internal combustion vehicles by 2035 (which the state calls "zero emission," which is misleading, again because tailpipe emission is not the only source of pollution), but it is an open question whether this is realistic.[139] The supply-chain problems wrought by the COVID-19 pandemic have intensified air pollution in the Los Angeles basin. While the goods movement crisis receives more attention, a public health crisis looms as well: "ships alone are pumping an additional 20 tons of smog-forming nitrogen oxides into the air each day—the equivalent of adding 5.8 million passenger cars to the region—while adding as much lung-damaging diesel particulate matter as nearly 100,000 big rig trucks."[140] The "solution" to the San Pedro Bay cargo ship traffic jam was to encourage ships to not queue immediately off-shore but wait further out at sea, dispersing emissions over a wider area farther from shore (but ultimately possibly reaching land anyway).[141] The socioeconomic geography of air here relegates communities neighboring distribution corridors to ill health and even death so that freight infra-structure may live.

ENTWINED STORIES

This chapter has charted a dynamic ebb and flow. There is a push-pull dy-namic between the local shoreline in San Pedro Bay and external forces that dictate where capital, labor, and commodities will flow: "Local actors across the United States responded to global restructuring by mounting vigorous campaigns to lure new investment, even as scholars doubted that they could harness and control capital's shifting tides."[142] As reported here, the ports of Los Angeles and Long Beach had a shifting relationship with bananas: a top twentieth-century commodity for them, but one that had largely departed for smaller ports by the turn of the twenty-first. As the scale and volume of port traffic increased, regular large shipments of this perishable commodity preferred to make dedicated facilities their point of entry, even as some significant portion of the bananas' next stop was warehouses and retail in Los Angeles. As of 2014, a facility in downtown LA operated North America's largest banana-ripening facility, adjacent to a wholesale produce distribution center.[143] Transporting and cooling bananas has been wholly reliant on petroleum, a more continuous presence in the harbor, though some energy shifts may be on the horizon.

Some key lessons emerge from the entwined stories of bananas and petroleum. In a single 2013 banana shipment, we can see the culmination of several trends. Dole and Chiquita had routed large Latin American shipments away from San Pedro Bay, but in the early 2000s, the Philippines applied for market access to the United States for bananas, and the first shipment, arriving in 2013, called at the Port of Long Beach. Dole was the exporter, shipping its premium Sweetio brand bananas from the Mindanao International Container Terminal in Tagoloan. The seven-ton shipment was highland-grown Cavendish, but exporters hoped that Americans might develop an appetite for Filipino varieties like lakatan and latondan. Presumably Filipinos and Filipino Americans would already be eager to consume them. The shipment was slated for distribution in the greater Los Angeles area and greeted with fanfare.[144]

First and most obviously, shipping bananas from the Philippines to the West Coast of the United States represents scale and containerization. For bananas to do well on this journey (at least twice as far from Southern California as the coast of Ecuador), containerization would be desirable: even traveling a further distance on a slower vessel, a well-regulated container can keep fruit from ripening for a long time.[145] Ultimately, though, the import of Cavendish from the Philippines was deemed impractical: the cost was not competitive with Latin American bananas. Discussion returned to marketing the lakatan as a specialty item, to command a higher price than Cavendish. The Philippines also continued to export processed (nonperishable) food made from bananas, like banana chips, to the United States, while sending fresh fruit to China, the Middle East, and Japan.[146]

Besides consumer tastes, another reason Dole was likely at least curious about diversifying the supply stream of bananas had to do with the fact that the Cavendish is, as noted earlier, a monoculture. Two fungal pathogens that affect bananas are black Sigatoka and Panama disease (more scientifically, Fusarium Wilt Tropical Race Four). An earlier strain of Panama disease (Race One) is the pathogen that decimated the Gros Michel. Sigatoka is airborne and Panama disease proliferates in soil.[147] The experience with the Gros Michel caused growers to incorporate fungicides to ward off pathogens as well as herbicides and fertilizers to boost yields.[148] First identified in Taiwan in the 1990s and then spreading to Southeast Asia and Australia, as of 2019 experts confirmed that the new strain of Panama disease had reached Latin America.[149] Of course, this does not mean that bananas will become extinct; there are thousands of varieties around the world.

The possible effects on the commercial banana industry, however, could be substantial. Only a few varieties of bananas "have the precise characteristics necessary to withstand the rigors of large-scale commercial cultivation, long-distance transport, and international marketing."[150] And the threats to producers in Latin America and elsewhere are manifold. To cease industrial Cavendish production would be devastating economically, but the disease affects other varieties as well, and bananas are an important food locally in places where they grow. The Cavendish is a more industrially produced commodity, planted more densely than the Gros Michel had been, which also means that pathogens can spread rapidly.[151] The loss of a food source and export commodity at the same time would be disastrous.[152] This is all to say that even if Cavendish crops afflicted with wilt were to rot away, commitments to scale and increased reefer containerization mean that existing infrastructure is already poised to entangle and sweep up new spaces in the capitalist system of accumulation, should there be a need to switch banana supply streams.[153] (Frequent natural disasters afflicting tropical regions have prevented even greater geographic concentration.[154] Environmental and other crises increasingly are themselves opportunities for capitalist expansion.[155])

The tightly choreographed pas de deux of scale and containerization is driven by the logic that capital must circulate in order to accumulate.[156] Bananas and petroleum are but two flexible and lively resources here, animated by labor. But this logic makes local control difficult to effectuate. In the Los Angeles harbor, air pollution regulations now require ships to run on shore power (the electrical grid) when they are docked, or to use a "fuel sock" to scrub the exhaust "clean," and there is movement toward electric- and hydrogen-powered transport and refrigeration.[157] Yet in practice, port ships are one of the biggest sources of pollution in the region. A cargo ship docked or idling for a 24-hour period can emit as much as the equivalent of 33,000 passenger cars on the road for that one day.[158] Movement toward lessening port emissions is insufficient for community members who are suffering from cancer and asthma at high rates; as of 2020, state regulations requiring ships to plug in or scrub their exhaust still only applied to something more than half of the approximately 8,000 vessels that dock each year.[159] And in summer 2020, when record heat waves gripped Southern California, the port complex received special dispensation to ignore air quality regulations, allowing the vessels and equipment to burn heavy fuel to reduce strain on the electrical grid: "State leadership has identified this temporary exemption to at-berth emissions control requirements because shutting off shore power is the single biggest means of reducing power *in a way that does not inhibit cargo movement.*"[160] As heat waves grow more frequent, longer, and hotter, the race to reduce energy consumption and make consumption more efficient runs afoul of the increase in movement of goods. Pausing or slowing the flow of cargo is apparently off the table, leading to a cycle where a state of exception due to heat leads to an exemption to pollute, which leads to increased heating, ad infinitum.

The ports' managers assume and act as though the solution to global warming, pollution, and other side effects of scale can only be mitigated by switching to "clean" technology and fuel sources, not slowing down or reducing goods movement. In other words, they represent the energy source and mode of delivery as the problem, not the scale of consumption itself. Nothing illustrates this more plainly than a 2003 episode in which Arnold Schwarzenegger, signaling his intent to run for governor of California, was criticized for driving a Hummer, a brand for which he had been a paid spokesperson. The Hummer symbolized violence, masculinity, and something like "energy dominance" (the energy policy of the Trump administration, several years later).[161] But his "vehicle aroused disgust among those who argued that carbon dioxide emissions from cars should be reduced."[162] Schwarzenegger's solution: a Hummer with hydrogen fuel cell technology. Lest this example seem dated, in 2021 President Joe Biden received acclaim when he took the wheel of a powerful (and grotesquely large) electric Ford pickup truck in a short video that showed him accelerating rapidly ("Biden went pedal to metal," said ABC News).[163]

These vignettes are quintessentially American and even quintessentially Californian: established structures of the system of growth, circulation, and accumulation are not held up for scrutiny, while a fantasy of *effortless freight* achieved using "clean trucks" and "clean shipping" propels the *pursuit of scale* and speed.[164] In late 2020, as the world was gripped by the COVID-19 pandemic, the ports saw record movement of goods, even to the point where the Port of Long Beach was using industrially zoned space in urban Long Beach, far from the port, as warehouse overflow, to the dismay of residents and city officials, who complained about truck traffic, noise, and pollution.[165] The ports also celebrated the long-awaited opening of an updated bridge over the harbor; massive capital investment went into tearing down the old bridge and building a new one, higher above the water, to accommodate the movement of even larger shipping vessels. (Rising sea levels will also necessitate the raising of port infrastructure here and globally.) According to Port of Long Beach executive director Mario Cordero, "This new bridge is another major milestone in the Port's ongoing commitment to remain the most advanced and most competitive port in the world. . . . It is much more than a convenient roadway. It is a critical link in the global movement of cargo."[166]

The trajectory of bananas in the LA harbor shows that capital is sufficiently flexible to first build up and then tear down the banana-handling infrastructure it built, and to reroute the bananas to other ports when cargo volume and congestion made it untenable to process them in Long Beach and LA's ports. But port managers and state officials are banking on the durability of other infrastructures, even when these investments present dilemmas. For one thing, it is literally impossible to tell whether the ports will be able to meet the state's emissions standards. And there is reason to doubt this: in spite of standards set by the federal Clean Air Act, California is routinely in "extreme non-attainment" status throughout significant parts of the state, especially in the inland San Joaquin Valley, though also in Los Angeles County and the Inland Empire.[167] New technologies are under development but barely out of prototype stages. The fact that the ports keep building infrastructure to scale up operations, while betting that "clean technology" will save the day, is curious; one might wonder if there is an assumption that enforcement will be lax or, at the very least, if states of exception will be granted as part of normal operations.

And how many of these decisions are truly under local control? Of course, the decisions to invest in additional infrastructure like the bridge, requiring environmental and revenue sign-offs, are effected at the state and city levels. But as a journalist describing the ports' clean energy plans writes, "If the ports' plan backfires, cargo ships could take their business to competing ports around the country and one of Southern California's most important economic activities could dwindle."[168] This statement that local officials cannot control where global capital will choose to ship goods is likely true. At the same time, it should not necessarily be taken at absolute face value: officials have made similar claims to advance an agenda for economic growth and regional development *that serve certain interests*, even when this growth and development comes at the cost of labor and environmental protections. In the period 1972–2000, the LA region doubled its share of US global trade while the New York region saw its share fall by about half, and this was in large part a result of decisions by officials in Los Angeles.[169] Yet the port complex truly does present a paradoxical challenge for those governing it: as a node in a system, to make local changes to promote local quality of life might do little to unseat the system as a whole, especially as far as carbon emissions are concerned. Like the bananas departing the San Pedro Bay complex for San Diego and Port Hueneme, the same goods, dependent on circulation, might just turn up elsewhere. Petroleum especially has multiple routes from suppliers to buyers, especially as the Arctic warms and new oil can be tapped beneath the ice.[170] And pollution and violence accompany the circulation of goods, at close and long range; logistics is driven by literally lethal force.[171] The US military, too, is interested in "clean" technology, but not in service of irenic pursuits.[172]

Another thing to note is that the flexibility of capital to reroute bananas from the LA harbor largely has to do with the fact that the intensity of investment in this infrastructure was not *so* great, by comparison. Bananas are flexible, virtually unprocessed once they leave the docks in the grower states. Conveyor belts, fabric pouches, and even refrigerated warehouses are less durable than highways and railroads or petroleum pipelines and refineries. Whether or not it proves feasible to transition to renewable power for the banana ships, containers, and trucks, the LA harbor is an undeniable petroleumscape. "In both growth and decline, changes to petroleum activities, and by extension, the ports that serve them, have had major impacts on cities. . . . Railways and roadways [survive] and shape later user patterns, but shipping networks [can] disappear with little trace," writes architecture and planning scholar Carola Hein.[173] At this point there is little that points definitively to Southern California's petroleumscape becoming a post-petroleumscape. There is an inertial quality to the petroleum infrastructure; the port facilities are almost unimaginable without both their petroleum operations and petroleum as a fuel source. But even if the petroleum did depart, would this reduce violence, or merely shift it out of local sight?[174] How would other shipping patterns and infrastructures be affected?

A multispecies ebb and flow of lively commodities moves into and out of the port: lively because it animates a system of capital flow, and lively because some of its components are organismic. But these lively commodities are deadly too, all along their commodity chains. Bananas are relatively unprocessed plants, sometimes accompanied by fungus and tarantulas, and always bearing the imprint of labor and managerial apparatuses; meanwhile petroleum is "paradoxical kin."[175] People and wildlife alike have been harmed by the chemicals used to control Sigatoka: applications of pesticides kill and maim fish, shrimp, possums, and skunks; they cause serious health effects including cancer, sterility, and death in humans.[176] Of the chemical dust sprayed on crops, workers and families, and wildlife, anthropologist Alyssa Paredes writes that "banana fungicides are so deeply embedded in the violence of everyday landscapes that they have become almost entirely banal."[177] The intensity of storms and droughts in tropical regions caused by global warming threatens to alter not only commodity crop production but food security and habitability; and of course there is

a history and present of extractive, colonial relationships and violent suppression of workers and political sovereignty in banana-growing locales
as well.[178] Extraction regimes conscript racialized bodies for harm: not as
an incidental side effect but as a constitutive dynamic.[179] The movement of
goods at scale requires road-building, an emissions-intensive process that
accelerates habitat loss and death.[180] Air pollution harms and prematurely
kills people in Southern California, near the ports and along inland logistics corridors. Industrial violence also kills and maims wildlife.

To the grocery shopper or smoothie drinker, bananas simply appear,
handy and ready to eat. The mechanized ballet is obscured from view. So
too have been the capital currents that swept bananas first into and then
out of San Pedro Bay, as its port complex strains to process ever more volume of cargo, year over year. If capital must move or die, and its movements are deadly and/or undead, what are the implications for life?[181] The
infrastructural vitalism that managers impute to freight movement and
petroleumscapes sets the terms of ecological relation that are possible not
only in San Pedro Bay but in spaces of industrial production along freight
corridors and commodity chains. The ports and the systems into which
they are notched drive habitat loss, climate crisis, pollution, extraction,
and even ecocide in myriad, shifting ways. And yet, they offer an opportunity for thinking about how things might be otherwise, if transspecies
supply-chain justice were to become an objective of trade policy and as-
serted in supply-chain governance.

3

COASTAL TRANSLOCATIONS

In May 2010, the Aquarium of the Pacific in Long Beach opened a new exhibit featuring sea otters. The otter habitat was funded by a gift pledged in 2006 by BP, the petroleum company, which donated one million dollars to the aquarium. In the weeks leading up to the opening of the new habitat, the partnership suddenly became quite awkward, as BP's massive Deepwater Horizon oil discharge fouled the Gulf of Mexico starting in April, a sudden and dramatic nightmare for the gulf. Though the Aquarium of the Pacific acknowledged the public relations difficulties, its president said that there had been no debate about removing BP's name, stating: "We're comfortable about the course we have taken. . . . The challenge is, 'What can we learn from this going forward?'" For its part, BP's West Coast representative offered to stay away from the opening of the exhibit, so as not to court controversy.[1] It is unclear whether the spill had yet been granted its eventual status as the largest oil discharge in the history of the industry (to date) when the Aquarium of the Pacific issued its statement.[2] The president of the aquarium added, "Life is filled with ironies."[3]

Life is, indeed, filled with ironies. Before delving into the ones here, it is useful to situate the Aquarium of the Pacific and its otters. In 2010, when the expanded otter habitat opened, the Aquarium of the Pacific was a little over a decade old. The City of Long Beach built the aquarium in hopes of attracting tourism revenue in its man-made harbor area. When the Aquarium of the Pacific opened in 1998, California sea otters (southern sea otters) were classified as threatened and hovering near endangered status.[4] The southern sea otter had been decimated by hunting in the eighteenth and nineteenth centuries, and, by the turn of the twentieth century, many believed them on the verge of extinction.[5] Hunting both fur seals and otters was regulated by international treaty in 1911.[6] California banned the killing of otters in 1913.[7] But the population there dwindled to around fifty individuals.[8] Conservation efforts began in the middle of the twentieth century, and the southern sea otter received additional protections when the National Endangered Species Act passed in 1973; it now lives a post-industrialized-commodity life.[9] Its numbers have been stable but have not achieved substantial growth; it is still listed as threatened. Speaking in 1999, a curator for the Aquarium of the Pacific said, "one big oil spill could easily wipe them all out."[10] The otters' presence in the aquarium in their initial and later, BP-funded expanded habitat was intended by aquarium managers to support a conservation mission as well as recreation and tourism.

Southern sea otters' arc, from all but extinct to protected keystone species at the center of conservation efforts with an ambiguous future, is situated within a mass extinction event. Their trajectory in San Pedro Bay shows a regime of conservation in tandem and in tension with that of infrastructural vitalism. The otters' aquarium habitat is an invitation to explore otters' lives and deaths in local context over the past few decades. This history includes the forcible relocation of wild otters in the 1980s and 1990s and the otters' subsequent participation in a "surrogacy" program intended to increase the number of otters in the wild; it includes the production of aquatic habitat for otters and other creatures using commodified seawater. Living on the harbor's shifting silt, animals in captivity are still burdened by the toxic accumulations that affect their wild cousins.

Otters in post-1970 coastal California dwell in a curious contradiction. Extensive conservation efforts define their lives: they are meticulously accounted for in field studies; they are presented as charismatic objects of conservation; and they have been transformed from pelt profit to exalted "keystone species"—according to some, though for commercial fisherfolk, they are still competitors for catches and thus non grata. At the same time, though California sea otters are no longer *themselves* industrial commodities, their lives are still bound up in commodification processes: they are a commodified (furry) face of conservation and expected to support other life-forms, all while staying out of the way of petroleum extraction and transport as well as commercial shipping. Otters taking up their former habitats in great numbers is limited by commitments to infrastructural vitalism along the California coastline and especially in San Pedro Bay. Sociologist Caleb Scoville writes, "credible claims of endangerment are often made possible by the fulfillment of the very engineering needs and extractive relations to nature that are understood to cause endangerment in the first place," and this statement fits the California otters' post-1970 situation extremely well.[11] In other words, otter *conservation* is not *in conflict* with infrastructural vitalism as much as it is perversely *supported by* infrastructural vitalism, which has drawn otters into conservation schemes while sharply delimiting their lives.

(NO) OTTER ZONE

By the 1970s, southern sea otter numbers had risen from near extinction, but they totaled only around 1,650. This was perhaps one-tenth of their estimated population in the nineteenth century.[12] They were listed as threatened in 1977, under the Endangered Species Act.[13] The otters, whose historical range was at least Oregon to Baja California, were now concentrated in the central California coastal region between San Francisco and Point Conception, a zone also containing a high volume of oil transport. Simultaneously, conservationists identified otters as a "keystone" species, and thus especially worthy of targeted conservation efforts.[14] What makes otters a keystone species is that they feed on shellfish, including purple sea urchins, which themselves feed on kelp's anchoring system. Otters keep urchin numbers in check, which in turn promotes kelp health, and kelp provides habitat for other creatures, including fish nurseries.[15]

Wildlife managers thus suggested relocating otters from their coastal range to a single island in the Channel Islands (an eight-island archipelago in the Southern California Bight). The island, San Nicolas, is toward the southern end of the archipelago and farther west into open ocean. It is farther south than the bulk of the otters' coastal habitat, but managers believed the island possessed "ideal habitat [kelp forest] within the historical range of the southern sea otter," and the idea was to have a protected and growing colony of otters in case of a coastal spill.[16] San Nicolas also had infrastructural support for scientists monitoring the otter colony: already in place courtesy of the US Navy were housing and dining facilities, roads, a landing field, and, less relevant for the otters, a missile testing site.[17]

In tandem with trying to coax otters to flourish on San Nicolas Island, regulators also declared much of Southern California an "otter-free zone." This seemingly contradictory stance is explained by the fact that fishing interests were hostile to regulations protecting otters. For the fishing industry, otters represented competition for shellfish, leading to antagonism toward conservation efforts, even to otters being shot.[18] Otters were also sometimes caught inadvertently in gillnet fishing, resulting in death.[19] The state tried to balance these considerations by promising fishing groups that coastal areas south of Point Conception (near Santa Barbara) would be free of otter-protection dictates. Otters found in the supposed otter-free zone were supposed to be captured and returned to designated habitat.

Ironically, San Nicolas, being further south, was at a similar latitude as the coastal otter-free zone.

The forced relocation project's outcome appeared ambivalent at best. Scientists released 139 relocated otters on San Nicolas between 1987 and 1990. This was a significant proportion of the total southern sea otter population, roughly 8 percent. Releases were deliberately skewed toward female and juvenile otters, in order to drive population growth through reproduction (otters are polygynous, in the parlance of biology).[20] However, at least thirty-six relocated otters returned to their prior homes, the coastal range in central California—no small feat, as it required traversing over sixty miles of open ocean.[21] Another ten were "captured in the no-otter management zone" in coastal Southern California. Several other otters simply disappeared and were not accounted for; some likely died and others perhaps dispersed elsewhere, like coastal Baja California in Mexico. Ambiguity regarding these otters' whereabouts was increased by the fact that not all the otters were radiotagged, and ones released on San Nicolas without tags were not recaptured for tagging. Thus, in spite of some success with otter births on San Nicolas, averaging five pups per year, between the otters' tendency to flee San Nicolas and also to die, sometimes at the hands of fisherfolk, the population there did not grow. Instead, it remained steady from 1990 to 1998, at around 140 individuals; this was verified through field study.[22] Scientists concluded, "We learned that the basic, underlying concept was flawed: that you can move sea otters in this mechanistic way and expect them to do what you want them to do."[23]

Overall, otter population growth in California even during the conservation efforts of the 1980s and 1990s did not exceed about 5 percent per year, which frustrated scientists; otter populations in Alaska, Washington, and British Columbia had seen growth exceeding 15 percent.[24] When the San Nicolas program failed to generate abundant otters, regulators abandoned the otter-free zone in 2012, meaning otters were "allowed" the full range of the Southern California coast.[25] The otters received extra advocacy in the form of lawsuits from conservation groups, and wildlife managers turned to other strategies to increase the otter population.

OTTER "SURROGACY": FIRST STEPS

For the Monterey Bay Aquarium (MBA) in Northern California, which opened in 1984 with a now-famous kelp forest exhibit, otter conservation has been a key institutional effort. Starting in 1984, one plank of MBA's otter conservation was rescuing and rearing stranded otter pups in order to return them to the wild. Otter pups are dependent on mothers for nearly the first year of life, and stranded pups will not survive on their own. How-ever, by the 1990s it was clear that many rescued pups did not fare well upon release: "Pups rehabilitated for release have been reared by methods that rely heavily on human care, contributing to release failures. From 1986 to 2000, 67% of unsuccessful pup releases resulted from failures to reinte-grate with the wild population and avoid interactions with humans."[26] In response to this setback, conservationists proposed enlisting captive adult female otters to rear the pups instead. Scientists believed this would offer the pups a clearer boundary with regard to humans and give them better skills for living in the wild. Though there was some precedent with oppor-tunistic "surrogate mothering" as a technique for rearing orphaned animal young in the wild and in captivity, the otters were the first instance of cap-tive female surrogate animals rearing orphaned young with the intention to return the young to the wild.[27] Starting in 2002, MBA introduced surrogate mothering and set out to compare the success rates of pups raised by sur-rogates versus other means.

The initial surrogate mothers were two female otters rescued in 2001. They were rescued from the central California coast exhibiting signs of dis-tress (illness or injury) and, after treatment and rehabilitation, deemed un-fit for release back into the wild. However, the scientists called on them to become surrogates because they "demonstrated maternal behavior" dur-ing their time in care.[28] (This maternal behavior was not specified in the research I reviewed. An Aquarium of the Pacific mammologist said of an otter named Chloe that she had demonstrated maternal behavior, and that this could include sharing food or interacting with another otter as if to carry it on her back.[29]) Scientists introduced the females to stranded pups and observed successful "bonding" after a short time (sometimes the pups and females needed more than one introduction to one another, some-times not, but neither surrogate rejected a pup) (fig. 31). The otter surro-gate mothers' edge over other methods of rearing stranded pups included their "species-specific mentoring and tactile stimulation while grooming and nurturing the pup. The surrogate also provided nourishment through food sharing and demonstrated feeding methods, such as dismember-ing crabs and cracking open hard-shelled bivalves using rocks as tools."[30] Otters not raised by surrogates were still offered simulated "ottering," in-cluding ocean swims with a free diver, grooming (by humans), and encour-agement in feeding on clams, mussels, and crabs.[31]

When scientists undertook systematic comparison, they concluded that surrogate-reared pups had an advantage over other pups whose care had been overseen more directly by humans. In research published in 2007, scientists compared surrogate-raised pups with pups raised exclusively by

FIGURE 31. Illustration in scientific paper showing the same otter (denoted with arrows), first as a pup in captivity with her foster mother in (a), and later in the wild, rearing a pup of her own, in (b). From Mayer et al. (2019).

humans in a cohort of other pups without adult otters, and pups raised by humans in "isolation," that is, without any otter contact.[32] Perhaps unsurprisingly, surrogate-raised pups had the most success: they demonstrated skills needed to survive in the wild and they avoided interactions with humans. They also learned "otter skills" more quickly, exhibiting developmental milestones such as "(1) pounding objects together on their chest, (2) foraging on (diving, searching, retrieving, eating) partially prepared/cracked open live-prey (mussels, clams, crabs), (3) biting open whole live mussels, (4) pounding open whole live clams, and (5) successfully feeding on live crabs" around two to three weeks earlier than their peers. Otters raised in otter pup cohorts had "mixed" release outcomes: they tended to learn these foraging and feeding skills, but they did not universally avoid interacting with humans, so some were relocated after initial release to more remote areas where interaction with humans was less likely. The pups raised in isolation, who numbered the fewest, fared the worst: one was recaptured and placed in permanent captivity soon after release since it was apparent that the pup did not have the skills for survival, and the other "disappeared" after a very short time in the wild. Scientists concluded that pups raised by surrogates had a one-year survival rate comparable to free-ranging (wild) juvenile otters (70–75 percent), while the survival rate of non-surrogate-raised juveniles was less than half that (31 percent).

The benefit of surrogate care to pups seems clear. Scientists speculated that there could be an evolutionary benefit for the "mothers" in surrogacy as well: "Adoption behavior . . . may provide a young female with experience necessary to, at some point in the future, increase survival of her own offspring," they opined.[33] In any event, they noted that adoption and "alloparenting" had been observed in wild southern sea otters (though the article makes reference to only one instance) and other marine mammals whose investment in young is high. For all these reasons, scientists concluded that surrogacy using captive adult females was a viable strategy. After this initial comparative exercise, they settled on continuing and expanding otter surrogacy.

Several years later, scientists evaluated the project of otter surrogacy, having had time to longitudinally follow surrogate-reared pups' success in the wild. They concluded that surrogate-reared and wild otters had similar rates of survival and reproduction.[34] This finding justified the expansion of otter surrogacy, including beyond Monterey Bay Aquarium. Now I will turn to the otters in Long Beach, first establishing the Aquarium of the Pacific in its local context, San Pedro Bay. Otter conservation here literally rests on land manipulated to form the ports and is funded by oil profits; conservation and infrastructural vitalism are complementary yet contradictory.

WATERY LIFE IN CAPTIVITY

The Aquarium of the Pacific was founded in the 1990s during a period of questions about what to do with Long Beach's harbor area. Much of the coast in San Pedro Bay is devoted to industrial use, and the entire shoreline is manipulated. On the far side of the port complex, near the border with Orange County, is a recreational beach. But the waterfront area right between the beach and the port, nearest to downtown Long Beach, had been subject to "ups, downs, and an identity crisis," in the words of a *New York Times* reporter writing in 2000.[35] In the very early twentieth century, the waterfront hosted the Pike, a Coney-Island-esque bathing area, boardwalk, and amusement park featuring rides and games, concessions, an elaborate hand-carved carousel, and, in a later era, tattoo shops (the buildup to World War II brought the navy to the harbor, and sailors brought demand for tattoos).[36]

In 1979, the Pike was formally shuttered, though it was well off its heyday before then. The area retained some tourist attractions, notably the docked RMS *Queen Mary* ocean liner, Howard Hughes's massive wooden plane, the *Spruce Goose* (encased in a custom-built geodesic dome), and an annual Grand Prix motor race, begun in 1975.[37] But the area was underutilized by urban development standards, and the city considered how to update it. The Disney Corporation managed both the *Spruce Goose* and the *Queen Mary* starting in 1988.[38] Around then, Disney expressed interest in siting a massive ocean-related theme park in the Long Beach harbor, to be called DisneySea; the entire complex was to include a research center and resort, and to be collectively called Port Disney.[39] Fantastical artistic renderings of the complex resembled the contemporary Biosphere 2 artificial environment, with a glistening science-fiction sheen evocative of the space age. (A space imaginary at the edge of the sea had precedent in Sealab; see chap. 4.) But these plans were short-lived; the park was never built.[40] The harbor nonetheless contained glimpses of futuristic fancy: a 1967 artist's rendering of an oil island at night rivals the Disney imaginary (fig. 32); and the *Queen Mary* and dome, although divested by Disney in the 1990s, still remain today (fig. 33).

Fantastical harbor flourishes aside, the 1990s hit Long Beach hard economically. The navy consolidated its Southern California presence in San Diego, closing a naval station and hospital as well as shuttering a shipyard in the Long Beach harbor. In turn, aviation manufacturing plants reliant on military contracts also closed. It was in this context that the city looked to cultivate tourist attractions, with or without Disney's involvement. (Simultaneously, the region pursued port development as an economic strategy.) It secured municipal financing to build an aquarium—albeit a more modest, far less spectacular one than the facility Disney had planned—and develop the harbor with a shopping center and refurbished convention center.[41] The aquarium was paid for through government funding and philanthropic contributions, although indirectly the municipal funds were tied to the city's oil revenues (fig. 34).[42] The city owns the aquarium, which is managed and operated by a nonprofit organization.[43]

Public institutions for the display of animals emerged in larger Euro-American cities in the nineteenth century, often with funding from scientific societies.[44] Projects of taxonomy and empire, displaying unfamiliar

FIGURE 32. Artist's rendering of an oil island at night, 1967.
Courtesy Port of Long Beach.

FIGURE 33. The RMS *Queen Mary* ocean liner with *Spruce Goose* dome. Long Beach, 2011.
Photo by David Jones, CC-BY 2.0 license.

FIGURE 34. Aquarium of the Pacific exterior, Long Beach Harbor, 2021. Note the cranes at the port on the horizon.
Photo by McKenzie Stribich.

animals from other locales, zoos and aquariums both satisfied and stoked public interest in animal life. Some early American zoos also bore the influence of the urban parks movement, emphasizing conservation of native species. Zoos often resembled amusement parks, offering children rides on ponies and Galápagos tortoises, transporting visitors around the parks on buses and trains, and dramatically exhibiting trained seals and chimpanzees to enthralled audiences, according to historian Pamela Henson. Not unlike circus sideshows, they emphasized the novelty and exoticism of their offerings, and they competed with other zoos, even to the point of keeping animal care regimens secret.[45] By the middle of the twentieth century, conservation emerged as a more consistent concern, and zoos were coming under fire for animal exploitation and poor conditions.[46] By the late twentieth century, zoos had brought conservation fully into their remit, including cooperating to serve as genetic reservoirs for endangered species, sharing information and resources, and addressing conservation in exhibits and mission statements.[47]

Both the Monterey Bay Aquarium and Aquarium of the Pacific's work with otters is in line with these trends. Zoos and aquariums conduct conservation work both in situ and ex situ, in field sites.[48] But aquariums, unlike zoos, often work closely with local wildlife officials too.[49] The aquariums' otter work involves housing a native (sub)species whose numbers have dwindled in the wild with the goals of educating the public and expanding the population, within the parameters of their own institutional mandates and constraints.[50]

As noted above, MBA has had ambitious otter conservation programs central to its mission since its inception. The Aquarium of the Pacific has also hosted otters since its earliest days. When it was founded in 1998, otters were not local to the immediate Southern California coastal area near Long Beach, due to the otter-free zone, though of course they were ecologically native to the area. The Aquarium of the Pacific immediately worked closely with MBA to host otters, offering housing and care for otters that could not live in the wild; this allowed the two institutions working together to care for more animals than MBA could alone. The Aquarium of the Pacific declared its first full summer in operation, 1999, to be "Sea Otter Summer," with a full public relations blitz. Its charismatic otters were Monterey Bay transplants, young animals who were not suitable candidates for release into the wild and instead resided in the Aquarium of the Pacific's Northern Pacific habitat (here Northern Pacific means essentially California and north, that is, the cooler water zone north of the warm-cold mixing in the ecotone that is the Southern California Bight). At least two of the otters were orphaned during El Niño storms in 1997 (rough water and wind can cause pups to get separated from mothers, and storms are a common cause of pup stranding).[51] Given the timing, these young animals would not have been candidates for surrogacy, which did not begin until 2001.

One of the Aquarium of the Pacific's otters, a young female aptly named Summer, featured in a heartbreaking and frankly bizarre *Los Angeles Times* article that accompanied the exhibition:

> A little girl named Summer arrived in Long Beach last month with what sounds like a Hollywood crisis: a lousy fur coat, a weight problem and a dependency issue. Summer, an 11-month-old sea otter at the Long Beach Aquarium of the Pacific, also would be distressed to know she's missing her spot in the limelight. This Saturday the aquarium will launch Sea Otter Summer, but the budding diva will be in rehab.[52]

Distressing anthropomorphism and peculiar pathologizing aside, the article paints a vivid picture of the struggles stranded otters and their human caregivers can face. When rescued by MBA, Summer's caregivers hoped to rehabilitate her for release into the wild, but over time, she failed to thrive: her coat did not come in with sufficient thickness to keep her afloat and warm, which was evident when human handlers took her on daily ocean swims as part of rehabilitation efforts. (Otters' coats are dense, and pups' fur actually helps them float because of how it traps air, which saves their bodies energy. The drive to commodify this lustrous fur is what led otters to be hunted to near extinction.[53]) Summer did not gain sufficient weight, probably because of being chilled. And her "addiction" to suckling towels was an unfortunate effect of her separation from her mother when she was only one week old.[54]

Aquarium curators laid out a comprehensive plan of care for Summer. Her towel suckling appeared to be a core cause of her failure to thrive. Without otters to care for pups, human handlers gave otter pups towels to suckle, cuddle, and groom themselves with, "a replacement for their moms." Handlers suspected the enthusiasm with which Summer took to snuggling and suckling towels was actually damaging her fur; according to laboratory analysis of her pelt, the fibers were twisted and damaged. So in addition to continuing to trying to get her weight up through attentive feeding, caregivers weaned the pup off towels: she went from one per hour to two per day, with the goal of being able to comfortably give them up entirely. Her handler said: "The rewards of the job are similar to those of parenting[.] I enjoy the satisfaction of seeing the otters hit certain milestones. I also think it's a responsible act. Summer couldn't survive in the ocean, but she's healthy. Why not give her a good life, while educating the public and us about how otters live so we can use the knowledge to help the environment?"[55]

Summer lived another eleven years at the Aquarium of the Pacific, though she never fully recovered from the health issues she experienced as a pup. Aquarium staff tried to diagnose and cure Summer, unsuccessfully; veterinary dermapathologists suspected her fur and thermoregulation issues perhaps ultimately derived from an immune-mediated condition, similar to an autoimmune disease in humans.[56] The causes of autoimmune disease are complex, but exposures to toxins are strong possibilities; effects of chemical violence are not necessarily immediate, even leading to epigenetic harms.[57] In spite of Summer's health problems, aquarium officials stated that she had led a "relatively healthy and apparently happy" life with her exhibit-mates at the Aquarium of the Pacific, until reaching a more advanced age when her health declined again, leading to compromised organ function. They determined that euthanasia was the most humane course, but Summer died on her own hours before the planned procedure, in September 2010.[58] Twelve years is a somewhat shorter lifespan than might be expected for a female otter in captivity, though not dramatically so. Her loss was mourned by aquarium staff and caregivers, many of whom had known her since her arrival.

Around the time of Summer's death in 2010, the Aquarium of the Pacific opened a new animal care facility. The 14,000-square-foot facility was unusual in one main regard: it included a large room for veterinary exams open to the public (through a pane of glass). On most days, aquarium staff perform veterinary exams and medical procedures on aquarium animals, in public view, with either a staff interpreter out in front of the window or one inside who explains what staff are doing over a public address system for viewers outside. Simulations of veterinary procedures are on display even when the aquarium is closed (figs. 35, 36).

One day in September 2019, two otter dental procedures were listed on a whiteboard: a root canal for Betty, age seven, and a tooth extraction for Maggie, age seventeen.[59] A curator said that there is treatment activity on public view at least a couple of days per week, and that the facility conducts nearly every procedure in public view (exceptions might be if no interpretive staff were available to narrate, or in case of a high-stakes procedure where the patient might be in danger of "crashing," in which case blinds would be drawn). An adult sea otter would get at least one exam per year, including blood draws, x-rays, and an ultrasound, all during regular business hours in full public view.[60] The aquarium holds around 11,000 animals (fish, reptiles, mammals, birds), so there is a lot of opportunity for routine exams that can double as public programming.[61] While the Aquarium of

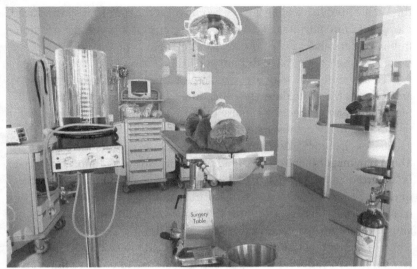

FIGURE 35. Plush toy otter "receiving anesthesia" on the surgery table, on display after hours. Aquarium of the Pacific, Long Beach, 2021.
Photo by McKenzie Stribich.

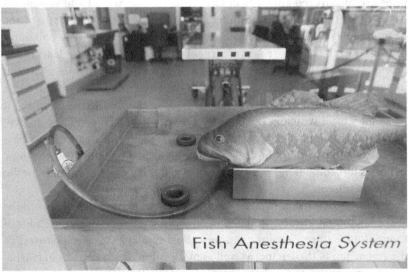

FIGURE 36. Display of "Fish Anesthesia System" with a toy stuffed fish. Aquarium of the Pacific, Long Beach, 2021.
Photo by McKenzie Stribich.

the Pacific's public viewing facility was novel at the time it was introduced, more and more facilities like it are being built; it is a trend that promotes public understanding of and transparency about the institution's activities.[62] (Though the curator did not spell this out, it also helps communicate to the public the expense associated with so much care for so many animals.) At the same time, the procedures with the aquarium's actual living animals, and especially the use of plush children's toys to stand in for wildlife, arguably domesticate these creatures, blurring boundaries. These spectacles also normalize "nature" in human care, or even on life support. Though managers act in pursuit of "autonomy" for wild animals, this state is "deferred and impossible to achieve," requiring dependence (especially in the case of highly managed creatures at the edge of extinction).[63] This has potential implications for how the aquarium's audience relates to these animals in the aquarium as well as outside of it.

As of 2020, the Aquarium of the Pacific could house up to six adult otters comfortably, but it was expanding its capacity in order to implement a surrogacy program. The agreement the Aquarium of the Pacific formalized with MBA in early 2020 solidified a commitment to create the conditions to be able to add as many as five adult females who could nurture and socialize pups. As many as ten to fifteen stranded southern sea otter pups are discovered annually in California, so this would add significant capacity for otter care. Like Summer, all stranded pups will first go to the Monterey Bay Aquarium for around eight weeks, and then some will move to Long Beach for longer-term rearing (six to seven months), learning to groom and feed and act like "regular" sea otters.[64] If a pup does well with its surrogate mother in the Aquarium of the Pacific, it will return to MBA for another month or two to socialize with peers, and then, assuming it is deemed fit, it will be released into the wild. Released young adults will be radiotagged with VHF transmitters and trackable for up to three years; scientists will no longer be able to track the otters once the transmitters' batteries die, though the tracking devices will remain in the animals for the rest of their lives.

Sea otters come ashore rarely and can perform all essential life functions at sea, including sleeping and giving birth. Charismatic representations of them often feature a mother and pup afloat in a kelp bed.[65] The otters of the Aquarium of the Pacific, as well as many other creatures, live in marine water that approximates their oceanic habitats. The aquarium's water supply therefore is a life-sustaining consideration of major consequence for the institution and its residents. It is sourced from the harbor just outside the aquarium's door, processed by a company that also supplies water to other aquariums and marine science facilities throughout the western United States and for which the Aquarium of the Pacific is a major customer.

Founded in 1988, Catalina Water Company commodifies a naturally occurring substance, ocean water.[66] In claiming water as a resource, processing it, and selling it, the company provides an environment to sustain ocean life in circumstances where it would not be found otherwise: in conditions of captivity and often in geographic locales far from the species' native environments. Tropical fish in home or institutional aquariums, otters in conservation programs, jellyfish in veterinary care, and mollusks in neuroscience research settings may all find themselves swimming in this water (or, in the case of mollusks, anchored in it). Commodification of ocean water is driven by the commercial trade of tropical fish: "The aquarium hobby could never have become what it is today without the business interests that were, and still are, involved."[67] Recent estimates are that 25–30 million animals from more than 2,000 species are traded annually, including fish and corals; animals are imported from the Philippines, Indonesia, the Solomon Islands, Sri Lanka, Australia, Fiji, the Maldives, and Palau, especially richly biodiverse reef ecologies; and domestic fish outnumber pet cats and dogs in both the United States and United Kingdom.[68] Most collectible animals are taken from the wild, and many marine species' needs for breeding in captivity are poorly understood.[69] Of course, this practice of removing animals from oceans for global hobbyist trade has ecological implications in their sites of origin. These accumulating environmental injuries are not the main focus here but bear notice as a significant effect of the commodification of marine life and seawater.[70]

Unsurprisingly, supplying conditions for marine life, let alone healthy marine life, is challenging. The Aquarium of the Pacific's water comes from the Pacific Ocean via Catalina Water Company, but another option for coastal aquariums is building a water intake system with pipes going out into the sea to take in and discharge water. (A curator at the Aquarium of the Pacific speculated that this would be hard to gain approval for in California's present-day regulatory environment.[71]) Facilities that are not coastally located are more likely to manufacture their water, mixing salt and fresh water. Catalina Water Company touts its product by stating, "All synthetic salt mixtures have one thing in common. They are attempting to duplicate real saltwater. Catalina Water Company provides real ocean saltwater, not a synthetic substitute. . . . Synthetic Saltwater, while being basically sound, simply can not provide all the subtle chemical benefits of true saltwater." The volume of water that the company sells for simulated ocean environments is at least ten million gallons per year.[72] The Aquarium of the

FIGURE 37. Truck delivering Catalina Water Company seawater ("Real Ocean Water")
to laboratory at California State University, Northridge, 2016.
Courtesy Mike Kaiser.

Pacific is a major client and takes several deliveries per week; its biggest
tank, as of 2012, was a 56,000-gallon quarantine tank, part of the Molina
Care Center, a holding tank for large animals that need to be kept separately.[73] Deliveries of fresh ocean water at the scale needed by aquariums
are delivered via truck in food-grade stainless steel tankers (fig. 37). Catalina Water Company also sells packaged seawater for home aquarium use
through the PetCo pet store chain.[74]

The quarantine tank leads toward a further consideration of the water itself. To become commodified, seawater must be processed. Catalina
Water Company notes on its website that it "starts with natural ocean seawater which is filtered, (fiber, sand, and charcoal) ozonated, and protein
skimmed."[75] Before using the water for its marine life, the Aquarium of the
Pacific also runs its own tests to make sure it is safe for the animals, and
filters it again.[76] The 1999 *Los Angeles Times* article about Summer the pup
also offers details about how seriously the Aquarium of the Pacific takes
its marine environment: "Before he climbs the metal ladder to the access
door of Summer's tank, [Summer's handler] steps in two bins of liquid, one
containing water and one a disinfectant. He'll step in them again when he

leaves. 'We're fussy about quarantine here,' he explains. 'I don't want to take any germs into her habitat or out to the rest of the aquarium.'"[77] Of course, extra precautions are indeed necessary for public health in congregate settings (as the COVID-19 pandemic recently showed when the virus cut a tragic, lethal, and preventable path through prisons and elder care facilities).

But this attention to hygiene, water filtration, and monitoring in the aquarium setting exposes an irony. Otters and other life-forms under custodial care of the aquarium are provided cleaner and safer water than their counterparts in the wild. As noted at the outset of this chapter, worries of otter annihilation in the wake of an oil discharge prompted conservation efforts in the 1980s, leading to, among other developments, the otter relocation to San Nicolas Island. The rationale was not only to prompt the settlement of a new territory but to have a population reservoir in a more protected locale, less vulnerable to spills than the near-coastal area the otters inhabited. And spilled oil is not the only source of chemical harm for otters: industrial agricultural fertilizers and other contaminants wash into the ocean from land, bringing toxins that can sicken and even kill marine otters.[78] Toxins should thus not be understood as mere "wayward molecules": they are substances whose patterned presences in land, water, and bodies are indicative of particular political and economic relations.[79]

"WHAT CAN WE LEARN FROM THIS?"

What can we conclude about southern sea otters and life in San Pedro Bay? The most obvious point is that there are no wild otters in San Pedro Bay now, even though it is within their historical range. Since the 1970s, otters have been protected, and significant efforts have gone into increasing their numbers in California. Though reasons are no doubt complex, at the core, scientists have determined that otter conservation from roughly 1980 through 2000 was hindered more by excess death than by failure to reproduce. Though conservation efforts succeeded in increasing the otter population from around 1,800 in the 1970s to a high of over 3,200 in 2016, their population has not increased as much as desired by wildlife managers.[80] Scientists observed that survival of "prime-aged" otters in the wild was declining. Causes of death included shark bites, fishing entanglement, and starvation. Infectious diseases including parasites are increasing as well.[81] They concluded that, overall, "conditions in central California have become less favorable for the survival and reproduction of sea otters over the past several decades."[82] Recent data bear this out: recovery appears stalled, dipping lower again to around 2,900 otters in 2019. In more favorable conditions, wildlife managers would likely have seen a stronger rebound, but to date southern sea otters have not attained a population where they might be candidates for delisting (removal from the Endangered Species List).[83]

This explains some of the measures chronicled above. For instance, scientists and aquarists focused more on increasing survival than, for instance, on forced breeding in captivity.[84] In fact, North American facilities housing southern sea otters have, in conversation with the US Fish and Wildlife Service, placed a moratorium on breeding captive otters in order to preserve institutional space for rescued nonreleasable otters.[85] The Aquarium of the Pacific is indeed expanding its space for nonreleasable otters, but some of those otters are also being put to work as surrogates, raising pups for wild release. Such a project maximizes preservation of individual members of an endangered species, while still adding to the wild population. Surrogacy research also continues, as wildlife managers hope to increase "the knowledge and experience necessary to successfully reintroduce sea otters in the event of a catastrophic decline in the wild population."[86] Otter surrogacy represents a flexible strategy that works with the needs of stranded pups and tendencies of adult female otters that contribute to life begetting more life. Even though surrogacy is not commonly observed in otters in the wild, this practice supports thriving pups who can later move into the wild. Juveniles move on from the maternal relationship when they normally would, and it does not seem particularly cruel or extractive to the surrogates the way forced breeding or even wet-nursing might. (One might however wonder why there is an insistence on calling this "surrogate motherhood," rather than, for instance, otter "foster parenting" or "adoption," or, less bureaucratically, godparenting or "auntie-ing." Surrogacy specifically refers to carrying a pregnancy and giving birth for another, not to practices wherein many creatures sometimes contribute part-time or full-time care for the young of another parent.[87] The term for this in biology is alloparenting, but, curiously, even in scientific papers about otters, the gendered and arguably misleading term "surrogate mother" is usually used.)

Since the morass of San Nicolas Island, another strategy scientists have pursued to further multiply otter life is releasing only surrogate-raised pups into new habitats: pups stranded on the open sea coast have been released into the Elkhorn Slough, an estuarial area south of Santa Cruz. Juvenile otters who learned "ottering" from surrogate mothers but were "naive" to the slough habitat took to it much better than adults who were captured and released in the San Nicolas episode. Tracking the introduced otters since release, scientists have concluded that they are doing relatively well there: as of 2019, the surrogate-reared otters and their descendants represent at least half of the otters in the Elkhorn Slough; their reproduc-

tion rates match those of wild otters; and the total population of slough otters would not have been possible to achieve without the introduced otters
and their offspring.[88] Scientists regarded Elkhorn Slough as a "degraded
ecosystem," so introducing "keystone" otters there was understood not to
be for the otters' sole benefit but for the wider ecosystem as well. In other
words, their lives matter not only for their own sake but also for the sake
of environmental futures.[89] Scientists concluded that releasing these young
otters into new habitat where they thrived was a "viable alternative to capturing and relocating wild sea otters."[90] (Certainly, capturing and relocating wild adult otters does not seem like much of an alternative at all, from
the perspective of either otters or wildlife managers!)

Yet even though southern sea otters in conservation are currently not
subject to the violence of forced breeding or forced relocation, all is not
well. The only known otters in residence in San Pedro Bay are residents of
the Aquarium of the Pacific, living in an artificial habitat, on infilled estuarial land. The tragic figure of Summer the pup offers an opportunity for reflection on important themes for life in San Pedro Bay. Though her health
problems were never definitively diagnosed, the possibility of something
like an autoimmune disease invites questions of whether Summer experienced toxic chemical exposures. Toxic substances transgress bodily boundaries with ease and can cause immune-mediated inflammatory diseases and
endocrine disruptions.[91] Her sparse and damaged fur would have spelled
the end for her in the wild; otters' fur keeps them insulated and buoyant.
This is why grooming is such an important behavior for survival and is also
(part of) why oil is so threatening, as oil can penetrate fur and wreak havoc
with otter fur's precisely evolved warming and water-repellent properties. Ingestion or inhalation of oil is obviously toxic as well and can happen
when an oiled otter grooms itself. In captivity in the Aquarium of the Pacific, Summer was protected from further toxic harm by rigorous hygienic
practices. There is no reason to doubt either the quality of abundant expert
care she received nor the sincerity of her handlers' affection for her; after
they determined releasing her back into the wild would be irresponsible,
she was given a "good life" in captivity.

And yet the care Summer received represents how the conservation
response to vulnerable wildlife is intervention in the lives of endangered
species, often in measures that are not matched with equivalent harm-
prevention efforts.[92] Wild otters, like other wildlife, are nakedly vulnerable.[93] Though oil is not the only source of toxic exposure for otters, it
deserves special scrutiny. Oil discharges are sources of acute toxicity, but
oil operations (including not only extraction and refining but fueling and
transportation) provide a lower-level backdrop of *constant residual toxicity*

for otters and other life-forms. In San Pedro Bay and along the California coast, there are deep linkages between bodily accumulation of toxins and shipping infrastructure. A warming earth, caused by the burning of fossil fuels, threatens oceans through warming and acidification, which unsurprisingly threatens otters and their ecologies. In 2020, scientists reported a massive kelp die-off due to a marine heatwave in California coastal waters between 2014 and 2016. Otters, of course, depend on kelp, and otters help keep kelp forest ecologies in balance due to their predation of shellfish.[94] Summer's handler, a father of human children, chided her for being a "kelp brat" when she yowled for food—and fed her promptly.[95] At present, if captive or wild otters were to yowl for kelp, their needs might go unmet: scientists now estimate that around 95 percent of the bull kelp in Northern California has died over the past decade, and they believe this is an abrupt event caused by sudden heating rather than a gradual loss.[96] And disappearing kelp is not the otters' only problem: warming waters have drawn sharks into waters that were previously too cold for them, and their predation on sea otters has increased dramatically. Warming waters also affect otter health by creating favorable conditions for parasites and harmful bacteria to thrive. According to research published in 2021, Monterey Bay has seen an 86 percent drop in the number of otters since 2014.[97] Disappearing kelp is also a problem for many other species, as it provides fish nursery habitat; without kelp, fish populations will suffer.

The dwindling opportunities for multitudinous life along the California coast should raise questions about the scale and aims of interventions. A tension between care for individual members of endangered species, or species-level intervention, on the one hand, versus broader responses to ecological threats like curbing the burning of fossil fuel or drawing back on monoculture cultivation in industrial agriculture, on the other, is subtly illustrated in the Aquarium of the Pacific's otter habitat description.[98] The Aquarium of the Pacific opines that "a caring public can make a difference" in the southern sea otter's recovery. Steps it recommends the public take are "clean up the land. You can help by reducing, reusing, and recycling and taking care to properly dispose of hazardous wastes."[99] On the face of it, these recommendations seem unobjectionable—but they promote personal consumer responsibility and draw attention away from industrial sources of pollution, regulatory frameworks, and larger political and collective problems. A personal responsibility framing is starkly apparent in this passage from the Aquarium of the Pacific otter habitat website:

> Oil has the potential to seriously harm or kill sea otters. Help keep oil or anti-freeze out of storm drains that lead to the ocean by not letting it spill

on the ground. Recycle used motor oil. Cut down on oil consumption and oil-based products. And use public transportation, walk, bike, or join a carpool.

Household chemicals and pet waste are some of the other pollutants that are harmful to sea otters and other marine life. Take a second look at everything you put down your drain since most of this waste makes its way back to rivers, streams, and the ocean. Dispose of hazardous waste properly.[100]

Though it recognizes oil's ability to maim or kill otters, the lengthy list of "helpful" things one can do places responsibility squarely on the consumer. Industrial waste and the petroleum industry go unacknowledged.

The Aquarium of the Pacific does not fully shy away from promoting legislative intervention: it urges the public to lend support for legislation to protect kelp forests, otter habitats, and marine protected areas. This is a larger scale, though given the crisis otters (and people) face, it is likely still inadequate to "solve" ecological catastrophe within small, bounded parcels of land and water, as opposed to speaking aloud of the systemic problem of infrastructural vitalism, which privileges extraction, shipping, and trade at scale (and drives ocean heating through fossil fuel consumption). Notably, the Aquarium of the Pacific also recommends members of the public support "legislation and community efforts to improve wetlands."[101] This seems to be of a piece with the other legislative recommendations, but in point of fact, present-day coastal California oil drilling permits are often granted in a complex offsetting scheme, whereby former extraction sites are returned to communities and often "developed" for wildlife use, in exchange for new permits to drill.[102] In other words, "support for wetlands development" may translate to tacit endorsement of expanding extraction activities. Given that the named sponsor for the otter habitat was BP, a founding sponsor for the Aquarium of the Pacific overall is automotive company Honda, and that the Aquarium of the Pacific was initially funded with municipal bonds related to oil revenue, a revenue source that continues into the present, this raises questions.[103]

Or maybe it doesn't. It is possible that the aquarium's messaging about otters and conservation would be identical without any petroleum industry sponsorship (which implicates municipal and regional leadership as well, as the ports and petroleum are their economic "lifeblood"). The problem is that petroleum industry sponsorship muddies (or oils) the water of an aquarium's mission, given petroleum's harm to life in general and sea life in particular. The argument can be made that philanthropy is corrupt and despotic. It rewards resource profiteering. Even if generous or well-intended, philanthropic giving is generally donor-directed in ways that cannot help being regressive and antidemocratic, especially compared to progressive taxation and democratic deliberation about where funds should be spent.[104] It is also often not transparent or accountable. Companies can set agendas to shape regulatory environments that favor their activities and then go on to engage in philanthropic distribution projects that shore up their reputations, presenting their industries and founders in favorable lights. Meanwhile public priorities go unmet or are held hostage to the whim of those with massive wealth. As stated earlier, it is not possible to claim that a greenwashing agenda was definitely at play with the BP Sea Otter Habitat—but that is precisely the problem. Though oil is acknowledged as a source of harm to otters, the oil industry's influence is unspoken, an inevitability. The sponsorship creates a conflict of interest, even if the Aquarium of the Pacific strives for integrity. To be provocative, if Summer was injured by oil toxicity, what does it mean that her rescue was philanthropically funded by the industry that harmed her? Does a "good life" in captivity fulfill its obligation to her, or her fellow kelp forest neighbors?

Contemporary zoos and aquariums are moving to recognize that different practices and ethical principles guide attending to ecologies and populations versus individual animals or even species.[105] Critics have charged that more could be done for conservation if such institutions closed and devoted resources and expertise to in situ efforts. Zoo and aquarium managers have responded that the bulk of their revenue comes from visitors (admissions, concessions, and merchandise, as well as memberships), so their operating budgets would be reduced without public facilities.[106] Institutions also "argue that once visitors learn to care about the wild animals they encounter in zoos, they will also be inclined to contribute to the conservation of their conspecifics (namely, members of the same species) in the wild," in the words of legal scholar and geographer Irus Braverman.[107] I personally find zoos and aquariums situated within mainstream conservation science and state (geo)politics to be politically and aesthetically troubling, but there is true ethical complexity here, and doubtless there is not a "one size fits all" solution either. Given that these facilities do exist, it seems desirable to approach their messaging with care and rigor; their relationships to sponsors, not least petroleum industry sponsorships, are worthy of sustained attention.[108] One might also wonder if such facilities could be explicitly reoriented toward consideration of how to share a future with nonhuman creatures amid mass annihilation.[109]

In a virtual tour of the Northern Pacific exhibition in late 2020, a cura-

FIGURE 38. Chloe the otter standing up, reaching toward her handler. Aquarium of the Pacific Virtual Otter Encounter, 2020.
Screenshot by the author.

tor explained how she hoped the take-home message for attendees was "biodiversity," which she defined as "life" plus "differences." She said that even though the tour had focused on individual animals (including young adult southern sea otter Chloe, fig. 38), attendees should think of the "ecosystem" as a *whole*. "With more biodiversity, we have more resilience. More species can occupy more niches. But they all depend on this cold-water ecosystem." She did mention climate change but did not name its causes. She said, "As humans, we can help; we have all this technology, and we are learning more and more every day."[110] As the tour had run long, her wrap-up presentation seemed rushed; she did not connect the dots between cold water and "helpful" technology—nor between warming waters and industrial activities. But notes of human exceptionalism and technological fixes rang out. She presented the Pacific habitat as an object for manipulation, not a site of shared present and future.

This being said, explicit consideration of habitat and "environment" was, if not a novel approach in 2020, indicative of a shift over time. The addition of the aquarium in Long Beach, some argued, represented something of a change in terms of how the city presented and perhaps thought about itself. Though in the perpetual shadow of Los Angeles, Long Beach has its own center of gravity, and in the late 1990s it was California's fifth-largest city.[111] Its main identity as a city for many years was as a port town with a large navy presence; putting on an "environmental" public face was not a self-evident move in light of the city's history. Writing in 2000, a *New York Times* reporter described "knowing one had arrived" in Long Beach when driving south from LA by the sight of a huge oil refinery.[112] Like Long Beach's human residents, it is nearly impossible to overstate the degree to which Aquarium of the Pacific creatures live within a petroleumscape, surrounded by oil extraction and major petroleum refining and shipping operations .[113] When planning the aquarium, officials remarked, "We had a mind-altering experience one day . . . when one of our consultants said 'well, you can't have an outdoor exhibit with sea lions and expect them to listen to race cars at the (Long Beach) Grand Prix.'"[114] The annual motor race continues to this day.[115] Officials opted to build the initial aquarium as an entirely indoor space, though subsequent modifications have added outdoor exhibit space, with only a few "noise-tolerant" animals, like jelly-fish and rays.[116]

In spite of this history, arguably Long Beach has shifted its image some-what. Around the time the Aquarium of the Pacific was built, the Port of Long Beach began a public relations blitz claiming to be a "Green Port," signaling its commitment to "improving the region's environmental qual-ity of life."[117] The Aquarium of the Pacific characterizes its commitment to clean water for its animals using clean air as an analogue: "Like the air we breathe, seawater needs to be clean and free of contaminants for aquatic animals to be healthy and thrive."[118] This is perhaps ironic: the air in Long Beach is notoriously contaminated by port and refinery emissions, and all of greater LA is famous for dirty air. But if one stops to think about it, one might conclude that this statement does, at least, productively undermine human exceptionalism.[119] If taken at face value, it points to an urgent need to attend to cleaner air and water. Animals in captivity should have no spe-cial claim to detoxified habitat.[120]

As the Aquarium of the Pacific moves to expand its otter operations, adding capacity for otter surrogacy (or auntie-ing), otters acting in place of biological parents will probably be able to rear more stranded pups and wildlife managers will release them back into the wild. The population on California's coast and estuarial sloughs may finally creep upward. Or it may not. Southern sea otters face an uncertain future. Though they have been revived after being on the brink of extinction, climate change threatens marine ecologies, and toxins additionally threaten marine habitats. The scale of extinction we are living through is "unknown and unknowable with any real certainty."[121] Global surveys show astonishing rates of vertebrate loss since 1970. California sea otters, along with other life-forms, face "the problem of living despite . . . ecological ruination."[122]

And yet the Southern California Bight may contain surprises. The species of kelp in Northern California's (heretofore) cooler waters is bull kelp (*Nereocystis luetkeana*). The species that has occupied warmer waters, forming canopies in Southern and Baja California, is giant kelp (*Macrocystis pyrifera*). A US Army Corps of Engineers (USACE) representative said that her understanding was that giant kelp was less stressed by heating than bull kelp,[123] and there seems to be some evidence for the potential of this kelp rebounding in Southern and Baja California waters. A 2018 biological survey of the ports' harbors revealed some increases in kelp canopy,[124] and a project off Palos Verdes (going north and west around the peninsula from the harbor) has recently cleared some "urchin barrens" in order to restore 200 acres of giant kelp.[125] In 2019, USACE made a recommendation to restore some kelp in eastern San Pedro Bay (over the objections of recreational boaters), while maintaining its ironclad commitment to commercial and industrial activity.[126] Because of biological life's potential to generate more of itself, there are latent possibilities for renewed organismic ecologies in the Southern California Bight. As bull kelp dies, San Pedro Bay and the southern Channel Islands archipelago could be an ideal place to regrow giant kelp, alongside noncaptive otters, fish nurseries, terns, eelgrass, abalone, and even some container cranes. Crucially, fast-growing kelp also sequesters carbon. Conservation managers attempt to prop up organismic ecologies, but many aspirations run afoul of commitments to infrastructural vitalism. Though conservation goals can coexist in uneasy tension with infrastructural vitalism, the latter is fundamentally inimical to thriving ecologies—and the balancing act whereby officials are trying to have both is precarious indeed.

4

AQUA NULLIUS

In spring 2020, during the initial period of global lockdown precipitated by the COVID-19 pandemic, economic data showed a major dip in global shipping. Factories in China were operating at reduced capacity and producing fewer goods for export.[1] Global supply chains experienced disruptions, and members of workforces across many countries stayed home due to either government orders or illness.[2] Chinese capacity returned, but the effects on supply chains continue to be felt; longer-term effects of the pandemic will perhaps include more diversified supply chains and adjusted patterns of global trade. In addition to the suffering caused by disease and bereavement, the caesura in commercial and industrial activity caused economic pain for many. Scientists, however, were grateful for what they termed an "anthropause," which offered them an unprecedented ability to study other life-forms with the usual hum and clang nearly silenced.[3] They observed a significant drop in low-frequency sounds associated with ships, which they characterized as a once-in-a-generation opportunity for marine scientists to listen: "We have a generation of humpbacks that have never known a quiet ocean. . . . I expect what we might see [now] is an opportunity for whales to have more conversation and to have more complex conversation," said a marine acoustician quoted in the *Guardian*.[4]

This chapter uses the 2020 anthropause and its effect on cetaceans who transit through San Pedro Bay and the Southern California Bight as a point of entry into thinking about infrastructural vitalism.[5] This anthropause occurred in a decades-long context where port managers and other regional officials had turned toward goods movement as an economic strategy. These officials had noted in the early twenty-first century that, unless attended to, increasing cargo movement and its accompanying air pollution "would create a 'major health crisis for generations.'" However, limiting the circulation of goods was not acceptable for politicians and economic managers. Rather, they concluded that "port growth and environmental protections '[could move] forward in lock step at the same time . . . [because] they should be viewed as one project.'"[6]

Like goods, cetaceans routinely transit in and out of the Southern California Bight and can often be found in the coastal waters between the shoreline and the Channel Islands, including San Pedro Bay (fig. 39). Though regional managers have presented the movement of goods and flourishing of coastal and marine life as a unified project, this chapter illustrates how biological lives are circumscribed by commitments that first and foremost promote the circulation of goods. It first surveys the history of the gray whale, which migrates along the North American Pacific coastline, as an example of a conservation effort that succeeded through international efforts and domestic legislation but is imperiled anew in the present. It then turns to consider the US Navy's 1960s experimental underwater habitat (for men) in the Southern California Bight that was "staffed" by a dolphin. The navy's interest in marine mammal physiology and bioacoustics sets up an irony, as it was through this work that marine mammal acoustic sensing came to be better understood by scientists—but in spite of this knowledge, acoustic harm has been on the rise in recent decades due to both military and commercial activity. Though cetaceans have largely ceased being industrial commodities, they and other life-forms off the California coast incur environmental injury because they occupy territory

FIGURE 39. Blue whale off the coast near the port complex; cranes visible on land; circa 2018.
Courtesy Port of Los Angeles.

that has been claimed for other uses, such as global shipping and every-day militarism. (Movement of goods as commercial activity cannot be fully disentangled from logistics as activity of empire.[7]) While scientific under-standing of cetacean acoustics has proliferated within a logic of industrial and state valuation of marine life that generates harm and industrial pollu-tion, considering the cetacean sensorium as a lively yet incommensurable feature of these animals presents an opportunity to consider transspecies sovereignty and flourishing. Anchored in San Pedro Bay, these stories also travel north and south along the coast, like the animals themselves.

CETACEAN CONSERVATION IN THE SOUTHERN CALIFORNIA BIGHT

The gray whale is a baleen whale, around fifty feet long and weighing up-ward of 60,000 pounds. Like the sea otter, its history as a species includes decimation due to commodification; both species now live *post-industrial-commodity* lives. An Atlantic gray whale population was exterminated entirely in the eighteenth century, due to whaling for oil and blubber for use as fuel. Today, the whales that migrate between Baja California and northern Alaska are known as the Eastern Pacific population. There is also a Western Pacific population that is quite imperiled. Whale hunting for commodity fuel has ended, though there are still pockets of commercial and subsistence whale hunting along with scientific "harvesting" of whales for research.[8]

The gray whales that transit through the Southern California Bight are in the more robust group, but they were hunted almost to extinction in the mid-nineteenth century and again in the twentieth century before pro-tections for them were imposed.[9] Gray whales are especially vulnerable to hunting because, unlike many other whales, they tend to stay close to the coast. Eastern Pacific gray whales calve in specific lagoons in Baja Califor-nia, which have the advantage of warm and placid waters but the disadvan-tage of being easily accessible to hunters. Mexico had passed protections for other marine animals by the 1920s, earlier than it did for whales, as "in-discriminate hunting, mostly by Americans" off the coast of Baja Califor-nia affected manatees, elephant seals, and Guadalupe fur seals there.[10] But these protections excluded whales, as whaling was seen as industrial activ-ity. Early international regulations protecting whales included prohibitions on hunting pregnant whales, nursing mothers, and their calves; these vol-untary guidelines were passed in 1931 and Mexico joined the convention in 1933.[11] For obvious reasons, hunting mothers and calves could decimate whale populations more quickly than hunting adults.

Given their migratory arcs, wrangling over regulations to protect whales is an international concern. In 1946, member nations in the International Whaling Commission (IWC) put forth a proposal to fully protect gray whales from commercial whaling, though there was an exception for scientific research. Mexico joined the convention in 1949, which was a significant measure for protecting the Eastern Pacific gray whale because the species' breeding and nursery areas are located within its territorial waters. By the 1960s, the population had rebounded significantly—which ironically opened up a conversation about hunting again. Geographer Serge Dedina writes that while US conservationists voiced loud objection to Mexico's considering commercial/sport whaling again (which, ultimately, it did not permit), they were more subdued in their reactions to lethal whale research in the United States and Canada. (He also points out that postwar scientific research in Baja California had a colonial cast to it, as it was easier for scientists in the United States, particularly at Scripps Institution of Oceanography in La Jolla, to visit the lagoons than for researchers from Mexico City to do so.[12])

Meanwhile in the United States, the 1960s saw a burgeoning environmental movement. This coincided with the oceans in particular being identified for increasing technocratic management. Nations zeroed in on oceans as sites of fishery and energy resources, while trade and maritime transport increased, as did national security and marine recreation commitments; "oceans were rising in importance for resources, economics, and public participation." The Marine Mammal Protection Act (MMPA), signed into law in 1972, joined other environmental regulations of this era. Its passage signified a shift in policy regarding wildlife: namely, to be considered *as wildlife*, rather than as "resources for the taking."[13] In other words, wildlife's existence and value could be articulated as distinct from any resource potential. Furthermore, the statute represented a shift in the regulatory approach to wildlife, as it began to consider effects on animals as parts of *ecosystems*: "such species and population stocks should not be permitted to diminish beyond the point at which they cease to be a significant functioning element in the ecosystem of which they are a part."[14] Though what constitutes an "ecosystem" can be difficult to define, measure, or regulate, the consideration of animals in ecological roles in habitats and ecosystems marked a break with earlier technocratic practices.[15]

Rachel Carson's landmark book *Silent Spring* was published in 1962.[16] "The environment" itself went from being "not a leading issue" in 1965 to the second-most worrisome public problem, after crime, in 1970.[17] Environmentalists made multiple arguments for protecting marine mammals, including that they needed to be managed for ecosystem repair and health, and on moral and ethical grounds due to their intelligence and concern about their abuse and exploitation. Conflict arose as to whether legal protections should favor "conservation," meaning species management, or "preservation," meaning a more absolutist protection. In spite of the fact that policymakers, scientists, and members of the public disagreed about "what conservation was all about," the legislative path was relatively straightforward.[18] Because "preservationists" were unable to persuade legislators that a "flat ban [on killing or taking animals for scientific management] would inevitably operate to the benefit of the animals concerned," they ultimately supported the same legislative solutions as their opponents in the "conservationist" camp: careful regulation with advice by scientists (in particular, those whose guidance was not corrupted by industry interests) and opportunities for public input.[19] (In the late 1960s, the US government had authorized a permit for killing a few hundred gray whales for "scientific research," but whose flesh was ultimately sold as pet food by a whaling company. Such conflicts of interest were decried by protectionists, who testified before Congress during the shaping of the MMPA.[20])

Public input was not a scarce commodity, and marine mammals were not mere objects of public concern. They quickly became *symbols* of "saving the planet" and the faces of environmentalism, especially whales.[21] A 1970 album of humpback whales' "song" became a surprise smash hit, going multiplatinum.[22] Conservationists played the record in congressional hearings in 1971 as part of their testimony: one said, "Having heard their songs, I believe you can imagine what their screams would be."[23] A portion of *Songs of the Humpback Whale* was reissued later in the decade on a "flexidisc" in an issue of *National Geographic*, giving it a very wide distribution to over ten million households.[24] In 1974, a Los Angeles teenager shocked by a magazine article about commercial whaling had t-shirts made that read "Save the Whales" and sold them through mail order, shipping them nationwide by popular demand.[25] There is also a strong link between the rise of "Save the Whales" and the spread of oceanariums, especially cetacean captivity and display on the Pacific coast.[26] According to a founder of Greenpeace, "The whale was the perfect species in danger that could stand for all of wild nature."[27] In media historian John Durham Peters's vivid description, "Within the course of a decade, from about 1965 to 1975, the dominant conceptions of whales and dolphins changed from long animate barrels of animal feed and lubricants to sea gurus soulfully singing of cosmic peace and harmony, showing humans the higher path of intelligence and coexistence, like age-old Yodas."[28]

Initially, whale conservation appeared to be a success story: it was "perhaps the greatest triumph of the postwar conservationist movement," writes philosopher Amia Srinivasan.[29] Commercial whaling was banned outright in 1982 by the IWC, and enforcement began in 1986, although the ban excluded whale-hunting rights for some Indigenous communities.[30] As populations rebounded, commercial hunting was debated again, and some nations even resumed whaling, amid controversy.[31] But whaling, however odious many find it, is no longer the main contributor to cetaceans' mortality. Ship strikes, entanglement in fishing equipment, and even starvation—as whales consume plastic pollution and their proper food sources become scarce due to warming and overexploitation of oceans—are bigger threats.[32] In addition, cetaceans are beset by chronic and acute sonic disturbances that constitute a potentially existential threat. In other words, even as conservation efforts showed proof of concept, large-scale industrial activities have imperiled cetaceans once more.

TUFFY: LIFE IN TERRITORY

In 1954, members of the US military stationed on a NATO airbase slaughtered a pod of over a hundred killer whales off the coast of Iceland. The whales' offense was annoying the Icelanders by competing with them for fish, and "bored" GIs fired upon them with machine guns, to the delight of the Icelanders; the massacre was described as very good for American-Icelandic relations. In the US press, the event was reported favorably as well; partisan on behalf of the Icelanders and soldiers, it described the whales as "savage sea cannibals up to 30 ft. long and with teeth like bayonets."[33]

Such an event would likely have been received very differently in the United States in 1975, after whales had been adopted as gnomic emblems of environmentalism and even mysticism. I relay it here to underscore how, even in the era after cetaceans were nearly exterminated through being commodified as lubricant and fuel, they dwelled within (and continue to dwell within) watery everyday militarism. By "everyday militarism," I mean the pervasive imprint of militarism on daily life, the ubiquitous traces of war and preparedness for war, as opposed to spatially and temporally bounded war itself.[34] In 1954, bored servicemen exterminated orcas with machine guns they happened to have ready to hand. Even as public sentiment toward whales has shifted, in the twenty-first century cetaceans are subject to maiming and even death from explosives and sonar testing.

In the intervening decades, some cetaceans and sea lions participated in a program conducted by the US Navy, its Marine Mammal Program. The navy took an interest in dolphins after World War II for two reasons: first, their ability to move through the water so swiftly and efficiently (which had potential application in submarine design), and second, their bioacoustic capabilities, including using sound to navigate.[35] By 1971, when Congress was debating the Marine Mammal Protection Act, scientists invoked the navy's work with cetaceans in a positive light, a "cooperative relationship with marine mammals in mutually beneficial projects," expressing support for the expansion of such projects.[36]

A key figure was neuroscientist John C. Lilly, who experimented on dolphins' brains, was convinced they shared communicative potential with humans, and whose ideas influenced the navy's research program in the early 1960s and popular conceptions of cetaceans a few years later.[37] Writing in a 1967 book, he declared, "Before they are annihilated by man, I would like to exchange ideas with a sperm whale. I am not sure that they would be as interested in communicating with me because my brain is obviously much more limited than theirs."[38] He went on to say, "Probably that which would excite the most respect for the human species in a sperm whale would be a full orchestra playing a symphony."[39] Lilly's controversial endeavors had lasting influence on not only the navy but also on public conceptions of cetaceans, according to historian of science D. Graham Burnett. Lilly's work was also memorialized in the 1973 film, *Day of the Dolphin*, which depicts a Lilly-esque figure in conflict with a military foil who wishes to train the peaceful and intelligent dolphin for war efforts; the film symbolized the Age of Aquarius in a showdown with the hydrogen bomb. (Lilly was not only rhapsodizing about cetacean language and symphony appreciation but also injecting dolphins with LSD in the mid-1960s.[40] Of course, the history of LSD is intimately tied to the military-industrial complex, making them complementary as well as conflictual, an instance of "inappropriate contiguity."[41]) "The dolphin as popular spectacle contributed not only to Lilly's fame, but to opening the military coffers for scientific research," notes historian of science Gregg Mitman.[42]

All of this is to say that while the navy was indeed sincerely interested in finding ways to "work with" the biological properties of marine mammals, the claim in a 1971 congressional hearing that these projects were "mutually beneficial" is worth interrogating. The navy's early work with marine mammals happened in Atlantic waters off Florida, the Bahamas, and in the Pacific off Southern California. In Florida, a facility called Marine Studios (later Marineland) trained and filmed animals for the entertainment industry, recreational viewing, and scientific research.[43] Their animals—and those in their Los Angeles facility, Marineland of the Pacific in Palos Verdes—were also of interest to navy researchers. In 1960, at Marineland of the Pacific, scientists who were interested in whether and how cetaceans used sound to navigate "succeeded in configuring dolphin 'blindfolds' and published the most compelling 'proof' of dolphins' active sonar," writes Burnett.[44]

The navy released a public relations film, *The Dolphins That Joined the Navy*, in 1964, detailing its work with dolphins in a naval air station at Point Mugu, near Santa Barbara. It situates the dolphin research, begun in 1962, by mentioning that space studies and missile experiments also take place at Point Mugu.[45] (The missile experiment range includes San Nicolas Island, to which the otters had been coercively relocated.) The film's narrator addresses the audience: "If you're wondering why the navy is so interested in dolphins, the reason is quite simple. The dolphin is an expert on sonar, high speed water travel, underwater communication, and maybe a number of other things the navy is quite interested in." Illustrating the navy's research, the film shows a number of dolphins being trained and going through drills. One of them is a bottlenose dolphin named Tough Guy (called that because his flank was scarred, possibly from an encounter with a shark), and the film depicts him training with the blindfolding technique: he swims through hoops with his eyes covered by plastic cups and also retrieves a weighted disk that had sunk to the floor of his enclosure, navigating using only his aural capacities. The film closes with another dolphin, named Buzz-buzz, being dramatically released into open ocean and then called back by her trainers using a buzzer tone she recognized; it concludes that Buzz-buzz prefers her life as an assistant to the navy to wild dolphin life because "she obviously likes it better here, with her trainer companions, who always have a pocketful of fish."[46]

In the 1960s, the navy built three experimental habitats for "aquanauts," men living for short periods on the sea floor. (This has an obvious parallel to ambitions for space exploration in that period.[47]) The project was called Sealab, and Sealab I was assembled in Florida and lowered off the coast of Bermuda, where the aquanauts lived for eleven days in the summer of 1964 at a depth of 193 feet and under nearly seven atmospheres of pressure.[48] For Sealab II and III, the navy moved across the continent to Southern California. Sealab's connection to San Pedro Bay is through the naval station in Long Beach (fig. 40). Sealab II (1965) was lowered 205 feet off the coast of La Jolla, with Scripps partnering.[49] The seabed off La Jolla was less inviting than that in Bermuda, as it was colder and the water was less clear, but naval researchers felt that this represented more "realistic" environmental conditions; La Jolla also offered ideal logistical and research support.[50] Sealab III (1969), assembled in San Francisco, moved to Long Beach for shallow-water tests, around 45 feet deep, before being lowered to a much greater depth (610 feet) off the coast of San Clemente Island in the southern end of the Channel Islands archipelago (fig. 41).[51] In the San Clemente

FIGURE 40. Sealab II dedication in Long Beach, before its submergence off the coast of La Jolla, July 1965.
US Navy, public domain.

FIGURE 41. An aquanaut leaps into the water in Long Beach, conducting premission tests for Sealab III, November 1968.
US Navy, public domain.

depths, an aquanaut died. The program was discontinued, though it lived on as a futurist cartoon, Hanna-Barbera's *Sealab 2020*, broadcast for one season in 1972, and in a more general sense as the Office of Naval Research's Undersea Medicine and Performance program in the present day.

Sealabs II and III also incorporated trained animals, one of whom was Tough Guy, now known as Tuffy (fig. 42). Prior to "enlisting," Tuffy had worked as a trained dolphin in an amusement park ("earning his living the hard way," according to *The Dolphins That Joined the Navy*). For the Sealab II project, the submersible craft was floated from Long Beach to La Jolla and then sunk to the seabed. Tuffy was airlifted from Point Mugu to a pen near the craft.[52] Initially upon arrival he fed and behaved "normally" and performed practice dives up to 170 feet well, so handlers expected him to perform "satisfactorily." But on his first day of service to the aquanauts, Tuffy balked and wouldn't dive. Handlers speculated that he was spooked

FIGURE 42. Tuffy presses an underwater buzzer on a boat in his training at Point Mugu, June 1969.
US Navy, public domain.

by the cables extending from the submersible craft. (If so, Tuffy was right to fear them: fishing gear entanglements are another cause of cetacean mortality.[53]) The following day, aquanauts who were to hand items back and forth with Tuffy moved to a less obstructed area about 100 feet away from the Sealab craft. There, Tuffy met them and performed "flawlessly," responding "quickly and correctly to every signal." Tuffy's main duty was to use his buzzer-training to ferry items between the surface and the craft on the seabed; these items included fish, tools, and Coca-Cola. Authors of a 1967 naval report reflected back on Tuffy's performance, concluding, "A porpoise can be trained to perform useful and even vital tasks in man-in-the-sea programs such as Sealab. It can adapt relatively quickly to a strange and in many ways disturbing environment, and once trained will perform with a high degree of precision and reliability." Furthermore, they recommended that "porpoise and/or pinniped personnel should become an integral part of the Sealab program" and urged testing of additional work functions for pinnipeds and cetaceans in future naval research.[54]

Tuffy's Sealab II support received attention in the press, as did that of a pinniped, a sea lion named Samantha. The *Los Angeles Times* reported Tuffy's refusal to deliver packages on his first day of duty with the Sealab crew under the headline "Porpoise Fails Sealab Tryout as Postman." In the story, a navy spokesman was quoted as saying that Tuffy had been beset by "claustrophobia": "porpoises are afraid of being trapped under water because they'll drown if they don't surface within five minutes."[55] Mainly, though, he was celebrated, alternately as a "pugnacious porpoise" (invoking his name, Tuffy, a "bodyguard, shark-fighter, and rescuer for divers"[56]) or as a faithful watchdog, as when the *LA Times* published an updated story the day after the claustrophobia report, saying the porpoise had "made good," coming through "like an old postman."[57]

The expansionist ambitions of Sealab were evident in many ways. "The [dolphin's] physiology is not much different from ours. . . . We want to find out what [its] adaptations [to living in the sea] are—they might provide clues that will help man *as he goes farther and deeper into the sea*," said a research veterinarian at the Point Mugu naval research center in a 1967 newspaper article.[58] We might refer to this as *aqua nullius*, a nod to *terra nullius*, "no one's land," the doctrine that European settler colonists used to justify claiming "empty" land in the so-called Americas and elsewhere.[59] This assumption is articulated even more explicitly in the 1964 film—"The sea is the home of the dolphin. It is also the domain of the United States Navy," intones the narrator, naval researcher Glenn Ford—and in a 1966 conference publication chronicling Sealab where the authors wrote, "We hope that the need for man to invade the sea will be clarified soon, and that more groups, both military and commercial, will augment the small body of men now carrying the burden of improving the technology."[60] The dolphins themselves were configured as ideal colonial subjects, foreign but capable of being domesticated: "The dolphin is admirably equipped to perform many services in the sea that will be of great value to man. . . . The extent of the use of the dolphin will rest on how well we establish a system of commands and responses. . . . We know that the dolphin is friendly, good-natured, and cooperative."[61] Geographer Rachael Squire writes that handlers "believed that Tuffy's 'native' body could 'hold clues to the mysteries' of the extreme context he called 'home.'"[62] In point of fact, both Buzz-buzz and Tuffy were actually captured in the Gulf of Mexico, not the Eastern Pacific; nonetheless, they were treated as "natives" to the sea without regard for whether they were in fact local to the waters the navy trained and worked them in.

Like the space race, undersea expansion was a Cold War project. But Sealab was not merely exploration; it was protosettlement, territorial expansion.[63] Not coincidentally, undersea oil drilling was growing into a major industry by the mid-1960s (fig. 43). The oil islands in San Pedro Bay are a local example, built the same year as Sealab II; and Sealab II was submerged near the continental shelf, an area of the earth's surface of great interest to geologists and prospectors. By the 1970s, commercial divers working in the offshore oil industry routinely conducted "otherworldly construction work," hundreds of feet beneath the ocean's surface.[64] The Sealab II aquanauts utilized experimental devices for taking samples of the seabed.[65] Sealab's colonization effort is instructive in the present day too, as the race to exploit resources in deep-sea mining is accelerating, especially as oceanic ice melts.

CETACEAN COMMUNICATION

Whales' calls, which so captivated people in the 1970s, have emerged as a matter of public attention again more recently. Or, rather, not whales' calls but interference in their transmission has become a matter of mounting concern. Sonic pollution caused by commercial shipping and other maritime operations is now understood to inhibit cetacean communication.

This concern has been evolving over time. In 1953, celebrity oceanographer Jacques Cousteau published a best-selling book entitled *The Silent World*; and the book and his 1956 film by the same name emphasized the visual elements of life underwater and presented the ocean as soundless.[66] Yet also as early as the mid-1950s, recordings of sea animals circulated; especially important for cetology was the 1962 record *Whale and Porpoise Voices*.[67] US Navy research propelled the understanding of ocean space as

FIGURE 43. Apparatus for undersea oil drilling built in Long Beach, mid-1960s. Courtesy Port of Long Beach.

populated by sound, and the navy was keenly interested in cetacean communication.[68] Whales' *song* was "discovered" later that decade, when a navy engineer named Frank Watlington was listening to recordings for sounds of explosions off the coast of Bermuda and found the sounds he was listening for obscured by whale vocalizations that, he recognized, contained patterns and repetitions quickly characterized as song.[69] He then used military hydrophones to record whale calls, and it was these recordings that were produced and released as *Songs of the Humpback Whale*.

While all cetaceans vocalize, their communication varies. At a minimum, they use sound to identify prey (in the case of toothed whales, including dolphins like Buzz-buzz and Tuffy); navigate; avoid predators; and communicate with and locate mates, companions, and young. Toothed whales emit and process auditory signals with a higher frequency range than baleen whales, and they have been subject to more scrutiny in echolocation and sonar research than baleen whales, whose lower-range transmissions are understood as communicative but not echolocative.[70] In the mid-twentieth century, military researchers interested in echolocation posited that the fatty "melon" in toothed whales' heads, prized by whalers in earlier periods, had acoustic properties, serving to focus and shape the sound beams they emitted. In the early 1960s, navy scientists in Point Mugu performed grotesque experiments with a dead baby dolphin, implanting it with a system to project sound in order to test its anatomical structure for acoustic lensing properties, hoping to reveal mechanisms at play in echolocation.[71]

Researchers were also interested in cetacean hearing, especially acoustic detection thresholds and how these were related to echolocation and sonar. How cetaceans perceive acoustic signals is shaped by their watery environment. Sound propagates quickly and travels farther underwater than in air, and how people might think of sound "sounding" based on experiences on land might be quite different from what other mammals experience underwater, even with some common anatomical features. Cetaceans lack external ears, and the structures that correspond to middle and inner ear in land animals migrated "outward" in their skulls. Their heads collect sound energy and gather it toward the structures that correspond to middle ears, and their sensing is more tuned to acoustic particles than acoustic pressure, which is distinct from hearing on land.[72] A likely mechanism for sound reception is perimandibular "acoustic fat" bodies in whales' jaws, which pick up vibration and enable it to travel for auditory processing. Researchers initially surmised that only toothed whales' anatomy contained these acoustic fats. But scientists have posited more recently that fatty sound reception pathways may not be unique to the toothed animals, in spite of significant differences in skull shapes between baleen whales and their toothed relations.[73]

Writing in the 1990s, a reviewer of bioacoustics research stated that hearing abilities had been studied in some toothed whales, hair seals, and eared seals, and limited data were available regarding manatees, but "direct measurements of the hearing sensitivity of baleen whales, walruses, and sea otters are lacking." Often, the audiograms in the scientific literature for a given marine mammal species were based on data from only one or two individuals.[74] Some of this dearth was in fact an effect of the 1972 Marine Mammal Protection Act, the passage of which made it harder to get scientific permits for research that "took" live animals, though the navy consistently received permits to renew the Marine Mammal Program.[75] The study that posited that baleen whales also had acoustic fats that aided in sound reception, published in 2012, relied on a combination of dissection of deceased stranded whales, magnetic resonance imaging, and computerized tomography. The authors noted that "the study of soft tissues in mysticetes [baleen whales] is particularly difficult due to the rarity of adequate specimens and the logistics of dissecting large animals, often on beaches."[76]

When the MMPA was passed, it regulated the "taking" of marine mammals including not only cetaceans but pinnipeds (seals, sea lions, walruses); otters; manatees; and polar bears. "Taking" here means hunting, killing, capturing, or harassing (or attempting to do any of these). And "harassing" can mean a litany of things:

> any act of pursuit, torment, or annoyance which—(i) has the potential to injure a marine mammal or marine mammal stock in the wild; or (ii) has the potential to disturb a marine mammal or marine mammal stock in the wild by causing disruption of behavioral patterns, including, but not limited to, migration, breathing, nursing, breeding, feeding, or sheltering.[77]

Though lawmakers were at this point aware of the fact that acoustic communication was important for cetaceans, sonic disruption was not among the concerns the legislation was meant to address.[78] But because "taking" included harassment, it was not a stretch to expand the regulatory purview to noise: by the 1990s, "noise-related disturbance [was] considered to be harassment." The MMPA could thus be brought to bear on any number of anthropogenic noise sources, including boats, aircraft, offshore noises emitted by the oil and gas industry (including airgun arrays, used in surveying the sea floor), icebreaking, sonars, marine construction, and explosions. The MMPA also applies to US citizens in international waters, so, for instance, it obtains in geologic exploration outside US waters by a US company.[79]

In spite of research attention to cetacean acoustic capabilities, the effects of environmental noise were not a central concern. At the same time, basic outlines of sonic disruption effects were certainly known. Writing in 2008, a bioacoustician pointed out that fully thirty-five years earlier, researchers had already observed that shipping noise had reduced acoustic communication range for baleen whales relative to preindustrial times.[80] There was a boom in bioacoustics research centering on marine animals in the first decade of the 2000s, culminating in an international conference in Denmark on the effects of noise on aquatic life in 2007.[81] One reason for this expanded focus on acoustic harm was the emergence of incontrovertible evidence linking navy sonar to beaked whale strandings in the Mediterranean Sea in the 1990s and 2000s.[82] Popular attention to this problem,

which is now ubiquitous, corresponds with the increasing research attention and employs familiar tropes about noise as "unwanted sound"; a 2005
public-facing write-up of marine acoustic research called the problem one
of "an increasingly *urbanizing* marine environment."[83] The same presentation likened acoustic noise to smog, also configured as an urban ill.[84] Other
marine life is harmed as well, including squid, octopus, krill, and tinier organisms like zooplankton, all of which are important for mutualistic marine relations, but whales are "the chief political delegates of ocean noise
'risk,'" writes geographer Max Ritts.[85]

But even as researchers coalesced around a general agreement that
acoustic phenomena greatly affected marine life, standardized knowledge
and consensus about specifics were harder to come by. Questions arose
about cetaceans' long-term exposure to sonic interference, not only acute
events: "the exposure criteria for single individuals and single-exposure
events are insufficient to describe cumulative and ecosystem-level effects
resulting from a repeated and/or sustained human input of sound into the
marine environment and interactions with other stressors."[86] Scientists
speculated that "masking" effects (i.e., background noise in frequencies
near the ones animals listen for, causing them to miss hearing the signals
they tune toward) could have population effects that were harder to identify and quantify.[87] "Ambient noise" sources in the ocean could include
wind, waves, surf, ice, organisms, earthquakes, distant shipping, volca-
noes, fishing boats, and more. Obviously only some of these are human-
caused, but understanding how sounds interact and propagate through water is complex, as this can be affected by water depth, source and receiver
depths, sea bottom slope and composition, sea surface conditions, temperature, and salinity.[88] Initial attempts to investigate subaquatic acoustics
were plagued by "the problem of snapping shrimp"—staccato taps, clanks,
rumblings, hammerings, croaks, and other eerie sounds that confounded
submariners—caused by small marine organisms who migrate through
ocean layers on daily and seasonal bases, reflecting sonar and drowning
out other sounds at shallow depths.[89] As specified in the MMPA, scientific
knowledge was needed to guide permitting with respect to sonic "harassment." As a researcher argued in 2008, "[current] regulatory practices may
be unnecessarily stringent, with little benefit to animals and significant cost
to human society, or insufficiently protective, with real costs to animals."[90]

Uncertainties notwithstanding, some standards on likely "thresholds for
harm" were published in 2008. They distinguished between (acute) injury
effects and "behavioral disturbance."[91] For acute harm, the US Navy was a
frequent offender, often seeking permitting to conduct sonar and explosives drills off the coast of Southern California and in Hawai'i. In 2012, as

it was looking ahead to permit renewal in 2014, a navy spokesperson said that as many as 2.7 million sea mammals could experience "temporary but nonlethal effects on their hearing and behavior," and roughly 2,000 could be injured or killed from explosive training tests in its upcoming planned five-year testing period. Environmentalists took to the courts, arguing that the navy ought to make a better effort, including avoiding areas with marine mammal density such as the coastal zone off Southern California, where dolphins had been killed by explosives testing the previous year (off Coronado, in San Diego).[92]

But "behavioral disturbance" from more ambient sound is also a major concern. Shipping itself is a source of sonic burden, as the noise from the synchronous collapse of bubbles created by ship propellers, as well as the rumbling sounds emitted by ships' engines, can mask cetacean communication and contribute to stress.[93] Commercial shipping may be responsible for approximately 75 percent of ocean noise, and noise from shipping is estimated to have *doubled every decade since 1950*.[94] Shipping in San Pedro Bay has only intensified over recent decades. Since the gray whales in the Southern California Bight were removed from the endangered species list in 1994, the port complex has increased its movement of goods significantly, especially as Chinese imports have grown from the mid-1990s onward.[95] As a researcher noted in 2012, "What we have is the abundance of whales has gone up, but also the number of big fast ships has grown."[96]

Sonic disturbance is likely a factor in ship strikes, which are more lethal to whales migrating along the California coast than previously understood. In 2018, at least ten whales were killed by ships in California waters, though this is almost certainly an undercount since not all vessels' crews are aware of ship strikes when they happen and many dead whales do not wash ashore. The number of recorded ship strikes rose fivefold in the Pacific Northwest in the 1990s and the 2000s.[97] Scientists speculated that the true number could be as much as ten to twenty times higher than the official count.[98] In 2012, researchers and regulators discussed altering shipping lanes in the approach to the ports of Long Beach and Los Angeles, which overlap with wildlife in the vicinity of the Channel Islands archipelago.[99] But nearly a decade later, ship strikes were still occurring at a sufficient rate that in spring of 2020, an environmental group announced its intention to sue regulators over ship strikes that continued to occur in shipping lanes approaching the ports in Los Angeles, Long Beach, and along San Francisco Bay (figs. 44, 45).[100]

One (almost perverse) proposed "solution" to the problem of ship strikes is to make noises to warn whales of oncoming ships.[101] Though research indicates that migrating gray whales will move around a stationary

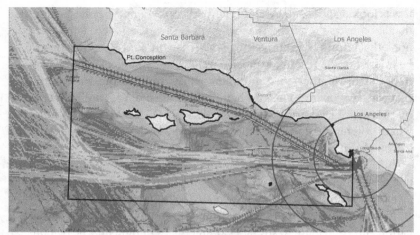

FIGURE 44. Graphic showing vessel density along the coast and at the port complex (the dot where traffic converges in lower right) in San Pedro Bay, 2017. National Oceanic and Atmospheric Administration, public domain.

FIGURE 45. Fin whale (presumably deceased) on the bulbous bow of a massive ship, Long Beach Harbor, October 2008. Courtesy Alisa Schulman-Janiger.

sound source emitting low-frequency active sonar sounds, indicating that utilizing sound this way could cause a whale to move to avoid a ship, even seemingly minor movement to avoid a source of sound can have larger effects on an animal's energy utilization. For instance, as few as ten days of lost foraging opportunities could lead to the loss of a pregnancy or calf, and with climate crisis, further disturbance to whales' feeding or navigational courses could multiply stress significantly, with population-level and even intergenerational effects.[102] While gray whales in the vicinity of the San Pedro Bay port complex are not considered endangered at present, blue whales, who are endangered, also frequent these waters near the Channel Islands in the summer.[103] Of course, a focus on endangered *species* can draw away from understanding broader ecological perils.[104]

Arguing for stricter protections for cetaceans from sonic disturbance, a 2017 paper proclaimed: "Absence of Evidence Does Not Mean Evidence of Absence—The Need for Precaution." The author opined that "management of cetaceans needs to be precautionary" because of the difficulty quantifying, and knowing with certainty, the degree and extent of harms that sonic disturbances could cause. Because whales and dolphins can be hard to study and the data are often limited, the ability to detect "trends" is hampered, even for the most thoroughly researched creatures; for instance, even in the best-studied dolphin populations, a population decline may take a decade or more before researchers detect it.[105] With more scarce or elusive animals, data can be similarly scarce and elusive. And even in 2020, "we know surprisingly little about the largest animal ever to live," said a Scripps Institution of Oceanography researcher about the blue whale.[106] On mainstream scientific grounds alone, there is probably good reason to be conservative in quantifying harm, not least because data lag changes in populations and their health; dissemination of scientific research lags data; and response lags research.[107]

More significantly, this "precautionary" standard represents an alternative to the paradigm that seeks to establish a threshold of harm, and then permits harm right up to the threshold. As anticolonial marine science researcher Max Liboiron notes, the threshold model naturalizes harm, seeking only to keep "strain" within "tolerable limits."[108] This establishes governance of pollution within a "permission to pollute" regime, that is, designating certain spaces (and their inhabitants) for contamination; such a governance scheme is on view in the discussion above, where researchers attempted to establish thresholds for acute injury and for behavioral disturbance.[109] *Precaution* is a more conservative standard, one which might *avoid* harm, or place the burden on the polluter to establish that harm is *not* being incurred. It also potentially opens up ways to think about cetaceans as creatures unto themselves, not just objects of scientific management within a context of industrial relations that are known to cause endangerment. In other words, to take precaution seriously would require confronting the potential incommensurability between ecologies of flourishing biological life and the infrastructural vitalism that animates the harbor's industrial function at scale. Should concern center around *minimum thresholds* for life to reproduce itself? Or can precautionary regimes offer alternatives to hegemonic managerial knowledge regarding wildlife, creating space to think about supporting creaturely sovereignty?

WHALE PRESENCE METRIC?

During the 2020 anthropause, "cute animal" memes and videos circulated, a balm for humans under orders to stay at home to arrest the spread of disease. This is an indication of how "animals have become safe and apolitical subjects," appropriate for polite conversation.[110] Though calls to "Save the Whales" are not apolitical, such politics of conservation have run up against certain limits. Cetaceans along the California coast have been given protections through legislation and international cooperation, have seen their numbers on the rebound (for many species, at least), and live in a secure post-industrial-commodity status. At the same time, industrial harm at scale to whales in the Southern California Bight persists and is worsening, with warming ocean waters, increased ship strikes due to ever-rising global trade, and the US military's insistent claims to both marine mammals' bodies and their aquatic surroundings. The "mystical" whale, wise creature of the deep, is an established trope, but is incapable of fending off these harms.

This is evident in the experiences of cetaceans in the Southern California Bight, who are subject to various kinds of violence. Some Eastern Pacific gray whales are simply starving as the climate crisis affects their food sources and the patterns of their continent-long migrations no longer coincide with abundant food; 2021 marked the third year in a row where scientists observed an unusual number of gray whales in very poor condition, or starving to death along their southern migration route, heading from the Bering Sea down to San Ignacio Lagoon.[111] The warming Arctic is causing a decline in the arthropods on which they feed, so a likely explanation is that they are leaving their feeding grounds without having gotten enough to eat. The same population had declined suddenly by around 25 percent in an earlier "unusual mortality event" in 1998–2002, so it is possible that a similar die-off is occurring now. Toothed whales, like dolphins, are high on the food chain, and their blubber is now loaded with mercury.[112] Though the impact on toothed whales has received more press attention, gray whales and other baleen whales are vulnerable to sonic pollution including military noise; some gray whale strandings have coincided with military exercises, and migrating gray whales will go out of their way to avoid sonar noise.[113] Sound masking can also upset predator-prey relations: gray whales might avoid vocalizing when in the presence of orcas (their predators), unless they fail to detect the orcas.[114]

And sonic pollution is not the only form that these cetaceans may encounter. In 2020, the *Los Angeles Times* reported that barrels and barrels of DDT, many leaking, had been identified in the deep water off Santa Catalina Island, which is a natural barrier between San Pedro Bay and the open ocean. Gray whales dredge the seabed when they feed, an unusual strategy for baleen whales, who usually eat nearer the ocean's surface (and gray whales are themselves versatile feeders, eating at surface and middle depths as well). In doing so, they stir up earth, microorganisms, and other life-forms in the seabed, transferring them between different layers of ocean water. Though they tend to graze farther north and at shallower depths than these barrels, they, and many other plants and animals, have likely been exposed to this industrial toxin for decades, as the Channel Islands ecology supports many life-forms. The *Los Angeles Times* story revealed that the source of the DDT was Montrose Chemical Corporation in south Los Angeles; its facility is now considered one of the most hazardous sites in the United States. Montrose had continued to manufacture DDT for export even after its use was banned in the United States, and it hired workers to put barrels on barges and sink them in the ocean to dispose of them. Sometimes workers took an ax or hatchet to the barrels to make them sink more quickly, and the story also revealed that sometimes they dumped the barrels closer to shore than they were supposed to, apparently to save time. DDT, like other toxins, stores readily in fatty tissue and could easily travel up the food chain from phytoplankton to zooplankton and larger animals.[115] It also remains stable without breaking down for decades and can even cause epigenetic harm across generations in humans.[116] Scientists are now positing that the startling rate of cancer in California sea lions—around 25 percent of adults and subadults have cancers—is probably related to DDT in the environment.[117]

But the above descriptions of sonic and chemical pollution do not fully capture the *processes and mechanisms* of environmental violence experienced by cetaceans. Capitalism regards land as a resource from which to extract resources. Under settler colonialism, land is also a place to put pollution; both of these mechanisms contribute to the creation of economic value. Seen this way, pollution is not so much a careless by-product of industrial processes as a designation that a given territory has been deemed acceptable to pollute in the process of generating value. In the Southern California Bight and elsewhere, the state grants permission to pollute the aquatic territory that blue and gray whales, dolphins, and sea lions live in and transit through. These state and industry uses of land disrupt other relationships to land—and we can extend this understanding to water as well.[118]

The experiences of Tuffy and Buzz-buzz, meanwhile, illustrate these processes another way. Actively configured as colonial subjects in the project of claiming the sea (and seabed) for state projects, they were not merely "collateral damage" for the expansion of empire or extraction of economic value in the same way as cetaceans exploded by bombs, poisoned by DDT, exposed to sonic pollution, or struck by ships are. These dolphins "actively shaped how the undersea environment came to be understood and inhabited by the U.S. military" in the construct of territory and extension of the US empire.[119] Furthermore, the very history of cetacean bioacoustics and underwater listening "reveals a coproduction of military strategy and animal science."[120] This provides a fuller context for the science around cetacean hearing and listening, which has become more salient and controversial in the twenty-first century.

In a 2012 *San Diego Union Tribune* article, a federal researcher said of ship strikes, "In my mind, a really great starting place is reducing that overlap between ships and whales."[121] Of course, on the face of it, this statement is unimpeachable and difficult to argue with. Scientists have recently proposed a system called "Whale Safe" that combines "oceanographic models that predict where individuals might show up, human observers on whale-watching boats spotting the animals as they surface, and a clever buoy that spies on the animals' calls." It uses a website and email alert system for cargo companies that notifies them of nearby whales, so vessel operators can be warned to slow down if whales are in shipping lanes. The buoy monitors whales in the Santa Barbara shipping channel, using a hydrophone to detect whale calls and transmitting notation of the whale audio to a human operator who makes a judgment call as to whether the signal is whales or, well, noise. At present, Whale Safe is essentially just a prototype, and its operation is dependent on voluntary buy-in from the shipping industry.[122]

But in taking an expansive view of the situation, one must acknowledge that preventing ship strikes is not, realistically, a matter of cleanly separating whales from ships. Ship strikes are happening in a context of rising vessel traffic with increasing global trade; projections for future vessel traffic suggest it will continue to increase.[123] The 2020 COVID-19 anthropause was short-lived; by the end of that year, infrastructural vitalism was ascendant once again. Shipping had roared back to life to such an extent that trade set new records and an "unusually high number of cargo ships" were anchored in San Pedro Bay killing time for days, waiting to dock and lining the horizon with a "thick brown haze" of exhaust.[124] Recall that in October 2021, a seabed oil pipeline burst just south of San Pedro Bay. Investigators of the leak's cause suggested that a strong possibility was a cargo ship's anchor striking and dragging the pipeline, which connected the Port of Long Beach to an offshore drilling rig.[125] Some birds and other marine life were oiled.[126] Research on how the cargo surge has affected local wildlife in general or cetaceans in particular has not been released as of this writing, but one can hazard an educated guess.

Within a threshold model of pollution, a high volume of (voluntarily) slower ships is designated an acceptable level of harm, even if it still generates sonic pollution that disorients, fatigues, and stresses whales. In this sense, the shipping industry still constitutes a form of state-sanctioned violence, on a continuum with dolphins being blown up or beaked whales stranding in response to acute sonic interferences. This becomes more apparent in conjunction with the fact that commercial vessels are forced to share the whales' preferred transit area, the lively waters between the Channel Islands and the mainland, because the military has claimed the open ocean on the far side of the islands for testing missiles. A researcher working on Whale Safe said, "[The Department of Defense] really do[es] not like when ships go back there, and they [the DoD] tend to be able to trump other proposals for whale protection."[127]

Indeed, the state claims a "right to maim" outright—it authorizes "incidental takes," granting that national security trumps the well-being of marine life.[128] As noted earlier, the navy's own spokesperson forecast that millions of sea mammals would suffer "temporary but nonlethal effects . . . or be killed or injured" from explosives or sonar during testing.[129] As courts adjudicate these matters, environmentalists have countered the navy's estimates of the number of animals it will harm: they held that the number of cetaceans "killed or crippled would be much higher," that is, either the military activity would harm more animals or cause more severe harm than was being disclosed.[130] The crux of the matter is whether and to what degree cetaceans should be rendered available for injury because they are in the way of capitalist profit-seeking or the expansionist tendencies of the US empire.[131]

Scientific knowledge is still emerging on how much nonlethal acoustic effluvia generated by sonar and shipping stress or harm whales. Furthermore, "nonlethal" addresses only acute events, not slower violence like lifelong exposure, let alone epigenetic effects.[132] Of course, there is an irony in the juxtaposition of the navy's insistence on its right to commit state violence against cetaceans with the fact that so much of what is known about cetaceans' bioacoustics and lifeways emerged from military-supported cetology.[133] Without the navy's interest in cetacean anatomy and navigation, less might be known about these creatures, including the harm being done to them by sonic pollution. Today some scientists are advocating for precautionary measures to be taken in the absence of greater certitude about the levels of pollution that stress whales to the point of infirmity, even death.

This seems useful, but it is necessary to tread (water) carefully. Scientists writing in 2019 continue to call attention to the unknowns here: not enough is known about ship noise, which is focused downward into the water and may transmit over long ranges.[134] Scientists lack controls for studying animal behavior, for vessel types, and for environmental conditions.[135] Et cetera. This is all true, but at a certain point it may be of equal if not greater value to review *what is known*: noise is caused by shipping, military exercises, and geologic surveying activities.[136] Noise masks whale expression between companions and family members, and dulls animals' perceptions of threats in their environments (including ships and predators). As much as 80 percent of communications among some species of whales is masked by noise. Noises emitted in geological surveys not only harm cetaceans, they kill krill and phytoplankton (baleen whales' food)[137] and disturb other marine life-forms as well.[138] Speaking to a journalist (and not in a peer-reviewed publication), a scientist said with certainty, "[Noise pollution is] ripping the communications system apart. . . . And every aspect of [cetaceans'] lives is dependent on sound, including finding food."[139]

Lilly's (and others') work to shape the perception of cetaceans as wise, garrulous creatures and potential interlocutors undoubtedly still bears an imprint in the present-day public outcry regarding cetaceans' sonic abuse at the hands of military and industrial actors. A 2016 documentary, *Sonic Sea*, claimed "our ocean is a symphony," and that "songs of whales are drowned out by man made noise."[140] This language (as well as the vivid invocation of cetaceans' "screams" in the hearings leading to the passage of the MMPA) is worthy of scrutiny. In spite of the way that this language sparks human empathy, it does not necessarily dictate that animal welfare will follow. It also subtly sets up an anthropomorphism that might be better left behind: the embodied realities of seeing and hearing cannot necessarily be translated across species, nor should whales singing or hearing "like people" be the prerequisite for conservation.[141] Furthermore, the five senses Euro-Americans often assume to be universal (sight, hearing, smell, taste, and touch) are rooted in culture; other possible ones include muscle sense, temperature sense, and movement sense.[142] One can only imagine that crossing species boundaries, embodied sensory experiences would be truly ineffable and incommensurable.[143] Media scholar Melody Jue, arguing against "terrestrial bias," notes that some "sea creatures would seem to possess modes of synesthesia that combine at least two of 'our' [human] senses." She offers examples of sensory regimes that would strain analogy with human experience: octopuses can taste with their tentacles; and mantis shrimp have more than five times as many types of light-sensing cones in their eyes as humans do, attuning them to a much broader range of the electromagnetic spectrum.[144]

The attempt to know with total certainty how cetacean acoustics function is part of what drew cetaceans into being objects of military research: "acoustics was part of a system of 'total war.'" The US Navy did recognize that the cetacean sensorium might differ from that of humans; some posited that cetaceans' sound waves might convey the internal emotional state of their sender and thus speculated that dolphins partook in telekinesis.[145] But this was still within a behaviorist paradigm that served as the grounds for further experimentation, trying to open up the cetacean sensorium to being abstracted, quantified, and used as a tool of war. Thus, recognizing cetacean communication as in some ways incommensurable with that of humans and even *unknowable* may open up space for the conduct of science at a greater remove from industrial and state relations that harm cetaceans (and other creatures, including people).

Both politically and ethically, anthropomorphizing the mystical whale or glamorous dolphin is undesirable—and, moreover, has likely hit its limits as a conservation strategy. And yet, there might be some utility in thinking about the unalienable freedoms that international law aspires to grant to people.[146] Article 19 of the Universal Declaration of Human Rights states that "Everyone has the *right to freedom of opinion and expression*; this right includes freedom to hold opinions without interference and *to seek, receive and impart information and ideas through any media and regardless of frontiers*" (emphasis added). The 2010 People's Agreement of Cochabamba builds on this (though it breaks with the Western liberal tradition) in a Universal Declaration on the Rights of Mother Earth, which stipulates that all planetary inhabitants also possess "the right to maintain their identity and integrity as differentiated beings, self-regulated and inter-related."[147] John Durham Peters has playfully suggested that dolphins may have an aquatic public sphere: "'Democracy takes time,' speculated one marine biologist, 'and they spend hours every day making decisions,'" he writes.[148] To be clear, I am not suggesting that cetaceans should be granted the right to communicate through any (watery) medium, regardless of frontiers (including those imposed by the settler expansion of the United

States) because they are *like us*.[149] But we might consider that they are *like them*, self-regulated and interrelated, and act accordingly, rather than fret about unknowns.

There are three main conclusions that can be drawn from cetaceans' uneasy life in the Southern California Bight. One, nonhuman lives can attune us to a fuller range of ideas associated with the frontier and exertion of colonial power.[150] Whales' calls, like their bodies, travel across distances and borders.[151] Two, cetacean sovereignty is here in conflict with land use and relations that claim land (and water) for generating value.[152] No longer being industrial commodities has been insufficient to insulate whales from industrial harm; trade and empire generate pollution, which threatens them "incidentally." The Southern California Bight is a site of struggle: infrastructural vitalism grants sovereignty to "stuff" and prizes the movement of goods, specifically commercial shipping and its closely linked cousin, imperialism; this threatens organismic flourishing and sovereignty. As scientists wrote of gray whales in 2019, "The coastal [migration] route may provide more protection from predators and opportunistic foraging but also has a greater risk of negative interactions with humans through entanglements, ship strikes, background noise."[153]

Could *transspecies supply-chain justice* provide a way into countering state and industry claims to territorialization and value extraction? If shipping and trade included audits for just resource extraction, human labor, and multispecies ecological effects, how might this change the lives of marine mammals, factory and dockworkers, miners, colonized people, farmed animals, and agricultural workers?[154] By contrast, discourse is now emerging about "saving the whales" on the grounds that they are carbon sinks. Economists at the International Monetary Fund estimated in 2019 that "each of these gentle giants [humpback whales] is worth about $2 million over its lifetime" and that the "entire global population of great whales [might be] a one trillion dollar asset to humanity."[155] This has led to calls for financialization: if conceptualized as whale-based carbon credits (and priced "correctly"), whales may become literally worth more alive than dead. But this logic is still very much in line with the state and industrial relations that got the whales where they are today in the first place.

Writing in 2020, marine biologists proposed the introduction of a "whale presence metric" for the Santa Barbara channel.[156] This was produced using the techniques that underlie Whale Safe: visual surveys, analysis of calls, and habitat modeling. The notion that "the acoustic lives of whales can be abstracted, mechanized, and to some extent automated" is (obviously) a vestige of military cetology.[157] The "whale presence metric" can reproduce the territorializing, extractive relations that harm whales

and ultimately undermine conservation strategies: scientists are interested
in the calls that indicate whale presence in a few congested shipping lanes,
in order to minimize conflict between whales and ships so that commerce
may proceed. But some of the lower frequency sounds emitted by baleen
whales can travel as far as 10,000 miles (and of course many calls are outside the range of human hearing). Thus being attuned to an expansive notion of "whale presence" can also potentially gesture toward how whales
and their utterances have *spatial and sonic logics of their own*.

The third point that cetaceans in the Southern California Bight draws
out is this: without endorsing anthropomorphism or *equivalence*, surfacing
creaturely voice (or creaturely audition, or creaturely sensing and communication that have no analogues in the human sensorium) may also begin
to surface *creaturely sovereignty* in productive ways.[158] This can orient us
toward relations that would promote flourishing, beginning with precaution and giving grounds to exceed it, such as contesting the capitalistic and
settler colonial relations that structure life in the Southern California Bight
now. How might the *presence* of whales' sensorium, their (unintelligible
to us) long-distance calls, speak to a potential for immersion in the multi-
sensory world, rather than violent control of it?[159]

FLUX

Bridging to Futures

A century after the industrial discovery of oil in the harbor of San Pedro Bay, port managers and city officials proudly announced the opening of a newly constructed bridge (fig. 46). High above the water, the Long Beach International Gateway bridge connects the port complex to the I-710 freeway (the "commercial spine of Southern California").[1] Boosters claimed that this $1.47 billion infrastructure project would "help define life in Los Angeles for generations." A decade in the making, the new bridge would allow for the smooth passage of extremely large cargo ships, which had gotten so massive that the largest ones were unable to pass beneath the previous bridge except at low tide, and some did not fit at all (fig. 47).[2] Engineers consulted with maritime experts to determine the likely specifications of *future* cargo ships, anticipating a continuing rise in cargo imports and ship dimensions. Officials repeatedly emphasized that the investment was worth the cost because it would serve the region for a century to come: "We're thinking of this as a 100-year bridge."[3]

What lessons are held in the contested ecological and industrial past, present, and future of San Pedro Bay? Energy systems, international trade, and logistics are global phenomena, but also local ones.[4] Present-day California may evoke the "shiny" software industry and Silicon Valley more than dirty petroleum, but it is home to both, and they are intimately tied. In fact, oil revenues spurred the development of the semiconductor and computing industries themselves; historian of engineering Cyrus C. M. Mody argues that the computing industry should be understood as an arm of the fossil fuel industry.[5] Petroleum and computing are also linked through logistics. California oil wealth drove trade expansion (as in Long Beach rolling its municipal oil profits into port improvements), facilitated

FIGURE 46. The new Long Beach International Gateway bridge, about 50 feet higher than the old bridge (visible on right), late 2020.
Courtesy Port of Long Beach.

FIGURE 47. The earlier Gerald Desmond Bridge, 2012 (opened 1968).
Photo by McKenzie Stribich.

by logistics science, itself facilitated by computing technologies that enabled new kinds of cost calculation.[6] As LA in the twenty-first century attempts to lure members of the "tech" industry south (dubbing itself "Silicon Beach"), it is worth noting that the substrate beneath Silicon Valley is actually Oil Beach.

San Pedro Bay's industrial infrastructure is a node in a world system that mobilizes sophisticated calculation techniques to circulate fuel, goods, and capital. In San Pedro Bay, the past half-century has seen an intensified pursuit of scale in trade alongside a host of projects to manage wildlife, all the while accompanied by the movement of petroleum. In recent decades, though the port complex here has seen modest expansions, its greater effect is arguably fueling (sometimes literally) infrastructural expansion elsewhere, through its participation in flows of capital and goods. For instance, China currently spends more on infrastructure than the United States and Western Europe combined, and in 2003–2008 it spent more on infrastructure than it had in the whole of the twentieth century; and Canadian companies operating on several continents annually extract billions of tons of resources used in fabrication of goods and infrastructure.[7] Thus a local snapshot may understate the effects of the port complex; we also need to account for the assemblages that have been mobilized on other continents to drive the influx of goods here. (The top five containerized imports into the Port of LA in 2020 were furniture, auto parts, apparel, electronics, and plastics, and trade with China was at least three times higher than with any other trading partner.[8]) Meanwhile, a warming earth, which is linked to fossil fuel emissions, is causing sea level rise, climate crisis, geopolitical crisis: threats to lives and ways of life for many.

But as I hope I have now made clear, harbors are spaces of flux. This space, the port complex embedded into San Pedro Bay, is a confluence where "universals and particulars come together to create the forms of capitalism with which we live," in the words of anthropologist Anna Tsing.[9] In the remainder of this book, I attempt to peer ahead to futures in San Pedro Bay. The new bridge, completed in late 2020, will no doubt "help define life in Los Angeles for generations," but not necessarily in the way harbor managers intend. In any event, there are better and worse potentials contained within this statement.

First, let's consider life and energy. Acting as delegates of the climate crisis, activists and civil society are pressuring states to transition toward more renewable, less polluting alternatives. Though there is a growing cry for so-called clean energy, it is not a given that transitioning *toward* cleaner energy sources would be accompanied by a transition *away from* fossil fuels. Earlier episodes in the history of fuel suggest that new energy

sources may increase demand for energy consumption, as opposed to leading to preservation of the prior fuel.[10] This actually happened with whales
in an earlier era: whales' journey through (and eventually past) industrial
commodification did not end with the shift away from using them as a fuel
source. In fact, as fossil fuel gained ascendancy, whaling turned toward
finding new efficiencies, according to environmental sociologist Richard
York. As whalers were already invested in the commodification of whales,
they took the opportunity of new fuel sources to innovate modern whaling
techniques in approximately the same moment that petroleum crowded
out whales as fuel. Steamships could hunt whales with greater speed than
sail-powered ships. Another innovation was whale processing at sea on factory ships, which did not need to return to shore until they had filled to
capacity. Whalers harvested raw whale materials at sea which they then
transported to shore and sold to be processed into new kinds of commodities, like glycerin and hydrogenated margarine, made possible through scientific innovation.[11] Perversely, what saved whales from extermination was
industrial whaling at scale: whale populations could not replenish themselves with the level of killing that was taking place, so the recognition that
all species that had been hunted were dramatically depleted provided im-
petus for conservation efforts in the mid-twentieth century.[12] Whales' near
extinction ironically made it easier for commercial whalers to step back,
as profitability had already fallen. Relative conservation successes notwithstanding, global populations of several species never rebounded from
intensive whaling.[13]

   All of this is to say that we should not expect that renewable energy
sources will necessarily topple petroleum per se. The port complex is curiously positioned here. To repeat, the petroleum infrastructure in the port
complex represents a long-term, fixed investment cemented in an earlier
era; massive refining and transport operations in the port can transfer petroleum from ship to shore and land transport (transshipment); and crude
oil represents approximately one-third of maritime cargo globally. Even
as state officials and other regulators pressure the ports to clean up ship,
truck, and rail emissions, the port complex is still a key intermediate node
in the import and export of petroleum. In 2020, the United States was a
net petroleum exporter, though most regions including California imported more fuel than they exported. (California's main sources of foreign
oil are Saudi Arabia, Iraq, Colombia, and Ecuador, as of 2021.[14] Foreign oil
is sometimes imported as crude and exported as a refined product, like jet
fuel. Recall that the United States also exports refined products that are
deemed too dirty for domestic consumption, like petcoke.)

   Even if Los Angeles, California, or the United States somehow turns away from producing or consuming fossil fuels *locally*, the investment in the port infrastructure for petroleum *transport* could linger. Coastal California has granted some new extraction permits in recent years, but the main action for drilling in California is inland; Kern County, the southern end of the Central Valley, plans to issue permits for around 43,000 new oil and gas wells before 2035.[15] Regulators are being urged to "phase out" extraction in California by 2045—more than twenty years from now.[16] All in all, unless states and countries commit to "leaving it in the ground" and banning its use, petroleum extraction and consumption may persist even with the rise of alternative energy sources.[17] (The petroleum industry is also renewing itself through plastics, as a hedge against a decline in fossil fuel use.[18])

Unlikely as it may be given the level of investment in the status quo, if the value of petroleum were to plummet to a level where it became no longer profitable as a commodity, petroleum infrastructure in the ports (and elsewhere) could become a noxious ruin. Around 135 operable refineries existed in the United States as of early 2020; in early 2021, at least seven large refineries had recently announced they were shuttering.[19] Though it is almost unimaginable that industrial petroleum could depart from Southern California, if it did, the port complex and the region would be haunted by its highly toxic chemical legacy.[20] Cleaning up and remediating a single large refinery site would take at least a decade and cost billions of dollars (and companies tend to not leave behind adequate resources to cover these expenses). On a smaller scale, idle and abandoned wells dot the landscape. Some of them have been sealed; many are insufficiently cared for and represent emissions and explosion risks to surrounding communities.[21] A small "pumpjack graveyard" on port land houses decommissioned apparatus, remnants of an energy regime in miniature (fig. 48).

Infrastructural commitments create path dependencies; this is their very purpose. Though the port complex imports and exports a large volume of petroleum, I argue its most important product is simply *scale*. And this is a key point for thinking about the recent past, present, and future of San Pedro Bay. Roughly concurrent with environmental regulation and conservation efforts that affected several creatures in this book was the rise of financialization, achieved through the deregulation of banking and financial services and the "invention" of complex financial instruments.[22] Capital, unbound, was swapped and bundled and electronically traded at high frequency, leading to well-documented malfeasance and volatility. But financialization also drove "massive investment . . . in the complementary sphere of commodity (rather than money) circulation, increasing the throughput of the transportation system and accelerating

FIGURE 48. Decommissioned pumpjacks on Port of Long Beach land, 2021.
Photo by McKenzie Stribich.

the velocity of commodity capital through a buildout in the form of tankers, port complexes, railyards, robotically-controlled distribution centers,
and the digital and network technology needed to manage the increased
volume and complexity of trade," writes literature and technology scholar
Jasper Bernes.[23] In other words, complex assemblages of credit and commodity futures trading accelerated a push for an ever-greater volume of
trade, overseen with the aid of integrated information systems that allowed
managers to see, expand, contract, and reroute supply chains quickly and
"responsively."[24] This pattern takes local form in many different places on
earth, driving extraction, fabrication, shipping, and other processes.

Scale is what drove bananas *out of* the port complex at the turn of the
twenty-first century; as a perishable commodity, bananas needed to be
routed to smaller, more specialized ports that could handle them without
the delays of the high-volume Long Beach/LA complex. Ever more cargo
passed through the ports. This has already had consequences: all of this
transport over land and sea has been fueled by petroleum, driving planetary heating that has affected crops, wildlife, and human life both locally
and elsewhere on earth. Banana cultivation is already being affected by
more intense storms, and heating and storms affect the lives and liveli-
hoods of many people in equatorial and tropical regions, forcing migration and causing immense suffering. Freight volume also exposes people

living near distribution sites and along freight corridors to toxic emissions, as well.

Over the past half-century or so, policymakers have instituted a series of regulations intended to respond to a regime of infrastructure building that had rapidly altered ecologies in San Pedro Bay and elsewhere. Especially since the turn of the twenty-first century, the port complex likes to present its "green" side: a 2018 biological survey touted modest gains in the number of species living in the outer harbor of the port complex.[25] Without discounting this finding, focusing on environmental gains—preservation or remediation—within processes of empire and commerce masks the broader context of social, political, and economic relations to which the port complex belongs and contributes, including mistreatment of people, landscapes, and wildlife locally and all along supply chains.[26]

What this book shows is that wildlife management practices run alongside logistics science and in effect work together to *stabilize* the assemblage that is the port complex. The past half-century of regulation has not *fundamentally* changed the relations that caused the ecological endangerment here. The production of scientific knowledge in this context helps build and maintain infrastructure: even if scientific knowledge is sometimes also mobilized to combat infrastructure's effects, governance of San Pedro Bay is guided by managerial commitments to infrastructural vitalism. Care for bird life has been paradoxically dependent on oil revenue to fund the facilities which tend to these animals. Individual birds may also go for inadvertent rides on shipping currents, which deliver them along with cargo to ports where, if they are noticed, they might receive attention that brings them into care and even home. Regulatory protections mean that individuals may be counted or even relocated with exquisite care. However, regulatory compliance is arguably as much *to meet legal requirements that will allow industrial activity to persist* as it is to allow birds, fish, crabs, eelgrass, and kelp to live in flourishing relation.

In Northern California, bull kelp that scientists imagine will live in reciprocal relation with otters is dying due to ocean warming. (Purple sea urchins are thriving, and hastening the kelp's demise.) In the Southern California Bight, wildlife managers granted otters only diminished access to their former coastal and open water habitat until 2011, and their survival depends now on inhabiting new ecologies like the Elkhorn Slough with the aid of otter foster parents and human managers. The only otters in San Pedro Bay today are in captivity, even though the bight was part of their historical range. Giant kelp, which grows in the warmer Southern California waters, is thought to be more resilient to heating.[27] If the US

Army Corps of Engineers and other parties reestablish more giant kelp in the southern waters, it might potentially be possible to reintroduce otters to help maintain this marine ecology, but USACE is not engineering its San Pedro Bay restoration project with this in mind. Rather, USACE has been clear that "restoration" will not affect the large-scale industrial functions of the harbor.

For whales, scale has led to increasing ship strikes and sensory disorientation.[28] Ocean noise has doubled each decade. Whales off the coast of California compete with commercial vessels for space in the corridor between the shore and the Channel Islands—and commercial shippers prefer this space in part because the US military has claimed the open ocean on the far side of the islands.[29] A multispecies account of San Pedro Bay shows that wildlife habitat can only be fashioned within established commercial and settler colonial relations that also drove infrastructural projects. And this short summary represents only a nonexhaustive account of the effects of this commitment to goods movement at scale on some of the most familiar and most charismatic creatures: that is, it almost certainly understates effects on organismic ecologies.[30]

The same regulators that ask the port complex to clean up its act recognize that it is a driving force in the region's economy.[31] Economic aspirations routinely undercut stated commitments to curbing emissions and limiting heating. When a heatwave in September 2020 knocked down the electrical grid, regulators gave the port a pass to run off generator and engine power. Greater LA residents, already sweltering and beset by choking wildfire smoke, now inhaled a higher volume of diesel particulates, all the while without electricity for lights or refrigerators, let alone air conditioning.[32]

But pausing trade was not an option. This underscores the "vitalism" of the port complex within a network of relations devoted to trade. Officials who frame it as a "beating heart" or "backbone" imbue it with a *liveness*.[33] In a 2021 snapshot of trade statistics, the Port of LA proudly proclaimed, "For the past 20 years, the Port of Los Angeles has been the busiest container port in the Western Hemisphere. With record volumes for containerized trade, economic activity generated by the Port . . . is a bellwether for the *health* of the overall U.S. economy."[34] This is not only a metaphor; it constructs a lively system where threats to circulation enact a biological politics, because the health and life of the system must be maintained.[35] For regional managers tasked with prioritizing the system's survival and resilience, there may be an uneasy question of *who is controlling what (or whom)*.[36] In the wake of the pandemic, surging cargo accelerated conversations about shifting to "24/7" supply-chain operation in the port complex, which was not in place, though some components were already in operation round-the-clock. In this, San Pedro Bay was "behind" major Asian ports.[37]

In devoting themselves to ensuring the circulation of the lifeblood that is trade, regional managers have perhaps boxed themselves into a corner: in the short and medium term, if the port and regional warehouse and distribution infrastructure cannot keep up with volume at a competitive cost, the region will theoretically lose business that will simply be routed elsewhere.[38] Seattle, Tacoma, Vancouver, and Oakland can all receive goods and in theory present alternatives to "overtaxed" Southern California.[39] So can New Orleans, Savannah, and Newark; the widened Panama Canal allows extremely large ships traveling from Asia or the Pacific coast of Latin America to pass through to the eastern United States and beyond. Other ports show the same trends as those in Los Angeles, making infrastructural adjustments geared toward increasing scale.[40] Goods can then travel by rail or truck to their ultimate destinations, just as they would after arriving in Long Beach or Los Angeles. Therefore, managers scramble to keep the ports in San Pedro Bay humming. It is clear whose transit and whose survival is being privileged here: that of goods and trade.

It is thus impossible to arrest the lethality of global trade without acknowledging that it is scale, not just "cleaner transport," that needs to be addressed. The circulation of capital coupled with the rise of logistics were designed to extract resources and labor, reducing the financial cost of this circulation while driving up its volume. Cleaner modes of transport could reduce tailpipe emissions from shipping, trucking, and rail.[41] But the production of many goods for trade is nonetheless still carbon intensive and otherwise exploitive with regards to resources and labor. For instance, cleaner shipping and refrigeration for banana boats does not address the exposure of workers, their families, and wildlife to fungicides and pesticides in the bananas' places of origin. Demand for inexpensive bananas in locations far from where they are grown drives extractive, neocolonial relationships with producer nations and harmful ecological and labor practices within them. And raw bananas are less resource intensive than goods whose fabrication requires mining, for instance. A (renewable and reconfigurable) dream of effortless freight obscures the true relations responsible for the movement of goods.[42]

To be clear, this is not an argument against global trade but rather *against exploitation*. In the 1990s, Zapatistas and other resistance groups specified that they were not opposed to "globalization" but to the terms of *corporate* globalization. Opposing the North American Free Trade Agreement (NAFTA) in the 1990s, they called for "alter-globalization," in a global justice movement that contested "market globalism."[43] The key here is to insist upon more just relations of trade, including labor and environmental protections along supply chains, but not those of commerce and empire. Rather, this is a political project that aims to support "on-the-ground struggles fighting for justice and the active acknowledgment of the value of all forms of life in the world."[44] In practice: enhance community self-determination (very much including Indigenous sovereignty); reject threshold models for pollution in extraction regimes; and generally include rights of refusal regarding lethal systems.

FLUX REDUX: TOWARD TRANSSPECIES SUPPLY-CHAIN JUSTICE?

Because of how it is implicated in multiple lethal world systems, San Pedro Bay is (perversely) an *especially good* place to imagine how relations here might be otherwise. "[T]ransformative responses to the threat of extinction" are urgently needed.[45] Port managers and state and regional leaders can acknowledge that business as usual is unsustainable sooner, or they can acknowledge it later. As a petroleumscape, San Pedro Bay offers an opportunity to think about "clean energy" and lowered emissions, as well as a just transition. To arrest climate crisis, petroleum needs to be "left in the ground," but this is not enough. Becoming energy efficient, switching energy sources, and curtailing consumption at the high end of the scale—where it is straining planetary boundaries—are within reach. This does not mean worsening standards of living for everyday people in rich countries, and it does not mean imposing scarcity in rich countries or (heretofore) poorer ones.[46] But leaders need to let go of a vision of a future that is simply a continuation of the present, imagining energy used to power freight movement changing only in source.[47] Unfortunately, this ignores the waste, carbon, and highly extractive relations implicated in producing new conveyances to move ever more cargo.[48]

Furthermore, leaders' fetishization of the gross domestic product (GDP) as a metric of economic health is fictive and harmful, as it leads to the pursuit of capitalist expansion that is literally terracidal.[49] Endless year over year growth is not sustainable, but living with what we have should be comfortable, and this would be ensured with increased provision of public goods, spaces, and services. Controlled economic rebalancing—what some would call "degrowth"—means scaling down the material throughput of the economy, rebalancing priorities.[50] Regional managers have been channeling currents of global capital which, I have argued, have been only somewhat within local control. Aggressively moving to scale back movement of both petroleum and other goods in San Pedro Bay is the wise choice to allow the region a habitable future.

In a context like the US empire, infrastructures are linchpins in political and economic domination. As such, opening up infrastructures for material and methodological scrutiny is fruitful for imagining how they might be otherwise.[51] In a historical study of the Port of Tacoma, political ecologist Amory Ballantine traces a trajectory similar to that of San Pedro Bay: colonization; industrialization; channelizing the Puyallup River; dumping of organic waste and highly toxic chemical contaminants like PCBs. Where the Tacoma story differs, however, is that members of the Puyallup tribal nation participated in civil disobedience actions in the 1960s and 1970s (the "Fish Wars"), forcing attention to and ultimately affirming treaty rights. The Puyallup tribe then sued the Port of Tacoma, railroad companies, and other polluting industries. Ballantine's account traces water quality from the mid-1800s to the present and correlates aquatic and estuarine habitat health to tribal sovereignty, arguing that the tribe's legal challenges to colonization made a positive impact on water quality.[52] Superior environmental stewardship that benefits settlers (let alone their GDPs) is not the main goal, of course. Rather, political and ecological phenomena are tightly twinned; the Puyallup tribe's successful contestation of the "legally vested system of advantages and rights" used to secure white settler property regimes also improved estuarine health.[53]

Metrics like GDP both obscure and drive the violence of infrastructure. "Following the infrastructure" will definitively reveal struggle and potentially open up space to think about other metrics to which infrastructures could be tied.[54] Research on railroads in North America, for instance, shows that their construction relied on not just enslaved labor but significant capital generated by enslaved labor. Thus studying the history and present of railroads yields insight into the workings of racial capitalism and presents a case for reparations.[55] Similarly, standing could be given to indicators of Indigenous sovereignty. These are moral calculations—but so is GDP, whether or not acknowledged as such. It is not impossible that *infrastructure could be "life-giving in its design, finance, and effects,"* if scripted differently.[56]

Knowing that relationships across "nature" and infrastructures will need to be managed in perpetuity does not resolve fundamental questions about what that will look like.[57] But conceiving of "the environment" as a space or set of relations in a manner that distinguishes the "natural" world from human spaces of living, working, and being has justified the adoption of managerial strategies applied to the distinct "natural" world as a separate space.[58] Such "environmentalism" turns away from acknowledging that

"global-scale forces of earth violence" have origins as projects of domination against Indigenous peoples in addition to landscapes and wildlife.[59]
Further, many of the originating managerial beliefs about environmental
stewardship were of a piece with the visions of global "mastery" claimed
by white supremacy and eugenics.[60] Planning for ceaseless growth through
the infrastructural forms of channel deepening, bridge raising, and freeway
widening represents commitment to infrastructural vitalism, which conflicts with organismic life.[61] The forces that conspire to gather the breath
and promote the "health" of the port complex do so at the behest of capital
managers and business leaders, local politicians, and, of course, agents of
the US empire, maximizing profit through resource extraction, labor exploitation, and colonial land (and water) relations.[62]

As a point of goods transfer, San Pedro Bay offers opportunity for con-
scientiously juxtaposing ecological relations with harbor functions. Major ports currently compete to prop up the violent system of expanding
global trade; this trend, visible in the LA harbor, is global. Endless growth
is likely to end badly—it is not an exaggeration to say the port complex's
new bridge is a bridge to terracide, if changes are not made. Rather than
simply supporting mindless growth, port infrastructure meant to support
the "frictionless" movement of goods could be reimagined as an audit
point for *transspecies supply-chain justice*. The ports' positioning in transshipment schemes could be applied toward monitoring labor and manufacturing processes and ecological impacts of goods that pass through
these ports, and shoring up fair labor and support for organismic ecologies at home too. Currently, goods that pass through this site may be accompanied by labor, anticolonial, or ecological struggles, but those struggles have been sufficiently detached from the goods to allow the goods to
pass through the port complex. However, given that a port is not a destination but a site to hand off goods, it is well positioned to *connect* goods
to struggle, not only sever them. Aiming for a fuller accounting of and
reckoning with the conditions of production, use, and post-use of what-
ever passes through this site opens up possibilities here. To accomplish
this would mean handling a lower volume of goods, for starters. But there
must be ways to undo scale and to execute goods movement that would
be better for local and distant economies and ecologies than growth for
growth's sake.

Transspecies supply-chain justice is *not* meant to be a technocratic, top-
down standard applied to current regimes of goods movement.[63] Rather, it
is a flexible idea meant to guide thinking about this space: the port complex, San Pedro Bay, and other spaces like them. What kinds of knowledge
and politics could run through them instead, if the annihilative power of

logistics could be subdued? In the United States, energy and the citizenship of goods are intimately tied, as the US military is reliant on affordable and accessible sources of energy. If residents of Los Angeles or the United States are keen to promote organismic ecologies, or resist the rise of fascist social orders that mobilize zero-sum logics of scarcity, it will help to have a clear-eyed analysis of what is at stake in San Pedro Bay. Though port officials have touted their goal of creating a "green port" and made some gains in combating air and water pollution locally, endless economic growth, predicated on resource extraction and the concentration of wealth, is not sustainable, for human or nonhuman life, in San Pedro Bay or elsewhere.[64] Business as usual for a very few is uncomfortably hot for many, and lethal for some. By spending less money on fuel and operations to secure access to petroleum (or post-petroleum energy sources), the United States could decrease military spending and reorient its economy away from imperialism.[65] (Note that even after the navy shuttered its San Pedro Bay shipyard in the 1990s, allowing the port managers to turn the space over to commercial shipping, the military fueling function remained in the harbor.) At the end of the day—or the beginning of a new one, we might hope—violent state orders that limit justice and sovereignty should be up for debate.

Such a reorientation may seem vanishingly unlikely. But "disparate lives of [labor and social] movements are connected through the infrastructures of logistics space."[66] It is worth drawing out the relationship between social movements (including those which mobilize around both political sovereignty and biodiversity): struggles over resource control and extraction in producer nations run through the port complex, whether or not they are acknowledged as such.[67] Logistics is far from an "apolitical" science of management.[68] Rather than accepting the violent mystification of commodities' origins in distant and distributed supply chains, local stewards, logistics managers, and regional planners could choose to invest in lively and life-affirming infrastructural engagement with the origins and intermediate points of passage of the goods that transit through ports and transshipment spaces, including human and nonhuman labor practices, toxic exposures, conditions of sovereignty, and fair recompense.[69]

Or activists and ordinary citizens could *force them to*.[70] It may be that accepting violence to life is simply realpolitik. But there are meaningful distinctions between systematized, industrial violence at scale and, say, the violence of the food chain. Working to "conserve" wildlife within a status quo of violence is not only paradoxical, it fails to confront root problems. Specifically, the violence which has so long been a by-product of petroleum companies and American imperial pursuits in port operations calls for reconsideration and resistance. This is already happening: civil disobedience to suspend fossil fuel extraction is a feature of Indigenous-led resistance movements across North America (and, as American Studies scholar and anticolonial organizer Nick Estes says, this is not merely a "fight *against* settler colonialism, but *for* Indigenous life and just relations with human and nonhuman relatives and the earth").[71] It is no coincidence that this resistance has centered on infrastructure: in the past decade in North America, attempts to halt pipeline construction have featured in struggles over the construction and operation of the Dakota Access Pipeline, the Keystone XL pipeline, and the Enbridge Line 3 pipeline.[72] In 2020, rail lines in Canada were met with blockades organized by protesters in solidarity with the Wet'suwet'en First Nation members who opposed a methane gas pipeline running through their land.[73] These inland struggles implicate and literally connect to coastal ports and refineries because ports and refineries are an ultimate destination for extracted fossil fuels (Canadian tar sands oil, like that in inland California, is especially heavy and dirty).[74] Infrastructure for the movement of goods, fuel, and the literal stuff of infrastructural expansion, like cement components, is a significant vulnerability in global capitalism and territorial regimes.[75] Writing of a 2011 blockade at the Port of Oakland organized by the Occupy! Movement in 2011, Jasper Bernes writes, "the quieted machinery of the port quickly became an emblem for the complex totality of capitalist production it seemed both to eclipse and to reveal."[76]

In California, on Friday, June 19, 2020 (Juneteenth), the longshoremen's union (International Longshore and Warehouse Union, ILWU) shut down all West Coast port operations (including Long Beach and LA but also Seattle and Oakland) in solidarity with the Black Lives Matter movement.[77] This unusual occurrence was sparked in reaction to the intertwined injustices of police brutality and killings, most recently the murder of George Floyd in Minneapolis, but also the COVID-19 pandemic, which was disproportionately infecting and killing people of color in the United States, especially Black, Indigenous, Latinx, and Pacific Islander people.[78] One reason for excess mortality in these communities was underlying respiratory illness caused by environmental racism; as noted earlier, poor and racialized communities are most likely to live adjacent to industrial polluters (highways, refineries, and in greater Los Angeles, the port complex itself).[79] Another was the designation of "essential worker": "essential workers have no choice but to put themselves at risk, working in industries—such as meat processing, agriculture, and logistics—where they keep supply chains operational so that others may work remotely. Those whose work is categorized as 'essential' are often those whose lives are most precarious."[80]

In greater Los Angeles, regional managers justify keeping the ports

humming and upgrading their infrastructure by citing their economic contributions, claiming that one in twelve jobs in the region are linked to the
ports.[81] However, there is reason to question whether these are good jobs,
or good for the health of the polity: racialized workers experience high
rates of contingent, hazardous, and low-wage work in logistics centers,
picking goods in warehouses, or driving forklifts, trucks, and delivery vehicles.[82] Warehouse work is difficult, hot, and dirty, and workers are commonly exposed to toxic chemicals in exhaust; as many as 40 percent report
either getting hurt on the job or feeling ill due to hazardous emissions.[83]
Many people also live near oil wells, freeways, and distribution centers
(sometimes in informal settlements).[84] Despite a low rate of unemploy-
ment, California has a very high rate of poverty.[85] Real estate and oil, both
implicated in the land management including and surrounding the port
complex, have concentrated wealth in the hands of a few at the expense of
many, along predictable patterns of racial domination.[86] Schoolchildren in
the poor neighborhoods of Los Angeles breathe polluted air daily at home
and at school; and one day in 2020, several of them in the small incorporated city of Cudahy were casually doused with jet fuel from above when
a passing airliner dumped fuel in order to meet its weight requirement for
safe landing.[87]

Without in any way minimizing the injuries to communities or individual people, the casual infliction of petroleum-based industrial violence
here in some ways has parallels with industrial harms visited upon wildlife,
particularly oiled marine life-forms. At the same time, because of media
and environmental movement fixations on charismatic wildlife, public outcry over an injured cetacean might be greater than that over a doused racialized child, which is plainly unjust (and a reminder of the noninnocence
of "care").[88] Environmental historian Gregg Mitman has commented that
Americans may care more about dolphins than ecosystems, with the aim
of revealing how the dolphin came to play a starring role in environmental
narratives.[89] His observation also carries the implication that privileging
a species over ecological relationships inhibits a discerning assessment of
ecological justice, reifying human exceptionalism for some (ironically including cetaceans, since the 1960s) while consigning others ("others") to
violence outside the frame.[90]

Taking a cue from the ILWU and the Movement for Black Lives, as well
as other anticolonial infrastructural conflicts like #NODAPL, port operations could be a site to imagine a commitment to life mattering, to sovereign accumulation of life.[91] "Beyond the accidental break-downs and stop-
pages that threaten just-in-time supply chains are more deliberate efforts
to interrupt the circulation of violence and remake environmentally and

socially just forms of provisioning and sustaining," write Charmaine Chua and her coauthors.[92] Rather than ports and logistics being implicated in deadly violence, what might it take to instead facilitate an infrastructural project of transspecies supply-chain justice, beginning with fossil kin; and including local and distant dock and warehouse workers; fabricators of goods in Asia and Latin America; as well as heron and sea lion neighbors?[93] Zoe Todd's conception of oil-kin is instructive: it reorients us to vitalism in a generative way, reminding us of the need to *tend to life*; and it looks for points of relation and coconstitution both upstream and downstream. What forms of accountability can be imagined and constructed to halt and repair the accumulative injury that occurs due to dwelling within industrial and militarized territories?[94] To be speculative for a moment, can sea lions, currently afflicted with cancer from industrial poisoning yet denied health insurance, form a union with the herons, schoolteachers, and warehouse and dockworkers—or add to the chorus calling for an anticolonial Green New Deal (or Red Deal[95])? In all seriousness, a chokepoint like the port complex in San Pedro Bay invites consideration of what might be possible at intersections of workplace democracy, antiracist organizing, and reversal of Indigenous dispossession.[96] As a potent site for violence, it is also a potent site for imagining liberation.

Logistics functions to promote unimpeded capital flows, entwining military and corporate logics to unleash violent and universalizing effects, often either aligning lives with profit-seeking or maiming them en route. Life-forms across species boundaries in greater Los Angeles bear evidence of this tendency. For life, there is no innocent space or essential nature to return to in San Pedro Bay.[97] Regardless of decisions made by harbor managers, gray whales, kelp, truck drivers, or activists, residents will be sitting (or swimming) with a toxic mess there for some time.[98]

Still, remediation and repair is needed. Some advocate for deliberately leaving industrial waste on display for interpretive purposes: its historical significance and the lessons it embodies about the past.[99] This seems fitting in a post-petroleumscape; if the "post" part is ever realized, it might be preferable to leave pipelines and pumpjacks on view. Perhaps an "oil island"—currently disguised to seem more like a more conventional island—could be modified to expose its industrial function and preserved as a monument to a past era. Or—recalling the informal housing referenced in the preface—land now devoted to petroleum could be thoroughly remediated and converted to other uses, including homes and ecological support for people and wildlife victimized by climate crisis and toxins, and dispossessed by the antidemocratic governance that accompanied the rise of oil.[100] Current agents of infrastructural vitalism are not ideal stewards of other uses, either. Though environmental planning here generally requires "consultation" with front-line community members and tribal members, consultation is not equal to consent. (Note that none of coastal Southern California is under tribal control in the present day.)

It is not the main goal of this book to offer prescriptions. But I sign off with a suggestion that thinking with "many worlds" can be helpful.[101] Industrial projects at scale, especially those involving capitalist expansion processes, are attempts at universalizing, drawing labor, resources, and knowledge together to fit them into a single world that aims to reach and remake everywhere (even if universal claims of science and capitalism "do not actually make everything everywhere the same" in practice[102]). This suggests that the challenge of San Pedro Bay is to imagine a port deliberately set to allow many worlds to transit through it—to pursue in solidarities a world within which many worlds (human, nonhuman, and their hybrids) are not only maintained but are *infrastructurally accommodated*.[103] Because of how the port complex is a node in lethal global systems, local choices here could arrest destruction elsewhere as well.

Anticolonial sciences can play an important role in evaluating and tending to the ecologies here. This means the exercise of sciences that neither "reproduce settler and colonial entitlement to Land," especially as a "sacrifice zone" for pollution, nor attempt to control land without regard for specific lines of ecological relation in San Pedro Bay.[104] This would mean sciences that can situate themselves regarding, and even critique and counter universalism as required by infrastructural vitalism, which mainstream conservation struggles to do.[105] This requires thinking about harm differently, and thus is distinct from the US military's provision of its missile testing site for otter habitat or its fueling facility for an endangered butterfly.[106] It is also distinct from the US Army Corps of Engineers' acknowledgment that it played a role in the destruction of San Pedro Bay, given that the "restoration" that USACE is now planning explicitly leaves intact the violent machinations of trade and empire. [107] The latter contain and constrain its ecological inquiries.

In other words, to meaningfully consider the future of San Pedro Bay requires standing to face the history and context that have caused endangerment and violence. Though regulations limit the level of pollutants that can be spewed into air and water locally, and industrial activities are not supposed to impinge on wildlife to the point of annihilation, it would be naive to ignore that goods circulation at scale is what is primarily accommodated in the harbor, and this circulation's destructive capacity is profound and not limited to wildlife. This chokepoint, which is a known "vulnerability" for trade, is also an opportunity for the assertion of alternative systems of knowledge and power. To appraise and contest infrastructural vitalism is to redraw boundaries between the dead and living, which is "revolutionary but profoundly practical work."[108] Nonuniversalizing but overlapping (even contradictory at times) sovereignties and logistical solidarities could conjoin and flow here instead. This might take the form of refusal, of stoppage, of breakdown. If logistics is "constantly confronted by events and processes that exceed its own logic," it is plainly in the interest of those who wish to live in more just relations with human and nonhuman relatives and the earth to hasten and intensify these confrontations.[109] Controlled economic rebalancing, heightened community self-determination, and capital and empire in retreat, all flowing through the port complex, would give not only terns but also their human neighbors in Wilmington (who currently dwell amid refineries and along "diesel death zone" freight corridors) the opportunity to perch less precariously and breathe more easily. It might result in colorful flocks of bananas alighting in San Pedro Bay once more.[110] Or it might not. Only life considered and in better relation with infrastructure—not the presence of a given species or commodity—is what can signify repaired and renewed lines of ecological and political relation in San Pedro Bay.

Acknowledgments

I first wish to acknowledge San Pedro Bay—land, water, and past and present inhabitants—with its complex legacy that precedes and will outlast my narrative or knowledge of it. Though this book focuses on the period after 1900 (when the ports were built), the setup for the emergence of infrastructural vitalism is the context of colonial dispossession and capitalist economics. These political and economic systems coalesced in prior centuries and persist into the present, as does the inhabitance of this area by its first residents, Gabrielino-Tongva people.[1] I moved to California in 2016 and in the course of getting my bearings had to contend with my ambivalently adopted state being on fire at a suddenly explosive scale—fire here was "normal" (especially so before European settlement and United States and California land management policy, when Indigenous people practiced controlled burning in their land stewardship), but this incendiary present and future were not. This was also a moment in which, in the region where I grew up, Indigenous activists and young people were protesting and even blockading petroleum infrastructure, confronting the Dakota Access Pipeline in the upper Midwest, which connected petroleum extraction to transshipment sites like the one I now found in my backyard. As a highly mobile settler on this continent, I'm not sure where I call "home," but San Pedro Bay represents a breathtaking (in more ways than one) site for thinking about histories, futures, and lines of relationality, and I am grateful to have had an unexpected opportunity to think and learn with it. My project with *Oil Beach* is in keeping with the research practice of "studying up" in order to denaturalize power relationships (here, "studying the colonizers" means identifying and historicizing relationships between conservation practices and port managers' belief in infrastructural vitalism).[2] This text is less a finished book than one opening in an ongoing conversation, but it is my hope that this book can help contribute to a project of "experimentally living together, feeling obliged to others, without a sense of safety or control that requires violent domination," locally and further afield.[3]

I was initially deeply puzzled by the seeming contradiction between California's reputation for environmental leadership and what I could observe firsthand, a lethal infrastructural sublime. Reconciling this contradiction did not have to result in a book, but in another sense, it perhaps did, because these political and ecological relations became all-consuming as I sought to find my footing in Southern California, propelling me into new reading in and across more and less familiar disciplines, subfields, and scholarly corners, ranging from multispecies, feminist, and anticolonial science and technology studies to anthropology, geography, political ecology, media theory, and environmental history. For his enthusiastic belief in a rather unorthodox book project, as well as stellar editorial support of the manuscript, I heartily thank my editor at University of Chicago Press, Joe Calamia. I also thank the "backstage" UC Press team, including Tamara Ghattas, Nick Lilly, Anjali Anand, and Michaela Rae Luckey; copyeditor Susan Olin; indexer Matthew MacLellan; and multiple anonymous reviewers and series editors for their careful readings, insights, and suggestions. All this effort is a tremendous gift even under ordinary circumstances: I can't begin to express my profound gratitude for everyone's help during pandemic times.

I am grateful to staff at the Aquarium of the Pacific; International Bird Rescue; and the United States Army Corps of Engineering for answering queries. A special thanks to invisible yet heroic Interlibrary Loan fairies who supplied me with documentary material throughout pandemic closures; and to Chris Berry at the Port of Long Beach for help with queries and documents. This book would not have been possible in this form without local newspapers: the *Long Beach Post, Los Angeles Times, Long Beach Press Telegram, Daily Breeze, Signal Hill Tribune, Daily Bulletin.* Independent media, environmental justice organizing, and frontline legal defense for water and land protectors will receive proceeds from this book.

On my campus, I first and foremost thank each and all of my comrades in USC-AAUP for solidarity and inspiration; and our growing STS community. For funding my time to research and write, I gratefully acknowledge the Berggruen Institute; an Advancing Scholarship in the Humanities and Social Sciences sabbatical grant from the Office of the Provost at the University of Southern California; and my former Annenberg School of Communication director, Josh Kun, and dean Willow Bay, with an assist from former provost Michael Quick.

McKenzie Stribich's photographs enliven and enhance this book—thank you. I am also grateful to photographers using creative commons licenses, allowing me to include some obscure images shot by strangers.

For literature suggestions and conversation both sustained and stray, I thank Morana Alaç, Steph Alarcón, Soledad Altrudi, Etienne Benson, Cynthia Chris, Juan De Lara, Jan Dutkiewicz, Scott Edgar, Megan Finn, Mel Gregg, Anna Lauren Hoffman, Lisa Onaga, David Parisi, Anne Pasek, Pam Perrimon, Venkat Rao, Camille Reyes, Tony Reyes, Cristina Visperas, and Ashton Wesner. For feedback that has strengthened this work, thanks are due to Cyrus Mody, Mike Palm; and to the Urban Ecosystems Working Group, Mihir Pandya, Andy Lakoff, Chris Kelty, Ashley Carse, and Nils Gilman. I also thank Andrea Alarcón for early research assistance. Omissions, distortions, and errors are mine alone.

For friendship, too much of which was lived through daily messaging during a very trying period for all of us, I am grateful for Biella Coleman, Brad S. Waskewich, Chris J. Smith, Christo Sims, Cody Hanson, Cristina Visperas, Cynthia Mason, Dan Thalhuber, Danny Anisfeld, Farzi Hemmasi, Felix Teitelbaum, Ian Petrie, Jack Bratich, Jason Livingston, Joe Mendelson, John Cheney-Lippold, Jude Webre, Judy Wajcman, Khaled Malas, Laura Forlano, Laura Portwood-Stacer, Lucas Graves, Marie Leger, Megan Finn, Meir Rinde, Mihir and Jessica Pandya, Mike Palm, M. Turkey Tidwell, Ned Diver, Paloma Checa-Gismero, Robert Davis, Ruth Rosenberg, Sarah Banet-Weiser, Scott Edgar, Steph Alarcón, Todd Wolfson, Venkat Rao, Victor Pickard, Wazhmah Osman, and Willy Schofield. Vicky Karkov and Bryce Renninger have been compadres in shared interests for some years now, and it delights me that I will be able to present this book to them. (I also thank some Internet people with whom I kept company while staying at home during a global pandemic; and I am acutely aware of my debt to essential workers who allowed me to do that. I'm sorry to anyone I forgot! The stressful blur of the past few years has taken a toll.)

Much of this book was drafted in the Hoversten household during frightful circumstances; I thank Peg for her kindness. Other elders including Kathy and Roger Later, Elaine Dunbar, Al Hester and Teresa Orantes, and Joe Allen wished me well from near and far. Anna, Pete, Dug, and Noodles strain kin categorization but are extremely important. I thank Erik for companionship and for materially supporting me and my work in so many ways including driving the car, cooking dinner, and washing the dishes too many times to count. I apprecialove you.

Timeline of Legislation and Events

1911	International Treaty protecting sea otters and fur seals
1918	Migratory Bird Treaty Act (US, in coordination with Canada)
1931	Geneva Convention for Regulation of Whaling
1964	New banana terminal built, Port of Long Beach
1964	Wilderness Act (US)
1969 (signed 1970)	National Environmental Policy Act (US)
1969	Santa Barbara oil discharge event
1970	California Endangered Species Act
1970	Environmental Protection Agency founded (US)
1970	National Environmental Policy Act (US)
1971	San Francisco Bay oil discharge event
1972	Clean Water Act (US)
1972	Marine Protection, Research, and Sanctuaries Act (also known as Ocean Dumping Act) (US)
1972	Marine Mammal Protection Act (US)
1972	California Coastal Commission founded
1973	Endangered Species Act (US)
1989	*Exxon Valdez* oil discharge event, Alaska
1990	Oil Pollution Act of 1990 (US)
1990	Lempert-Keene-Seastrand Oil Spill Prevention and Response Act (CA)
1991	State of California opens Office of Spill Prevention and Response
1994	Eastern Pacific gray whale removed from endangered species list (US)

1998	Aquarium of the Pacific opens, Long Beach
2000	Estuary Restoration Act (US)
2001	Los Angeles Oiled Bird Care facility opens
2003	"Green Port" resolution adopted, Long Beach and Los Angeles
2010	BP Deepwater Horizon oil discharge event, Gulf of Mexico
2012	Otter-free zone lifted (CA)
2019	US Army Corps of Engineers proposal for habitat restoration in San Pedro Bay
2020	Long Beach International Gateway bridge opens

Notes

PREFACE

1   Mongelluzzo, "LA-LB Proves Ability."
2   Nelson, "710 Freeway."
3   Scott, "Homelessness in Los Angeles County." Homelessness jumped 12.7 percent in one year and rose three of the past four years.
4   This includes imports and exports (statistics from Port of New York and New Jersey, "Port of New York and New Jersey Ends 2020"; *American Journal of Transportation*, "Port of Long Beach"; Port of Los Angeles, "Container Statistics").
5   A social media post in April 2019 read, "Neighbors, Need your help in contacting the [Redacted] Oil Company again due to homeless encampment at [address in residential area, Long Beach]. There is a large cart with bags and a tent. Here is the contact information for the oil company . . ."
6   The recreational area and dedicated wildlife habitat is new, laid atop of a pre-existing "spreading ground." The restoration is part of a master plan for the LA River (Los Angeles County Public Works, "Los Angeles County Flood Control District"). Dillon ("Civilizing Swamps in California") notes that today wetlands are valued as ecologically diverse and unique environments, contrasting this with nineteenth-century attitudes that regarded them as unhealthy, and arguing that the through-line here is land management as a racialized project. As a white settler, my own access to restored wetlands like the Dominguez Gap for recreation fits within these historical patterns.
7   Nelson, "710 Freeway."

INTRODUCTION

1   Belcher et al., "Hidden Carbon Costs"; Crawford, "Pentagon Fuel Use"; see Marzec, *Militarizing the Environment*.
2   See Netburn, "A Retired Teacher."
3   See Volcovici and Kearney, "150 Years of Spills."

4   Rock, "Fossil Fuel Companies Profited."

5   This is an allusion to artist Natalie Jeremijenko's "Mussel Choir," which was
     shown at the 2012 Venice Architecture Biennale and later installed in the harbors
     of New York City and Melbourne, Australia (Creative States, "What If We Could
     Translate Other Species' Language"). The Aquarium of the Pacific in Long Beach
     is currently trying to reseed the coastal area with endangered white abalone (field
     notes, December 11, 2020).

6   In 2021, the Federal Emergency Management Agency designated LA County the
     most vulnerable in the nation to natural disaster. This score combined vulnerabil-
     ity to natural phenomena like earthquakes, fires, and tsunamis with social vulner-
     ability, the susceptibility of groups like poor, elderly, and racialized residents to
     the hazardous effects of these phenomena (Associated Press, "Riskiest Place").

7   I present this clumsy fiction because, in the words of Ruha Benjamin, "The facts,
     alone, will not save us" ("Racial Fictions, Biological Facts," 2).

8   Güttler, "'Hungry for Knowledge,'" 240. My thanks to an anonymous reviewer for
     this reference.

9   Güttler, 247.

10   The percentage of freight entering greater LA is even higher when air travel is
     taken into account (Erie, *Globalizing LA*, 13).

11   United States Army Corps of Engineers, Los Angeles District (hereafter USACE,
     LA), "East San Pedro Ecosystem Restoration Study Integrated Feasibility Report
     (hereafter IFR), 2–6.

12   Alagona, *After the Grizzly*, points out that the modern rationale for conservation
     emerged in the 1910s, not in the 1960s.

13   Cowen, *Deadly Life of Logistics*, 227.

14   Mitchell, *Carbon Democracy*.

15   Sekula and Burch, "Notes on *The Forgotten Space*.".

16   Curwen, "Officials Knew of Potential for 'Catastrophe.'"

17   Pugliese, *Biopolitics*, 4.

18   Escobar, *Designs for the Pluriverse*, 12.

19   Escobar, "After Nature"; TallBear, "Why Interspecies Thinking Needs Indigenous
     Standpoints"; see also Cronon, "Trouble with Wilderness."

20   Cf. Truscello, who writes of "infrastructural brutalism: the historical context in
     which industrial capitalism has met the limits of its expansion and domination"
     (*Infrastructural Brutalism*, 4). I agree with his critique, but my analysis is more
     concerned with biological vitality and the interplay between infrastructure and
     "conservation." Pasek ("Carbon Vitalism") describes a rather more intimate vital-
     ism, carbon as the stuff of life, in the repertoire of climate denialism. Like infra-
     structural vitalism, carbon vitalism sustains rhetorical and material connections.
     Thomas ("Enduring Infrastructure") argues that "beyond the more visible and
     well-documented violence associated with infrastructural *construction, abandon-
     ment, and deterioration*, infrastructure also metes out gradual, accretive violence
     in the course of its *normal functioning*" (emphasis added). See also LaDuke and
     Cowen, "Beyond Wiindigo Infrastructure." Thanks to an anonymous reviewer for
     pushing my thinking here.

21   Enns and Sneyd, "More-Than-Human Infrastructural Violence," 483.

22   See Star, "Ethnography of Infrastructure."

23   See Edwards, "Infrastructure and Modernity"; Carse, "Keyword."

24 Weber, "Life."

25 Normandin and Wolfe, "Vitalism and the Scientific Image," 3.

26 Cowen and LaDuke, "Beyond Wiindigo Infrastructure."

27 Hughes, "Technological Momentum"; Normandin and Wolfe, "Vitalism and the Scientific Image"; Bennett, *Vibrant Matter*.

28 Port of Los Angeles, "Annual Facts and Figures Card."

29 Pierrepont, "Roundup."

30 Weston, "Lifeblood, Liquidity, and Cash Transfusions," S25.

31 Weston notes that the metaphor can also "flow" in the opposite direction: blood banking ("Lifeblood, Liquidity, and Cash Transfusions").

32 Collier and Lakoff locate the origins of a "vital systems security" historical ontology in the exact moment the Los Angeles harbor was built up as a major port. They write, "Vital systems security arose at a later conjuncture in the evolution of biopolitical government [than Foucault's advent of biopolitical modernity], beginning in the early 20th century. With the intensification of modernization and industrialization processes, planners and policy-makers recognized that collective life had become dependent upon interlinked systems such as transportation, electricity, and water" (Collier and Lakoff, "Vital Systems Security," 21). Cf. "oil for life" biopolitics as discussed by Huber, "Oil for Life."

33 See Cowen, *Deadly Life of Logistics*, 3.

34 Enns and Sneyd, "More-Than-Human Infrastructural Violence."

35 Normandin and Wolfe, "Vitalism and the Scientific Image," 11–12.

36 Port of Long Beach, Harbor Highlights Report, 1971, emphasis added.

37 Tejani, "Dredging the Future," 12.

38 Tejani, "Dredging the Future"; Tejani, "Harbor Lines."

39 Cunningham and Cunningham state that the earliest plan for a breakwater was in 1864 but a small one connecting Deadman's Island and Rattlesnake Island was completed in 1871 (*Port Town*, 90, 97). The expanded breakwaters that comprise the modern ones were built by USACE in the 1920s.

40 De Lara, "'This Port Is Killing People.'"

41 Crandell, "The L.A. River's 'Natural' History." The same was true of the San Gabriel River which now also empties into San Pedro Bay, and the Santa Ana River which empties in Orange County. Together the three rivers made the area into extensive marshlands.

42 Los Angeles County Public Works, "Los Angeles County Flood Control District." See Price "Remaking American Environmentalism."

43 McNeil, *Something New under the Sun*, 189. Since the 1970s, US wetlands have been afforded legal protection under Section 404 of the Clean Water Act, and some have been "restored," like the Dominguez Gap. Thanks to Ashley Carse for references and discussion.

44 Features of the environment here "provided habitat to a range of resident and migratory biological life, including fish, marine and land mammals, and birds of the Pacific Flyway" (Tejani, "Dredging the Future," 12), so uselessness is plainly a matter of perspective.

45 Tejani, "Dredging the Future," 12.

46 Crouch, Paquette, and Vilas, "Relocation," 475.

47 The estate of Rancho San Pedro is in present-day Compton. Mexico had itself gained independence from Spain in 1821, and the modern-day state of California

was the province Alta California until it was ceded to the United States in a treaty following the Mexican-American War or, as it is known in Mexico, the "US Intervention in Mexico."

48 Knatz, "Marine Biological Laboratory," 96.

49 Cunningham and Cunningham, *Port Town*, 155.

50 Tejani, "Dredging the Future," 9, 16, 10. Around two thousand acres remain, in only three main sites (Tejani, 39).

51 Cunningham and Cunningham, *Port Town*, 122–24.

52 San Pedro is not only the name of the bay but of a village, later incorporated into Los Angeles, on the Palos Verdes peninsula west of the bay. It is remote from other centers of the action in greater LA (though LA is inarguably a decentralized city to begin with). Cunningham and Cunningham write, "Los Angeles is not a port town. Los Angeles is a city that happens to have a port" (*Port Town*, 8).

53 Carse, *Beyond the Big Ditch*, 16.

54 Tejani, "Harbor Lines."

55 Erie, *Globalizing LA*; Knatz, "A Century of Marine Science"; Tejani, "Harbor Lines."

56 Knatz, "Marine Biological Laboratory," 96, 97. Marine research on Catalina Island continues today, administered by the University of Southern California.

57 Cunningham and Cunningham, *Port Town*, 220. They add that automobiles in California jumped from 150,000 to 500,000 between 1915 and 1920.

58 Cumming, "Black Gold, White Power," 86.

59 Cunningham and Cunningham, *Port Town*, 270; Sabin, "Beaches versus Oil," 96.

60 Field notes, May 9, 2019.

61 Khalili, *Sinews of War and Trade*, 1.

62 Quoted in Cooke 2017: 70.

63 Cooke, "Energy Landscape."

64 Hacking, "Fine Long Beach Port"; Cunningham and Cunningham, *Port Town*, 347.

65 Levinson, *The Box*; Carse, *The Dredge*; see also Tejani, "Dredging the Future."

66 Khalili, *Sinews of War and Trade*, 3.

67 Cunningham and Cunningham, *Port Town*, 271, 279.

68 World Wildlife Federation, "A Warning Sign."

69 Oxford University zoologist Michelle Jackson, quoted in Carrington, "Migratory River Fish Populations."

70 Using "we" very occasionally in this book is a literary device meant to enroll the reader—but it comes at a loss of precision in language. I do not mean to imply that there is ever a universal "we," full stop. Crucially, people are not experiencing climate crisis and ecological collapse in universal ways, nor are they equally or universally responsible for causing them (see Toussaint, "Ecocide," on how ecocide is defined and potentially prosecuted). While it is popular to call this increasingly catastrophic era the Anthropocene, this is not a "human-made" era so much as one formed by the brutal and extractive relations of racial capitalism and colonialism, including settler colonialism. Following Kyle Powys Whyte, I here regard the present and future as a specific epoch in "a cyclical history . . . anthropogenic environmental change catalysed by colonialism, industrialism and capitalism—not three unfortunately converging courses of history" (Whyte, "Is It Colonial Déjà Vu?," 16; see also Pulido, "Racism and the Anthropocene").

71   Curwen, "Officials Knew of Potential for 'Catastrophe.'"

72   Ritchie, "Do Rich Countries Import Deforestation?"

73   Harvey, "Globalization and the 'Spatial Fix,'" 25.

74   See Riofrancos, "What Green Costs."

75   Liboiron, *Pollution Is Colonialism.*

76   Cowen, *Deadly Life of Logistics*, 4, 12; see also Collier and Lakoff, "Vital Systems Security."

77   See Brown, *Plutopia*, on the toxic legacy of plutonium production in the United States and USSR.; Truscello, *Infrastructural Brutalism*, on China's infrastructural expansion; and see Liboiron for general discussion of capitalism versus colonialism (*Pollution Is Colonialism*, 13). Thanks to an anonymous reviewer for the reminder that ecological destruction is a trait not only of capitalism.

78   Poisonings (pesticides, heavy metals, and the like) have carcinogenic and endocrine disrupting effects (Alexander, "Bioaccumulation, Bioconcentration, Biomagnification").

79   Bodies, of course, are porous; lungs carry airborne toxins straight into bloodstreams (or, for animals with gills, waterborne toxins) (Tuana, "Viscous Porosity"; Davis, "Imperceptibility and Accumulation"; Murphy, "Alterlife"). Faced with noxious by-products of industrial processes, bodies are figuratively and sometimes literally naked flesh (Fiske, "Naked in the Face of Contamination").

80   Nixon, *Slow Violence*. Arguably this is not only "slow" violence: the century-plus of change to landscapes in San Pedro Bay, and the biological harm that accompanied it, is very fast in geologic and evolutionary time. "Slow violence" is a heuristic for drawing attention to nonspectacular forms of injury, but multiple overlapping temporalities are obviously in play (Neimanis, "'Chemists' War'").

81   Cf. Cooper, *Life as Surplus*; Helmreich, "Species of Biocapital"; Sunder Rajan, *Biocapital*; and Cooper, *Life as Surplus* (again) and Gilmore, *Golden Gulag*, on surplus.

82   Davis, "Imperceptibility and Accumulation."

83   Tejani, "Dredging the Future," 7.

84   Carse, *The Dredge.*

85   Port construction itself also contributed to subsidence: deep well operations to support the construction of dry docks caused shifts in pressure in underwater geological strata (Cunningham and Cunningham, *Port Town*, 323). But the main culprit was earth settling after the removal of petroleum.

86   City of Long Beach, "Energy Resources: Subsidence." The total area of subsidence was around twenty square miles (Cunningham and Cunningham, *Port Town*, 327).

87   Cunningham and Cunningham, *Port Town*, 330–31.

88   Sara Pritchard writes, "envirotechnical systems include what both actors and analysts might usually label 'nature' and 'technology.'" She advocates for this term because it "acknowledges that nonhuman nature, however altered physically and mediated discursively, did come first" (*Confluence*, 19); see also Pritchard and Zeller, "Nature of Industrialization."

89   Root, "This Is Why Oil Turned Negative."

90   Krauss, "'Is Exxon a Survivor?'"

91   United States Energy Information Administration, "Despite the US"; see also Aronoff, "Obama's Climate Legacy."

92   See Mitchell, *Carbon Democracy*; Shulman, *Coal and Empire*; Van de Graaf and Sovacool, *Global Energy Politics*.

93   For instance, even in spite of the COVID-19 pandemic, the winter of 2020–21 saw record-breaking imports at the port complex; the Port of LA saw its highest volume of trade in its 114-year history (Littlejohn, "Port of LA").

94   De Lara, *Inland Shift*; Urry, "The Complexities of the Global."

95   "Recently" here refers to primarily settler and Western scholarship in hegemonic Euro-American traditions. Scholars oriented to other epistemic traditions, especially Indigenous epistemologies, are not coming to acknowledgment of nonhuman life-forms "recently" (see TallBear, "Why Interspecies Thinking Needs Indigenous Standpoints"; Todd, "Indigenous Feminist's Take"; Watts, "Indigenous Place-Thought"). These lines of thinking becoming more mainstream is a recent development, however.

96   Todd, "From Fish Lives."

97   Benjamin (*Captivating Technology*, 10) quoting Alexander Weheliye; see Wynter, "Unsettling the Coloniality of Being/Power/Truth/Freedom"; Todd, "Indigenous Feminist's Take"; Pulido, "Racism and the Anthropocene"; Jackson, *Becoming Human*; see also Banerjee, "Anthropology's Reckoning"; Büscher, "Nonhuman Turn"; Mitchell and Chaudhury, "Worlding."

98   TallBear, "Why Interspecies Thinking Needs Indigenous Standpoints."

99   Giraud, "Animal Studies."

100   Jackson, *Becoming Human*, 14, 12. Jackson adds, "racialized gender and sexuality [are central to] the very human–animal binarism that scholars are looking to problematize or displace" (13).

101   Landscapes or terrestrial formations are life-forms in some cosmologies, especially Indigenous ones, and they are certainly parts of living ecologies (TallBear, "Why Interspecies Thinking Needs Indigenous Standpoints").

102   Belcourt, "Animal Bodies, Colonial Subjects."

103   Dillon, "Civilizing Swamps in California." Racialized labor is used to clean beaches after oil discharges, including use of prison labor, at least since the 1969 Santa Barbara spill (LeMenager, *Living Oil*, chap. 1).

104   Dillon, "Civilizing Swamps in California."

105   Alimahomed-Wilson, "Unfree Shipping"; Cowen, *Deadly Life of Logistics*; De Lara, *Inland Shift*; Khalili, *Sinews of War and Trade*. Surf culture enforces racial exclusion in Southern California (Duane, "Long, Strange Tale"). Thanks to a reviewer for helping draw this out.

106   Lorimer writes, "recent thinking in both the life sciences and political ecology . . . [seeks] to rescue biodiversity from the tyranny of [fixed and timeless] Nature and to pluralize and animate conservation as a political ecology for a multiplicity of biodiversities" ("Multinatural Geographies," 606); Escobar ("Whose Knowledge, Whose Nature?") emphasizes the mobilization of biodiversity within social movements, emphasizing cultural autonomy as an alternative to dominant deployments; see also Raby, *American Tropics*. Taxonomists face considerable ambiguity in trying to define "species" and notes that new species identification is accelerating along with severe endangerment and extinction (Scoville, "Hydraulic Society," 9, and see Jackson, *Becoming Human*, again, for an entirely different critique of "species"). On endangerment, see Braverman, *Wild Life*; Lakoff, "Indicator Species"; Vidal and Dias, *Endangerment, Biodiversity and Culture*; and Scoville,

"Hydraulic Society." This quote on conservation is from Soule 1985 (in Lorimer, "Multinatural Geographies," 594). For a nonexhaustive series of anthropological treatments of life in the life sciences, see, e.g., Cooper, *Life as Surplus*; Helmreich, *Alien Ocean*; Paxson and Helmreich, "Perils and Promises"; Sunder Rajan, *Biocapital*. Lastly, both *ecology* and *environment* have rich genealogies as well (see LeMenager, *Living Oil*; Benson, *Surroundings*).

107 There are admittedly limitations to primary analytical engagement with "dominant structures of knowing," including "replicating erasures" contained in scientific research (Murphy, *Economization of Life*, 7), but to not engage with these findings would significantly limit this study in other ways.

108 Van Dooren, *Flight Ways*, 8–9.

109 See Lorimer, "Nonhuman Charisma."

110 Lorimer, "Multinatural Geographies," 600; he adds that the species concept "is especially problematic when species and habitats are understood as fungible units in emerging markets for biodiversity offsets and trading." It is not clear that any given animal in this account is an "indicator species" for anything else (Lakoff, "Indicator Species"). What can perhaps be concluded is that if charismatic, visible, and highly "conserved" whales, otters, and birds are failing to flourish, undoubtedly so are many others that are less celebrated and attended to.

111 Nor, even, will the end of fossil *fuel* necessarily portend the end of petroleum harms, as the industry has cannily pivoted towards plastics (McKay, "Fossil Fuel Industry Sees the Future").

112 See Bauer, Güttler, and Schlünder, "Encounters in Borderlands," on the violence of infrastructural borderlands (drawing on Anzaldua) in life-technology intersections; Carse et al., "Chokepoints"; Chua et al., "Introduction: Turbulent Circulation"; Toscano, "Mirror of Circulation"; and Truscello, *Infrastructural Brutalism*, on chokepoints.

113 Chua et al., "Introduction: Turbulent Circulation," 623, emphasis added.

114 Cowen, *Deadly Life of Logistics*, 227. By making this argument, I do not mean to imply that logistics is a "neutral science" that can simply be applied in different fashions. Rather, because of the port complex's implication in multiple lethal world systems, it is a generative site for imagining "otherwise" configurations.

115 Cowen and LaDuke, "Beyond Wiindigo Infrastructure."

CHAPTER ONE

1 Wright, "World-Class Oiled-Bird Rescue Center."

2 Care is not only an affective state but an ethical and potentially political orientation, albeit a slippery one (Duclos and Criado, "Care in Trouble"; Martin, Myers, and Viseu, "Politics of Care"; Puig de la Bellacasa, "Matters of Care"). Care should not be mistaken for an "innocent" stance, nor does care imply or endorse the possibility that such a stance is possible or desirable. Productive engagements with care often single out the contradictions of enacting care: sometimes deadly contradictions. As anthropologist Eben Kirksey notes, "Killing often becomes necessary when one makes commitments to others within ecological communities. Taking a stand for creatures one loves means taking a stand against enemies that present existential threats to them" (*Emergent Ecologies*, 218; see also Bocci, "Tangles of Care"). For both practitioners and analysts, a "politics of knowledge

cannot be disarticulated from a politics of care" (Martin, Myers, and Viseu, "Politics of Care," 631). In the context of this chapter, to critically assess the contradictory situation of care and support for birds harmed by industrial activity is not to yearn for either a prelapsarian past or a "state of innocence" for either caregivers or analyst.

3   Tejani, "Dredging the Future," 12.

4   Audubon Society, "Pacific Flyway."

5   Ebird.com, "Dominguez Gap Wetlands."

6   US Fish & Wildlife Service Coastal Program, "Urban Restoration."

7   Braverman (*Wild Life*) and others have observed that so-called wild nature may need to be managed in perpetuity.

8   Tsing, *Mushroom at the End of the World*, viii, emphasis added. Similarly, Michelle Murphy writes of "alterlife": "Alterlife is resurgent life, which asserts and continues nonetheless" ("Alterlife," 500).

9   Davis, "Imperceptibility and Accumulation," 191, emphasis added.

10 Cooke, "Energy Landscape," 68.

11 This data is all from the United States Energy Information Administration, "Profile Analysis." The emphasis on oil is mainly narrative, but this does not create a meaningful distortion as it is such a significant fuel and so important in the context of this place. (In inland California, oil and gas are both extracted through hydraulic fracking, but California gas output is vastly less than oil.) Likewise, birds stand in here for other forms of life and wildlife, though they are also special in terms of the amount of mediated attention to them as charismatic victims of oiling. For instance, there is not only a social media feed for the International Bird Rescue organization, there was also a 2011 HBO documentary about an oiled pelican, *Saving Pelican 895*, produced after the massive BP Deepwater Horizon spill in the Gulf of Mexico in 2010; and, as noted in the text, Dawn dish soap ad campaigns have used oiled birds for decades.

12 Rapier, "California's Oil Hypocrisy." California imports oil mainly from Saudi Arabia, Iraq, Colombia, and Ecuador (United States Energy Information Administration, "Profile Analysis").

13 Khalili, *Sinews of War and Trade*, 1.

14 Curwen, "Officials Knew of Potential for 'Catastrophe.'"

15 Port of Long Beach, Harbor Highlights Annual Report, 1966.

16 "Oil menace" is from a 1930 account, quoted in Camphuysen and Heubeck, "Marine Oil Pollution," 444.

17 Carter, "Oil and California's Seabirds."

18 LeMenager offers an excellent account of the ambivalent significance of this event (*Living Oil*, chap. 1).

19 Carter enumerates the 1972 US Clean Water Act; 1972 US Marine Protection, Research and Sanctuaries Act; California Water, Fish and Game, and Harbors and Navigation codes ("Oil and California's Seabirds,": 2).

20 Wright, "World-Class Oiled-Bird Rescue Center."

21 Berkner, "Genesis of International Bird Rescue."

22 Churm, "Tanker Spills Crude Oil."

23 Wright, "World-Class Oiled Bird Rescue Center."

24 Jessup and Mazet, "Rehabilitation of Oiled Wildlife," 574.

25 Comparative research funded by the American Petroleum Institute in 1978 indi-

cated the utility of the recently introduced Dawn soap for gently cleaning wildlife (Newman et al., "Historical Account of Oiled Wildlife Care," 60).

26 Carter, "Oil and California's Seabirds," 3.

27 All referenced in Jessup and Mazet, "Rehabilitation of Oiled Wildlife."

28 Henkel and Ziccardi, "Life and Death," 297.

29 Estes, "Concerns about Rehabilitation," 1157.

30 Henkel and Ziccardi, "Life and Death," 297.

31 Estes, "Concerns about Rehabilitation," 1157; Henkel and Ziccardi, "Life and Death," 298.

32 These facilities have separate histories and funders, but are sited together on public land that was formerly in military use (Fort MacArthur).

33 A shockingly large proportion of sea lions in California have cancer. Scientists speculate that this may be a result of DDT exposure, or DDT/legacy chemicals in combination with viral causes (see CBSLA, "'Overwhelming'"; Xia, "L.A.'s Coast"; Xia, "DDT's Toxic Legacy"). Commercial fisherfolk do not take kindly to sea lions, or otters, stealing their catch (Casteneda, "Sea Lion Found with Gunshot Wounds").

34 Wright, "World-Class Oiled-Bird Rescue Center."

35 International Bird Rescue via Twitter, September 1, 2020.

36 International Bird Rescue, "Heroic Efforts."

37 Field notes, September 9, 2020.

38 The bird cam mediates the facility and the birds, drawing the viewer out of the context of the facility and especially its heavily industrialized locale. See Chris, *Watching Wildlife*; Mitman, *Reel Nature*, on televisual and filmic representation of wildlife; and Altrudi, "Connecting to Nature through Tech?," on app-based nature viewing and collecting.

39 International Bird Rescue, "Heroic Efforts."

40 USACE, LA, IFR, 5–2.

41 "[It] is expected that the existing habitats within the project area will become increasingly vulnerable and less resilient to the effects of [climate] stressors (e.g., exacerbated loss of existing habitat, decreased viability of existing increased chances of wetland/habitat type conversion, submergence of transitional habitats)" (USACE, LA, IFR, xv).

42 USACE, LA, IFR.

43 USACE representative, interview, May 7, 2021.

44 Dunbar-Hester, "Average, Annual?"

45 Porter, *Trust in Numbers*, gives an elegant summary of the rise of cost-benefit analysis as a USACE managerial technique; USACE, LA, IFR, 4–25.

46 USACE, LA, IFR, xxiv.

47 USACE representative, interview, May 7, 2021.

48 Field notes, December 9, 2019.

49 US Fish and Wildlife Service, "Least Tern." The California least tern is considered a subspecies of the least tern.

50 Port of Los Angeles, "Harbor Habitat: Our Biological Treasures."

51 Science Applications International Corporation, "Final 2008 Biological Surveys," 9–7.

52 Caleb Scoville writes, "Credible claims about endangerment rely on the shared perception that a species is in decline, and these perceptions must be supported

by documented measurements showing a trend approaching extinction. Anteced-
ent still (and even more essential) is the classification of endangered species as
distinct taxonomic entities in the first place" ("Hydraulic Society," 4). See also
Alagona, *After the Grizzly*; Lakoff, "Indicator Species."

53 Life has a tendency to gather itself together to create more life, a capacity for ad-
ditive or multiplicative growth ($1 + 1 = 3$) (Murphy, "Reproduction," 288, quoting
historian Martina Schlünder). Of course, life has numerous other reproductive
"formulas" as well.

54 Van Dooren, *Flight Ways*, 12.

55 Port of Los Angeles, "Harbor Habitat: Our Biological Treasures," 18, 21.

56 USACE, LA, IFR, 7–1.

57 Science Applications International Corporation, "Final 2008 Biological
Surveys," 9–7.

58 MBC Applied Environmental Sciences and Merkel and Associates, "2013–2014
Biological Surveys," 9–9.

59 US Fish and Wildlife Service, "Least Tern."

60 USACE, LA, IFR, xviii.

61 USACE, LA, IFR, 1–11.

62 USACE, LA, IFR, 5–84.

63 USACE, LA, "Appendix D," 3–28. The snowy plover was scarcely present in the
2008 survey and not observed in the 2014 one, but the 2014 report notes that the
plover had been present in the 2008 survey.

64 USACE, LA, IFR, 5–87.

65 USACE representative, interview, May 7, 2021.

66 Woodward, "Military Landscapes," 51.

67 Cunningham and Cunningham, *Port Town*, 271. Gilmore notes that by 1940,
10 percent of all federal spending was in California (*Golden Gulag*, 35).

68 Cunningham and Cunningham, *Port Town*, 270–71, 211.

69 Terminal Island is a mostly fabricated island made of infill from dredging the
harbor.

70 Cunningham and Cunningham, *Port Town*, 272; Knatz, *Port of Los Angeles*, 191.

71 Cunningham and Cunningham, *Port Town*, 274; Knatz, *Port of Los Angeles*, 192.

72 Cunningham and Cunningham, *Port Town*, 279.

73 Knatz, *Port of Los Angeles*, 193.

74 Kurashige, *The Shifting Grounds of Race*, 122.

75 Reish, Soule, and Soule, "Benthic Biological Conditions."

76 Schoell, "The Marine Mammal Protection Act."

77 Schoell, "Marine Mammal Protection Act," 48.

78 Schoell states that in 1985, the entry-level wage for cannery workers in San Diego
was $6.63, but only $2.94 in American Samoa. He adds that another factor in the
departure of the tuna industry from Southern California was a 1976 change in
fishing regulations that extended the US territorial waters for fishing from twelve
miles offshore to two hundred miles. In reaction the expansion of US claimed territory, other nations began enforcing their own territorial waters with increased
vigilance, requesting licensing fees from US boats and seizing those out of compliance ("Marine Mammal Protection Act," 49).

79 Los Angeles Conservancy, "Star Kist Tuna Cannery Main Plant."

80   In the 1990s, the navy consolidated its Southern California presence in San Diego,
      shuttering a naval base and hospital in Long Beach.
81   Cunningham and Cunningham, *Port Town*, 466.
82   Crouch, Paquette, and Vilas, "Relocation," 474.
83   I am not sure whether the herons in the Navy mole are migratory or whether
      they live year-round in coastal California, as the black-crowned night herons with
      whom I am acquainted do. Given the location, it is not possible to observe this
      colony as a member of the general public.
84   Crouch, Paquette, and Vilas, "Relocation," 474, 475.
85   Crouch, Paquette, and Vilas, "Relocation," 477, 478.
86   Port of Long Beach, Annual Report, 22.
87   Field notes, May 9, 2019.
88   Per *Encyclopedia of Life* (https://eol.org/pages/45511338, accessed March 13,
      2022).
89   Staff veterinarian, International Bird Rescue, correspondence with author,
      May 20, 2021.
90   Staff veterinarian, International Bird Rescue, correspondence with author,
      May 20, 2021.
91   USACE representative, interview, May 7, 2021. Emphasis added.
92   Nixon, *Slow Violence*, 6. But the devastation is very rapid in geologic time: over
      mere decades, San Pedro Bay has been transformed into a noxious industrial site.
93   As of late 2021, setbacks for homes and schools near extraction sites were finally
      moving toward regulation, but that would not go into effect until at least 2023
      (Herr, "An Oil Well Right Next to Your House?"). Meanwhile California air quality
      is worsening with increased heating and increased movement of goods.
94   USACE representative, interview, May 7, 2021.
95   Crouch, Paquette, and Vilas, "Relocation," 475.
96   Anthropologist Hugo Reinert points out that monitoring endangered species is
      fraught: "Collect insufficient data and the species may die out, through the failure
      to act correctly and in time; collect too much, and risk pushing the tiny, super-
      exposed population over the brink, crossing some invisible threshold" ("The Care
      of Migrants," 12).
97   Thanks to an anonymous reviewer for helping me draw this out.
98   Berkner, "Genesis of International Bird Rescue."
99   Berkner, "Genesis of International Bird Rescue."
100   Henkel and Ziccardi, "Life and Death," 296–97.
101   Bell, "Dawn Dishwashing Detergent."
102   Davis, "Imperceptibility and Accumulation"; Todd, "Fish, Kin and Hope"; Liboi-
      ron, *Pollution Is Colonialism*.
103   Cowen, *Deadly Life of Logistics*. This work's focus is not environmental concerns, but
      the argument extends to them (see also De Lara, "'This Port Is Killing People'").
104   Rust, "How the US Betrayed the Marshall Islands."
105   Belcher et al., "Hidden Carbon Costs."
106   US Department of Defense, "Report on Effects of a Changing Climate."
107   Tamkin, "Is It Imperialist to 'Green' the Military?"
108   Militarism can be defined as "an ideology that prioritizes military force as a
      necessary resolver of conflict" (Woodward, "Military Landscapes," 41). Deborah

Cowen "insists on the precarity of the distinction between 'civilian' and 'military'" in the context of goods movement (*Deadly Life of Logistics*, 4). She is correct to flag that the construction of a boundary between the two is worthy of political and historical attention.

109 Astrida Neimanis writes, "we could follow [bombs dumped in the sea, which leach pollution in the present day] back to the rise of industrial chemistry and its suturing of militarisation to everyday marine pollution" ("'Chemists' War,'"11).

110 Neimanis usefully troubles the slow-spectacular binary of violence ("'Chemists' War'").

111 Cunningham and Cunningham, *Port Town*, 89. The most famous site of this "oil tar" is the La Brea Tar Pits in Los Angeles, a fossil discovery site and popular tourist destination.

112 Henkel and Ziccardi, "Life and Death," 297.

113 Todd, "Fish, Kin and Hope," 104, 107.

114 Whyte, "Is It Colonial Déjà Vu?," 6.

115 See LaDuke and Cowen, "Beyond Wiindigo Infrastructure."

116 The United States stands alone among rich countries in not providing universal health care of any kind to its human citizens.

117 Wigglesworth, "A Generation of Seabirds"; Wisckol, "Oil Wells in Bolsa Chica Reserve."

118 Pinho, "Bird Rescue Operation," emphasis added.

119 Wigglesworth, "A Generation of Seabirds."

120 Pinho, "Bird Rescue Operation."

121 Wisckol, "Oil Wells in Bolsa Chica Reserve."

122 See Bocci, "Tangles of Care"; Kirksey, *Emergent Ecologies*; van Dooren, *Flight Ways*.

123 Pierrepont, "Roundup."

CHAPTER TWO

1 Hacking, "Fine Long Beach Port."

2 But the container itself was forged in the crucible of war; the US military's use of it in World War II led to its standardization (Cowen, *Deadly Life of Logistics*, 41).

3 Cunningham and Cunningham, *Port Town*, 359.

4 Bucheli and Read suggest using the idea of the commodity chain as a unit of analysis ("Banana Boats and Baby Food," 207); see also Tsing, "Supply Chains and the Human Condition."

5 Nixon, *Slow Violence*, 2.

6 Cowen, *Deadly Life of Logistics*; Khalili, *Sinews of War and Trade*.

7 Todd, "Fish, Kin and Hope."

8 Gerasimchuk et al., "Zombie Energy"; Todd, "Fish, Kin and Hope," 104n4.

9 Carse et al., "Chokepoints."

10 LaDuke and Cowen, "Beyond Wiindigo Infrastructure."

11 Chua et al., "Introduction: Turbulent Circulation,": 623, emphasis added. I do not mean to imply that this would be a simple or primarily technocratic process (also see Freidberg, "Calculating Sustainability").

12 Cunningham and Cunningham, *Port Town*, 358. They call the Port of LA "an appendage to a metropolis" (361).

13   De Lara, *Inland Shift*, 4. De Lara's site of study is a corridor contiguous with the ports; he traces warehouse work in an inland industrial landscape.

14   Barboza, "Port Ships."

15   One occasionally sees fruit on (introduced) banana palms in people's yards in Southern California, but they are not a commodity here, and the fruit is far less abundant than yard citrus fruits or loquats.

16   Port of Long Beach, Harbor Highlights Annual Report, 1966.

17   The Port of Long Beach operates as a landlord to users of its facilities, contracting berth space for finite leases.

18   Port of Long Beach, Harbor Highlights Annual Report, 1967. This ranking reflects tonnage, not revenue.

19   Port of Long Beach, Harbor Highlights Annual Report, 1967.

20   Arthur, "Shipboard Refrigeration."

21   Paddleford, "On United Fruit Boat."

22   Port of Los Angeles, "United Fruit Company: The Product, 1."

23   Port of Los Angeles, "United Fruit Company: The Product, 2." See Colby, *Business of Empire*, for a detailed explication of labor, race, and the transnational trajectory of the banana industry in Latin America through the 1930s.

24   Port of Los Angeles, "Berth 147."

25   Port of Los Angeles, "United Fruit Company: The Trend, 2."

26   Bucheli and Read, "Banana Boats and Baby Food," 210.

27   Port of Los Angeles, "United Fruit Company: The Product, 2."

28   Arian, Port of Los Angeles Oral History.

29   Port of Los Angeles, "United Fruit Company: The People, 1–2."

30   Bucheli and Read claim that an event that is most prominently attached to United Fruit's brutal reputation, the 1954 CIA-led overthrow of the democratically elected Guatemalan president Jacobo Arbenz Guzmán, ironically offers scant evidence of direct involvement by the company. They argue that in the context of the Cold War, the US government was concerned that labor unrest among agricultural workers was a contributing factor in the spread of communism, motivating the State Department to intervene on its own; the government had also invested in shipping and communications infrastructure (including highways and air post) during World War II that made it less reliant on United Fruit's infrastructure, and therefore United Fruit's interests were less strategically important to the United States in later years (Bucheli and Read, "Banana Boats and Baby Food," 217, 218, 221). In the case of the Guatemala coup, this is likely a distinction without a difference, however, as the State Department's extremely close ties to United Fruit meant that the US and United Fruit interests could not be cleanly separated.

31   Bucheli and Read, "Banana Boats and Baby Food," 207.

32   Bucheli, "United Fruit Company," 96.

33   Bucheli and Read, "Banana Boats and Baby Food," 211.

34   United Fruit held Standard Fruit shares for a period of time in the early twentieth century, but the former was forced to divest them in the Standard Oil era of trust-busting, ca. 1908 (United Fruit Historical Society, "Chronology").

35   Karnes, *Tropical Enterprise*, 274.

36   Port of Long Beach, 1976 Annual Report.

37   Port of Long Beach, Harbor Highlights Annual Report, 1966.

38   Soluri, *Banana Cultures*, 14, 7, 10.

39   Arduino, Carrillo Murillo, and Parola, "Refrigerated Container versus Bulk," 230.

40   Carse, *Beyond the Big Ditch*, 134.

41   Soluri, *Banana Cultures*, 16.

42   Karnes, *Tropical Enterprise*, chap. 12.

43   Soluri, *Banana Cultures*, 11.

44   Port of Long Beach, Harbor Highlights Annual Report, 1966.

45   Port of Long Beach, Harbor Highlights/The Action Port, Fall 1979.

46   Port of Long Beach, Interport Annual Report, 1987.

47   Port of Long Beach, 1990; Port of Long Beach, Interport Annual Report, 1998.

48   Port of Long Beach, Interport Annual Report, 2005.

49   Port of Long Beach, Interport Annual Report, 2006. This would include fresh/ perishable and processed items.

50   Didion, "Trouble in Lakewood," 1993.

51   De Lara, *Inland Shift*, 14. Cumming ("Black Gold, White Power") traces the dynamics of racially segregated housing back to decisions about land use during the oil boom.

52   De Lara, *Inland Shift*, 162.

53   Complicating the container-centered narrative, others have suggested that dredging (Carse, *The Dredge*) or pallets (in Cowen, *Deadly Life of Logistics*, 44) are also key infrastructural interventions. Deregulation of the transport sector is also hugely significant (Cowen, *Deadly Life of Logistics*); certainly, no single artifact or technique drives the growth of complex systems like the ones running through the ports.

54   Port of Long Beach, Harbor Highlights, 1962; Cole ("The Tip of the Spear") studied how the International Longshore and Warehouse Union in San Francisco responded to containerization, showing that it led to fewer workers but not loss of unionized status for the remaining jobs.

55   Port of Long Beach, Harbor Highlights, 1962.

56   Carse and Lewis, "New Horizons," 3.

57   Port of Long Beach, Harbor Highlights Annual Report, 1969.

58   Levinson, *The Box*, 233, 234; Pandya, "After Automation."

59   Levinson, *The Box*, 234–35.

60   Levinson, 269.

61   De Lara, *Inland Shift*, 31.

62   Port of Long Beach, Harbor Highlights, Spring 1982.

63   Barsness, "Maritime Activity."

64   De Voss, "A Comparative Analysis," 87–89.

65   Coffey, "Dole's Productivity."

66   De Voss, "A Comparative Analysis," 87.

67   Reed 1991.

68   Paddleford, "On United Fruit Boat"; not to be confused with a group of US Navy battleships with the same nickname.

69   Bucheli, "United Fruit Company," 80.

70   Posner, "See No Evil."

71   Wang, "Meet Dole."

72   Levinson, *The Box*, 233.

73   Wang, "Meet Dole."

74   Linn, "Ports Add Reefer Facilities." A recently retired longshoreman in Tampa,

Florida, relayed that only the biggest companies use refrigerated containers even
in 2020. Thanks to Camille Reyes and Tony Reyes for discussion.

75 Sanchez, "Un-Banana Boat."
76 Sanchez, "Un-Banana Boat."
77 Levinson, *The Box*, 316; see also Danyluk, "Fungible Space."
78 Linn, "Ports Add Reefer Facilities."
79 Carse and Lewis write, "[Dredging the Panama Canal] is a hemispheric environmental standardization event that is implicated in place-based dynamics, giving
rise to complex forms of landscape change" ("New Horizons," 4).
80 Mongelluzzo, "Sweet Deal."
81 Showley, "Port Extends Dole Lease."
82 Port of Los Angeles, "California Petroleum Company: The Trend, 2."
83 Cooke, "Energy Landscape," 67.
84 Marathon Carson (opened 1938); Marathon Wilmington (1923); Phillips 66 Wilmington (1917); Valero Wilmington (1969); Valero Wilmington Asphalt (1980);
Shell Carson (refinery from 1923 to 1992; now a distribution terminal). This list
excludes a few other active refineries just a bit farther inland, in El Segundo,
Torrance, and South Gate; and at least two that are idle or closed (Long Beach).
The distinction between the refineries in the harbor and the ones further inland
is fairly arbitrary as there is extensive linkage between refining and distribution
in the form of pipelines running all throughout the LA Basin. California Energy
Commission, "California Oil Refinery History."
85 Cooke, "Energy Landscape," 82; emphasis added.
86 Wilson and Younes, "Oil Companies Are Profiting." They point out that though
coastal oil discharges receive more attention, the majority of extraction and spills
in present-day California are inland—farther from population centers, charismatic
seabirds, and media attention.
87 There is no reason to think that petroleum was not also the main export from the
1930s onward, but the port did not list commodities with as much detail in the
earlier reports I was able to review.
88 Field notes, May 9, 2019.
89 Port of Long Beach, Annual Report, 2009.
90 Data from Alameda Corridor Transportation Authority, Annual Report, 2013. Dry
bulk is likely chemicals like potash or materials used to make cement. See Slaton,
Reinforced Concrete; Truscello, *Infrastructural Brutalism*, on cement in industrial
infrastructure.
91 Alameda Corridor Transportation Authority, Annual Report, 2013.
92 In 1985, liquid bulk accounted for 23 million MRTs; it was down to 13.4 million
MRTs in 2019. By contrast, general cargo was 19.3 million in 1985 and 193.1 million
in 2019 (Port of Los Angeles, "Tonnage Data (1971–2019").
93 Wilson and Younes, "Oil Companies Are Profiting."
94 Embrey, "Los Angeles County Forms Just-Transition Taskforce."
95 Wang, "Managing China's Petcoke Problem."
96 Port of Long Beach, Interport Annual Report, 1998.
97 In 2013, the US Environmental Protection Agency stopped issuing licenses to
burn petcoke domestically (Wang, "Managing China's Petcoke Problem").
98 Wang, "Managing China's Petcoke Problem."
99 Shawn, "DLA Energy's Pacific Pivot." As of this writing, some of this fueling

facility is in limbo: a portion of the facility was shuttered around 2017 but officials debated reopening it soon after (Littlejohn, "Military Launches Study"; Reyes, "Navy's Plans to Revive a San Pedro Fueling Facility"; US Navy "Draft Environmental Assessment").

100 Shawn, "DLA Energy's Pacific Pivot."
101 Littlejohn, "Military Launches Study." Peter Harris argues that "the unparalleled seclusion that militarization imposes upon delineated geographic spaces can create safe havens for plants and animals that would otherwise suffer from human encroachment" can serve as a resource for "greenwashing" militarism ("Militarism in Environmental Disguise," 19).
102 Shawn, "DLA Energy's Pacific Pivot."
103 Oscar E. Anderson, quoted in Freidberg, *Fresh: A Perishable History*, 11.
104 Twilley, "Spaces of Banana Control."
105 Port of Long Beach, Harbor Highlights Annual Report, 1966.
106 Heavy fuel oil is a by-product of petroleum refining left over after lighter hydrocarbons are extracted.
107 Arduino, Carrillo Murillo, and Parola, "Refrigerated Container versus Bulk," 234, 233, 232. They note that even after the global financial crisis of 2008, worldwide trade in perishable goods was growing again by 2010.
108 Murray, *Moveable Feasts*, 37–38.
109 Baker, "Ditching the Diesel."
110 Murray, *Moveable Feasts*, 37.
111 Luske, "Comprehensive Carbon Footprint Assessment Dole Bananas." Refrigeration here includes both fuel and refrigerant components.
112 Cowen, *Deadly Life of Logistics*; Truscello, *Infrastructural Brutalism*; see also Mody, "Spillovers from Oil Firms."
113 Cowen, *Deadly Life of Logistics*, 56.
114 Simons and Zhuplev, "Comparative Analysis of International Business Practices," 21.
115 South Coast Air Quality Management District, "Clean Port."
116 Becker, "Shape Up or Ship Out."
117 Rapier, "California's Oil Hypocrisy." Though COVID-19 initially reduced demand for fossil fuel in the transportation sector, it rebounded fully. The Russian invasion of Ukraine shortly before this book went to press has also introduced volatility in energy markets.
118 Barboza, "Southern California Smog Worsens."
119 De Lara, "'This Port Is Killing People,'" 539.
120 Price, "Remaking American Environmentalism," 544.
121 De Lara, "'This Port Is Killing People,'" 545. Just-in-time logistics' full carbon footprint should also include the energy consumption and resource extraction of data centers.
122 Jake Alimahomed-Wilson ("Unfree Shipping") argues that racialization has accelerated the negative labor impacts related to the logistics revolution across warehouse and port trucking industries in Southern California, based on his study of low-wage, nonunion Latinx workers.
123 De Lara, "'This Port Is Killing People,'" 546.
124 Barboza, "Port Ships."
125 "How Hydrogen Trucks Are Shaping the Future," *Forbes*.

126 "How Hydrogen Trucks Are Shaping the Future," *Forbes*.

127 See Riofrancos, "What Green Costs"; Riofrancos, *Resource Radicals*.

128 Carpenter, "Toyota, Kenworth and Shell."

129 Ewing, "World's Largest Long-Haul Truckmaker"; Edelstein, "Hyundai Will Test Semis in California"; Halvorson, "Toyota Will Make Hydrogen Fuel-cell Modules."

130 See Andasan ("Port Pollution Sickens My Whole Neighborhood") for an eloquent account of frontline communities' experiences and the activism of groups like East Yard Communities for Environmental Justice; Port of Long Beach, "Port Exempts."

131 Quoted in Hersher, "Dawn of Low-Carbon Shipping."

132 Collins, "Hydrogen 'Can Power Virtually All Container Ships.'"

133 Pratt, "Maritime Fuel Cell Generator Project."

134 Baker ("Ditching the Diesel") writes that some are coming to market now. Solar is currently practical for the refrigeration component of the container but not for the whole rig (including the semi) because of the energy requirements to move the weight of a truck.

135 Keating, "Shell Steers Course toward Net-zero Shipping." Since methane emissions produced in the course of gas extraction are amplifying global warming considerably, 15–20 percent may be optimistic.

136 Princeton University Office of Engineering Communications, "For Hydrogen Fuel Cells, Mundane Materials."

137 Hsu, "Study Shows Hydrogen Made from Natural Gas."

138 Hersher, "Dawn of Low-Carbon Shipping."

139 Regardless of fuel or energy source, producing a new electric vehicle is very carbon intensive: sourcing and fabricating components, plus shipping it to the consumer. (The port complex handles automobile imports.) Increasingly, it is also acknowledged that tire particulates are toxic respiratory irritants and waterway pollutants.

140 *Los Angeles Times*, "Editorial: Supply Chain Issues."

141 Dean, "Is the Ports Logjam Really Getting Better?"

142 De Lara, *Inland Shift*, 12.

143 Center for Land Use Interpretation, "Refrigerated Nation."

144 *Filipino Reporter*, "PH Bananas Available in U.S. Finally."

145 I have been unable to fully verify whether this shipment was in containers but it seems extremely probable as Long Beach's fruit-handling breakbulk facilities were gone, and a whole reefer ship carrying fresh food was unlikely to have been sent on this long of an ocean voyage.

146 David, "Philippines Not Yet a Viable Source."

147 According to Paredes, because Panama disease has potential to wipe out crops and is "incurable," unresponsive to chemical, cultural, and biological control measures, it has gained infamy. She argues that Sigatoka is widespread, damaging, and costly to the industry, but relatively unknown because control measures for it have been widely adopted and are a routine feature of banana cultivation ("Chemical Cocktails").

148 Soluri, *Banana Cultures*, 206–7.

149 Karp, "Banana Is One Step Closer to Disappearing."

150 Karp.

151 Soluri, *Banana Cultures*, 206.

152 Karp, "Banana Is One Step Closer to Disappearing."

153 De Lara, *Inland Shift*, 18.

154 Bucheli and Read, "Banana Boats and Baby Food," 220. They add that the need to occasionally switch where bananas are sourced favors the operation of concentrated multinationals.

155 Büscher et al., "Towards a Synthesized Critique," 7.

156 See Cowen, *Deadly Life of Logistics*, 214, echoing Marx.

157 Barboza, "Port Ships."

158 Vock, "Can America's Biggest Ports Go Green?" And not only cargo ships: a single cruise ship in port for twenty-four hours can burn enough fuel to equal 10,000 cars on the road (Barboza, "Port Ships"). Both Carnival and Princess cruise lines operate out of the LA harbor, in Long Beach and San Pedro, respectively.

159 Barboza, "Port Ships."

160 Port of Long Beach, "Electric Grid Demand and Shore Power," emphasis added.

161 This was a continuation of the Obama administration's "energy independence," which overturned a forty-year ban on the US exporting crude oil (Aronoff, "Obama's Climate Legacy"); Cara Daggett has termed the historic role of fossil fuel systems in buttressing white patriarchal rule *petro-masculinity* ("Petro-Masculinity: Fossil Fuels and Authoritarian Desire").

162 Martin Hultman calls this "ecomodern masculinity," a refusal to acknowledge in realistic terms the limits of resources and the costs of orienting toward technological growth and consumption (that is, in his argument, compatible with hegemonic masculinity ["Making of an Environmental Hero," 89]). Thanks to Anne Pasek for this reference.

163 Nagle, Gomez, and Cathey, "Biden Floors Electric Ford Truck."

164 Sovacool et al., "Imagining Sustainable Energy," 650. See also Rajak, "Waiting for a Deus Ex Machina," for discussion of oil executives' "suspension of disbelief" over whether there is a conflict between endless growth and combating climate catastrophe.

165 Richardson, "Council Members Livid."

166 Clark, "Officials Tout New Port of Long Beach Bridge."

167 United States Environmental Protection Agency, "Current Nonattainment Counties for All Criteria Pollutants." Thanks to Kaitlin Stack Whitney for pointing me to this.

168 Vock, "Can America's Biggest Ports Go Green?"

169 Erie, *Globalizing LA*, 9.

170 North America's exportation of petcoke to China notwithstanding, much of the oil that has fueled China's growth is from the Middle East. The petcoke has no domestic consumer base because it has been deemed too dirty a fuel in the United States. In other words, it is essentially waste in North America (see Liboiron, *Pollution Is Colonialism*).

171 Cowen, *Deadly Life of Logistics*.

172 See chap. 1 for more on the Department of Defense's interests in climate change and national security.

173 Hein, "Between Oil and Water," 446.

174 Nixon, *Slow Violence*; Hultman, "Making of an Environmental Hero."

175 Todd, "Fish, Kin and Hope," 107.

176 Soluri, *Banana Cultures*, 211–12; Paredes, "Chemical Cocktails."

177 Paredes, "Chemical Cocktails."

178 Sarah Murray writes, "Without the well-traveled banana and the economic clout it brought American fruit companies, Guatemala may never have come to the attention of the U.S. administration" (*Moveable Feasts*, 131). I would not underestimate the US appetite for imperialism, but at the very least it is true that banana trade informed the specific trajectory of US intervention in the region.

179 Alimahomed-Wilson, "Unfree Shipping"; De Lara, *Inland Shift*; Tsing, "Supply Chains and the Human Condition"; see also Colby, *Business of Empire*, for a specific look at racialized labor in the transnational Latin American banana industry. Ecological justice will not be possible without racial justice, and analysis needs to consider them as coconstitutive (Pulido and De Lara, "Reimagining 'Justice'").

180 Truscello, *Infrastructural Brutalism*, 4–5. He notes that cement production alone accounts for 5–10 percent of global carbon emissions (13). The ports move material used to make cement through their dry bulk facilities; cement components, along with petroleum transshipment, are fixers of infrastructural modernity.

181 Cowen, *Deadly Life of Logistics*.

CHAPTER THREE

1 Boehm and Sahagun, "Recipients of BP Aid Face PR Dilemma."

2 As of this writing in late 2020, the BP Deep Horizon spill was estimated to be 8–31 percent bigger than the largest prior spill, per Wikipedia (https://en.wikipedia .org/wiki/Deepwater_Horizon_oil_spill, accessed November 29, 2020). But this tally was likely completed later than the otter habitat dedication, as the leaking well was not sealed until September 2010.

3 Boehm and Sahagun, "Recipients of BP Aid Face PR Dilemma." BP was not listed as a donor in the aquarium's 2019 or 2020 annual reports. It did appear in 2013, though in the range of $25,000, far less than the million dollars pledged for the otter habitat. From viewing archived webpages from the Aquarium of the Pacific's website, it seems that BP's name disappeared from the "Sea Otter Habitat" page between 2017 and 2019.

4 Jameson, "She's One Happy Pup."

5 Ravalli, "Near Extinction," 186. He adds, "the species was brought closer to total extinction at the dawn of the twentieth century than at any time at the busiest era of the trade" (181).

6 Ravalli states that this treaty (between the "Pacific world" of Japan, Russia, and the United States, "with the United States increasingly at the region's political and commercial center" post-1850, was primarily focused on sealing, and the protections were essentially too late to do much good for otters whose numbers had already plummeted ("Near Extinction," 181, 197).

7 Ravalli, "Near Extinction," 189. He notes that sea otters in California were easier to hunt than their Alaskan counterparts, because they were accessible from the shoreline (whereas in Alaska, they were often scattered about in less navigable islands). He also clarifies that hunting did not cease after 1913, just legal hunting.

8 Aquarium of the Pacific, "Southern Sea Otter." This number, which is not precise, seems to come from the "discovery" of a colony of them in Monterey Bay in 1938. Publicized as the "Phoenix-like appearance" of a creature thought to have been

more or less exterminated, it laid the groundwork for conservation (Ravalli, "Near Extinction," 189). According to Ravalli, it was more surprising that there was a large colony than that there were any otters at all.

9   The term "conservation" is a contested one, for both its semantic entailments and its relationship to an environmental movement with undeniable racist and eugenicist goals—and these cannot be cleanly separated (Purdy, "Environmentalism's Racist History"). Its appearance in this book is as an actors' category, as it is the common term for wildlife managers' work. "In the 1970s and 1980s biologists, who became alarmed by threats to species and ecosystems, adopted the label conservation biology for their work, which coincided with a related movement to concentrate efforts on protecting biological diversity," writes Bryan Norton ("Zoos and Sustainability," 241).

10 Jameson, "She's One Happy Pup."

11 Scoville, "Hydraulic Society," 6.

12 There were an estimated 16,000 otters in the nineteenth century (as reported by Barboza, "Wildlife Officials"), but this is assumedly a much smaller population than prior to European contact, because otters had already been quite exploited by then (Ogden, *California Sea Otter Trade, 1784–1848*; Gibson, *Otter Skins, Boston Ships, and China Goods*).

13 Rathbun, Hatfield, and Murphey, "Status of Translocated Sea Otters," 322.

14 Mayer et al., "Surrogate Rearing a Keystone Species."

15 Field notes, January 3, 2021.

16 Mayer et al., "Surrogate Rearing a Keystone Species," 8.

17 Rathbun, Hatfield, and Murphey, "Status of Translocated Sea Otters," 322.

18 Rathbun, Hatfield, and Murphey state with palpable frustration that "a certain amount of cooperation from the fisherman who have been largely unsympathetic with the translocation effort would help resolve these issues [of otters being entangled in lobster traps]" ("Status of Translocated Sea Otters," 326).

19 Rathbun, Hatfield, and Murphey, "Status of Translocated Sea Otters," 326.

20 Rathbun, Hatfield, and Murphey, "Status of Translocated Sea Otters," 324.

21 Mayer et al., "Surrogate Rearing a Keystone Species," 8.

22 Rathbun, Hatfield, and Murphey, "Status of Translocated Sea Otters," 324, 326, 325, 326. The most recent data on otters on San Nicolas states that there were around 100 animals living there as of 2019 (Marine Mammal Commission, "Southern Sea Otter").

23 Lilian Carswell, southern sea otter recovery coordinator with the US Fish and Wildlife Service, quoted in Barboza, "Wildlife Officials." See Bocci, "Tangles of Care"; Parreñas, *Decolonizing Extinction*; and van Dooren, *Flight Ways*, on violent care.

24 Rathbun, Hatfield, and Murphey, "Status of Translocated Sea Otters," 326.

25 Weiss. "U.S. Scraps 'Otter-Free Zone.'"

26 By the early 2000s, MBA had cared for more than seventy orphaned pups; Nicholson et al., "Effects of Rearing Methods," 313.

27 At least according to Nicholson et al., "Effects of Rearing Methods," 314.

28 Again according to Nicholson et al., "Effects of Rearing Methods," 314.

29 Field notes, January 3, 2021. The mammologist added that "maternal behavior" could vary, and they really did not expect to know how an adult otter and pup would get along until their introduction. Partly because the Aquarium of the

Pacific-MBA surrogacy collaboration was delayed due to COVID-19, staff were not sure whether Chloe would be a surrogate mother or not. They did, however, describe her as a "free-spirited, happy-go-lucky 'chill' otter."

30 Nicholson et al., "Effects of Rearing Methods," 314.

31 Nicholson et al., "Effects of Rearing Methods," 315–16, 317.

32 For reasons that were not explained, only male pups were used in the research. All were radiotagged and fitted with color-coded flipper tags.

33 Nicholson et al., "Effects of Rearing Methods," 318.

34 Mayer et al., "Surrogate Rearing a Keystone Species."

35 Sterngold, "Long Beach." His statement is about Long Beach generally but it fits the waterfront area well.

36 As of 2020, parts of the carousel and vestigial Pike games are on display at Looff's Lite-A-Line on Long Beach Boulevard.

37 The *Queen Mary* docked permanently in Long Beach in 1967. The *Spruce Goose* was housed there only from 1980–92, but its dome remains and is currently used as Carnival Cruise Lines' dockside cruise terminal.

38 Kopetman, "Spruce Goose to Be Moved."

39 Addison, "Long Beach Lost."

40 Various factors were responsible. Disney requested things the City of Long Beach was unable to deliver single-handedly, like highway modifications. Addison, "Long Beach Lost," notes that Long Beach was hard to build in both politically and financially since local, state, and federal approvals were all required; Disney instead reinvested in and expanded its Anaheim (Orange County) operations.

41 Sterngold, "Long Beach."

42 Johnson, "Long Beach, Calif., Gets a Boost." The "tidelands grant" the state issued the city to develop the harbor stipulated that revenue from oil profits drilled from the Wilmington and Long Beach oil fields, located in the tidelands, be reinvested in the tidelands area (and overseen by the state).

43 Kingsley, "Aquarium of the Pacific Turns 20 Today."

44 Young, "Zoos and Aquariums."

45 Henson, "American Zoos," 65, 70, 66.

46 Young, "Zoos and Aquariums"; Henson, "American Zoos," 72.

47 Henson, "American Zoos," 66; Braverman, *Zooland.*

48 Henson writes, "as 'natural environments' become more stressed through development and climate change, the line has become blurred between ex situ, or zoo- and aquarium-based, research and conservation and in situ, or field-based, biological research and conservation practice" ("American Zoos," 66); see especially Braverman, *Wild Life,* for more on this troubled boundary.

49 Muka, "Conservation Constellations."

50 The California or southern sea otter is classified as a subspecies of an otter whose range used to be the entire Pacific coast from Baja California to Alaska. It is now only found from about Point Conception, just north and west of Santa Barbara, to San Francisco; in other words, just north of the Southern California Bight into which San Pedro Bay is nestled.

51 Morris, "Long Beach Aquarium."

52 Jameson, "She's One Happy Pup."

53 Further north in the Pacific Northwest, Russian traders established a sea otter fur trade with China in the mid-eighteenth century (Gibson, *Otter Skins, Boston*

Ships, and China Goods). Otter hunting in fact drew Russians eastward from Siberia. Spanish colonists in California did not initially recognize the value of otter pelts in "their" territories but soon also entered the otter fur trade with China, and these otters were members of the southern or California sea otter subspecies. In both cases, Indigenous people also participated in these markets as hunters, though they often were resistant to hunting on the scale desired by merchants (Ogden, *California Sea Otter Trade, 1784–1848*, 43). Overhunting of otters is part of what pushed American maritime traders toward beavers in the nineteenth century (Gibson, *Otter Skins, Boston Ships, and China Goods*).

54 Jameson, "She's One Happy Pup."

55 Jameson. The journalist noted that the handler was himself a father of two, tying his parental duties with the otter to those with his human young.

56 Segura, "Long Beach Aquarium's Beloved Otter Dies." In humans, poisons like PCBs and dioxin have been detected in blood, breast milk, and urine (Murphy, "Alterlife," 495).

57 Murphy invokes a stencil by Métis artist and activist Erin Marie Konsmo depicting lungs filled with transformer towers connecting to underground fracking, accompanied by the statement "Violence from Fracking [and Pipelines] is Violence on Our Bodies" ("Alterlife," 500–501). Though the image depicts human lungs, the statement fits animal bodies as well—though chemical violence is not limited to fossil fuels, of course. See also Fiske, "Naked in the Face of Contamination"; Tuana, "Viscous Porosity."

58 Segura, "Long Beach Aquarium's Beloved Otter Dies."

59 Field notes, September 2019.

60 Aquarium of the Pacific curator, interview, December 7, 2020.

61 Aquarium of the Pacific, "Aquarium Animal Care."

62 Aquarium of the Pacific curator, interview, December 7, 2020.

63 Parreñas, *Decolonizing Extinction*, 155; van Dooren, *Flight Ways*.

64 Aquarium of the Pacific curator, interview, December 7, 2020.

65 Mothers will even wrap pups in kelp to hold them in place and keep them afloat while they go off to forage (e.g. Kranking, "Floating through Life").

66 The company is presumably named for the island that Spanish settlers dubbed Santa Catalina, one of the Channel Islands, just offshore from Los Angeles and Long Beach. It hosts tourism and marine research, and its rock is the source material for many modifications in San Pedro Bay.

67 Brunner, *Ocean at Home*, 140–41.

68 Brunner, "Through a Glass Sadly."

69 Brunner, *Ocean at Home*, 141. This is probably less a function of breeding being impossible to do and more that there is little profit motive to attempt it.

70 Brunner notes that only one in ten fish caught for aquarium trade survives the shipping and trade process and ends up in a hobby tank ("Through a Glass Sadly"). Toxic injury is also relevant here: Brunner adds that poisons are sometimes used in the water to numb or stun fish and make them easier to capture, and excess poison remains in the water after stunned fish are captured. The habitat effects call to mind Nixon's description of "delayed destruction" (*Slow Violence*, 2; see also Neimanis, "'Chemists' War'").

71 Aquarium of the Pacific curator, interview, December 7, 2020. The curator added that Monterey Bay Aquarium, built in the 1980s, has such a system.

72 Catalina Water Company, homepage.
73 Aquarium of the Pacific curator, interview, December 7, 2020; Aquarium of the Pacific, "Molina Animal Care Center."
74 Catalina Water Company, homepage.
75 Catalina Water Company, homepage. Punctuation per original.
76 Aquarium of the Pacific curator, interview, December 7, 2020.
77 Jameson, "She's One Happy Pup."
78 Aquarium of the Pacific, "Sea Otter Conservation." Parasites can also wash out from land.
79 Liboiron, *Pollution Is Colonialism*, 82; Murphy, "Alterlife."
80 Marine Mammal Commission, "Southern Sea Otter."
81 Estes et al., "Causes of Mortality in California Sea Otters." The authors noted that the microbes and pathogens killing otters were not ones for which otters were usual hosts, and they therefore questioned whether infectious disease in the southern sea otter should be considered a "natural" phenomenon (213). An Aquarium of the Pacific mammologist stressed how toxoplasmosis (a parasitic disease of domestic cats) can affect otters and suggested that people dispose of cat litter-box waste in household trash, not toilets, because of how wastewater would eventually reach otters (field notes, January 3, 2021).
82 Estes et al., "Causes of Mortality in California Sea Otters," 213.
83 Marine Mammal Commission, "Southern Sea Otter." Field surveys were interrupted by the COVID-19 pandemic, so aggregated data over three years (which scientists consider more reliable than any given single-year count) is lacking for the most recent period.
84 See Parreñas's discussion of forced copulation in orangutan conservation, or "how saving members of a species from extinction inflicts new forms of violence." She asks, "Could rescuing wildlife facing extinction bring about a life worse than death?" (*Decolonizing Extinction*, 84). See also van Dooren on "regimes of violent care" (*Flight Ways*).
85 Reed-Smith and Larson, "Otters in Captivity," 575. They note that sea otters have bred in captivity successfully, but they do not distinguish between southern sea otters and other subspecies.
86 Nicholson et al., "Effects of Rearing Methods," 318.
87 Parreñas, "Reproductive Labour of Migrant Workers," offers insight into the complexity of the global commodification of this labor.
88 Mayer et al., "Surrogate Rearing a Keystone Species," 7.
89 Which are tied to economic futures (Murphy, *Economization of Life*).
90 Mayer et al., "Surrogate Rearing a Keystone Species," 8.
91 Tuana, "Viscous Porosity."
92 Parreñas, *Decolonizing Extinction*, 11.
93 Fiske, "Naked in the Face of Contamination."
94 Woody, "California's Critical Kelp Forests."
95 Jameson, "She's One Happy Pup." Here I ambivalently reproduce the journalist's glib description of Summer's communication and her handler's interpretation of it.
96 McPherson et al., "Large-Scale Shift"; Stephens, "Collapse of Northern California Kelp Forests."
97 Carrington, "Climate Crisis."

98   Parreñas, *Decolonizing Extinction*, 11.
99   Aquarium of the Pacific, "Sea Otter Conservation."
100 Aquarium of the Pacific, "Sea Otter Conservation."
101 Aquarium of the Pacific, "Sea Otter Conservation."
102 Cardozo, "'Wetlands Protectors' vs. Big Oil."
103 "Long Beach, CA, Aquarium Revenue Bonds"; Kingsley, "Aquarium of the Pacific Turns 20 Today."
104 INCITE, *The Revolution Will Not Be Funded*; Reich, *Just Giving*.
105 Braverman, *Zooland*, 16; Norton, "Zoos and Sustainability," 244.
106 Norton, "Zoos and Sustainability," 242.
107 Braverman, *Wild Life*, 65.
108 Dolly Jørgensen has explored the trend of aquariums displaying decommissioned offshore oil rigs as artificial reefs, which she argues naturalizes the viewpoint that "American oceans are a harmonious meeting place of oil and water" ("Mixing Oil and Water," 285). Given the actual history of the oil industry's relationship to wildlife in San Pedro Bay, along the California coast, and more broadly, the portrayal of this relationship as beneficial seems vexed.
109 Parreñas, *Decolonizing Extinction*, 19.
110 Field notes, December 26, 2020. The tour was virtual because of the pandemic.
111 Shuit, "Running the Show in Long Beach."
112 Sterngold, "Long Beach."
113 Hein, "Between Oil and Water."
114 Kingsley, "Aquarium of the Pacific Turns 20 Today."
115 And arguably exerts a terrible influence on local driving culture.
116 Kingsley, "Aquarium of the Pacific Turns 20 Today."
117 Port of Long Beach, Annual Report, 2004.
118 Aquarium of the Pacific, "Molina Animal Care Center."
119 Van Dooren, *Flight Ways*.
120 This refers to the animals in captivity that are the subject of this chapter, but also it also invokes patterns wherein rich people in both Global South and Global North contexts have begun filtering their air and paying for exclusive access to clean water, while their poor neighbors take on toxins and contaminants.
121 Van Dooren, *Flight Ways*, 6. He adds, "Biologist Richard Primack (1993) estimates that the current rate of extinction is likely 100 to 1,000 times greater than would be expected as a result of normal 'background extinction'" (6).
122 Tsing, *Mushroom at the End of the World*, 19.
123 USACE representative, interview, May 7, 2021.
124 Richardson, "Marine Life Flourishing in San Pedro Bay"; Stolzenbach et al., "2018 Biological Surveys."
125 SeaTrees, "Palos Verdes, California Giant Kelp Forest Regeneration."
126 Field notes, January 19, 2021.

CHAPTER FOUR

1   In early March 2020, Adrian Economakis, head of market intelligence service VesselsValue, stated, "China really is the driver of the shipping industry. We are so dependent on Chinese demand and also Chinese exports, so demand for raw

material, exports of a finished product for driving cargo volumes and cargo demands" (Berti, "Impact of Covid-19 on Global Shipping").

2 Many mariners also got stuck at sea, which escalated into a humanitarian crisis as crews were not permitted to leave ships, "forced to continue working despite being under-resourced, over-stretched and separated from loved ones for over a year in thousands of cases" (Degnarain, "Global Toxic Ship Fuel Controversy").

3 Scientists made a point to acknowledge human pain arising from this boon to research, however: "While this is no doubt a valuable research opportunity, it is one that has only come about through tragic circumstances. Scientists who prepare to study lockdown effects on wildlife, and on the environment more generally, should be sensitive to the immense human suffering caused by COVID-19 and use appropriate language to describe their work" (Rutz et al., "COVID-19 Lockdown").

4 McVeigh, "Silence Is Golden for Whales."

5 An earlier anthropause presented itself when global shipping halted following the 9/11 attacks in 2001; scientists assessing stress hormone levels in whale excretions in the Bay of Fundy, near Halifax in Canada, noted that when ship traffic fell, whales became less stressed (Robbins, "Oceans Are Getting Louder").

6 De Lara, "'This Port Is Killing People,'" 542.

7 Cowen, *Deadly Life of Logistics*.

8 All of this is controversial, and it is beyond the scope of this work to give much comment. There is growing scientific agreement that nonlethal research on whales is a perfectly acceptable alternative, though some nations continue to request whaling permits for scientific activities from the International Whaling Commission (Pynn, "What's the True Scientific Value of Scientific Whaling?").

9 Marrero and Thornton, "Gray Whale."

10 Dedina, *Saving the Gray Whale*, 12, 47. Dedina presents marine mammal protection as anti-imperialist, embodying the ideals of the Mexican Revolution, "Mexico for Mexicans" (48). But he also says that even as managers agreed they were protecting wildlife from "foreigners," the "utilitarian" notion that marine wildlife is a "resource" has led to conflict between those officials interested in resource protection (for exploitation) versus others interested in biodiversity and preservation (46).

11 Dedina, *Saving the Gray Whale*, 47, 48.

12 Dedina, *Saving the Gray Whale*, 49, 51, 54.

13 Ray and Potter, "Making of the Marine Mammal Protection Act," 523, 522.

14 United States Code §1361 (2) (1972).

15 Ray and Potter, "Making of the Marine Mammal Protection Act." Pringle, "Tech Ecosystem," helpfully points out that emphasis on "holistic ecosystems" can be allied with eugenicist beliefs and practices, so "ecosystem" as a concept should be approached with a critical lens.

16 See Alagona, *After the Grizzly*, chap. 4.

17 Ray and Potter, "Making of the Marine Mammal Protection Act," 524. See Benson, *Surroundings*, on the history of the concept of "environment." And see Gilmore, *Golden Gulag*, on how California responded to the perceived threat of crime.

18 Benson, "Endangered Science," 42. Ray and Potter, "Making of the Marine Mammal Protection Act," 524.

19 US House Committee on Merchant Marine and Fisheries, 1971, quoted in Benson, "Endangered Science," 43.

20 Benson, "Endangered Science," 40–42. Zelko adds that for some protectionists who had fully committed to a "mystical whale" outlook, the managerial compromise that took hold was a rather bitter pill to swallow: "the idea of turning whales into semi-domesticated stock was possibly even worse than hunting them on the open sea" ("From Blubber and Baleen," 104).

21 Philosopher Amia Srinivasan notes that whales are somewhat unusual as charismatic subjects for humans to care about: "Animals that win human sympathy tend to be readily anthropomorphized (elephants, chimps, dolphins), or cute (baby tigers, pangolins), or—the holy grail of animal conservation—both (otters)." Conversely, whales are not cute, and are generally too large to be perceived in their total mass, let alone infantilized. But, she says, they are perceived to be "like us" in their familial bonds and communicative sociality ("What Have We Done to the Whale?").

22 Srinivasan, "What Have We Done to the Whale?"

23 Quoted in Srinivasan, "What Have We Done to the Whale?"

24 Grimshaw, "Calls from the Deep."

25 This led to the creation of a nonprofit organization of the same name, which still exists today (and a marine biology career for the young woman) (Grimshaw, "Calls from the Deep").

26 Mitman, *Reel Nature*.

27 Grimshaw, "Calls from the Deep." At its founding, Greenpeace was actually an anti-nuclear-weapons organization but shifted its focus to whales (Zelko, "From Blubber and Baleen," 101).

28 Peters, *Marvelous Clouds*, 69.

29 Srinivasan, "What Have We Done to the Whale?"

30 International Whaling Commission, "Commercial Whaling."

31 Norway, Japan, and Iceland have most consistently flouted international agreements.

32 Though commercial fishing is regulated to prevent excessive harm to cetaceans, regulations are frequently ignored. Subsistence fishing using illegal equipment also harms cetaceans, like the near-extinct vaquita. Gumbs argues that capitalism is the source of suffering for both the humans catching the vaquita in the gillnet because they will otherwise starve and the vaquita who is killed by illegal fishing (*Undrowned*, 102–3). See also Moore, *We Are All Whalers*.

33 This vignette is lifted in its entirety from Zelko, "From Blubber and Baleen," 91.

34 Neimanis writes, "we could follow [bombs dumped in the sea, which leach pollution in the present day] back to the rise of industrial chemistry and its suturing of militarisation to everyday marine pollution" ("'Chemists' War,'" 11).

35 Evans, "A Short History," 368–70.

36 Benson, "Endangered Science," 41.

37 Burnett, *Sounding of the Whale*, 602. Lilly's research was funded by National Aeronautics and Space Administration, Department of Defense, the Office of Naval Research (ONR), and National Science Foundation (Burnett, "A Mind in the Water," 44).

38 Quoted in Burnett *Sounding of the Whale*, 623.

39 Quoted in Burnett *Sounding of the Whale*, 624. Lilly further speculated that a

sperm whale might "modify the music and even further elaborate it beyond any human conception of music." Lilly focused on sperm whales, as they possessed the largest brains, in what Burnett calls a "flat-footed cortical reductionism" (622).

40 Burnett, *Sounding of the Whale*, 602, 621, 616.

41 Bryld and Lykke, *Cosmodolphins*, quoted in Ritts and Shiga, "Military Cetology," 201. Lilly also speculated about extraterrestrial life and drew parallels between space and the sea as sites of exploration and conquest (Mitman, *Reel Nature*).

42 He adds, "In nature as entertainment, science and spectacle are never far apart" (Mitman, *Reel Nature*, 177).

43 Mitman, *Reel Nature*, 159.

44 Burnett, *Sounding of the Whale*, 541n32.

45 Thackrey, "Porpoise Shows Man How to Live under Sea."

46 US Navy, "Dolphins That Joined the Navy."

47 Sealab II was in fact headed by Scott Carpenter, the second Mercury astronaut to orbit the Earth (Mitman, *Reel Nature*, 177).

48 Hellwarth, *SEALAB: America's Forgotten Quest*, 109.

49 Thackrey, "Porpoise Shows Man How to Live under Sea."

50 Pauli and Clapper, "Project Sealab Report," 1.

51 US Navy, *All Hands*, 4.

52 Pauli and Clapper, "Project Sealab Report," 408.

53 NOAA tracks whale mortality events due to entanglement. More deaths are concentrated in southern and central California, but this may not reflect the locations of entanglement events. Gillnet and Dungeness crab gear are most commonly implicated (Saez, Lawson, and DeAngelis, "Large Whale Entanglements").

54 Pauli and Clapper, "Project Sealab Report," 408, 409.

55 *Los Angeles Times*, "Porpoise Fails Sealab Tryout as Postman."

56 *Hartford Courant*, "Pugnacious Porpoise." Of course, animals have a long history in war, including dogs and horses; pigeons have been used in wartime communication (Phillips, "Pigeons in the Trenches").

57 *Los Angeles Times*, "Porpoise Makes Good."

58 Thackrey, "Porpoise Shows Man How to Live under Sea," emphasis added.

59 "*Aqua nullius*" appears in some Australian legal studies literature, mainly to refer to Indigenous claims to inland water rights. It does not seem to be widely used in the sense I am using it here, oceanic territory. See Hendlin, "From *Terra Nullius* to *Terra Communis*," for a review of the history of *terra nullius* as a concept and legal principle.

60 Marine Technology Society, "Transactions."

61 US Navy, "Dolphins That Joined the Navy." It is fruitful to bring the animal lives here into dialogue with decolonial critiques like that of Belcourt, who writes that "domestication of animal bodies as colonial and capitalist subjects . . . [deploys] animal bodies as settler-colonial utilities" ("Animal Bodies, Colonial Subjects," 3). See also Parreñas, *Decolonizing Extinction*. Further underscoring the settler colonial fantasy, a 1966 news story speculated that in the future, trained porpoises would be able to "ride herd" for "large-scale farming operations in the sea" (United Press International, "Lassie in the Sea?").

62 Squire, "Companions, Zappers, and Invaders," 5. Squire argues that Tuffy's body was drawn into the masculine ideals of the undersea experiment, as his name referred to scars that the Navy represented as souvenirs of encounters with sharks

in which he emerged the victor—natural and geopolitical norms projected onto this male dolphin and onto soldiers (5). Also according to Squire, Tuffy's own body was a territory, ripe for conquest by the American men who trained him and populated Sealab's environment (6).

63 See Squire 2016; Adler 2020.

64 Hellwarth, *SEALAB: America's Forgotten Quest*, 200, 201.

65 Pauli and Clapper, "Project Sealab Report," 20–21.

66 Peters, *Marvelous Clouds*, 73.

67 Burnett, *Sounding of the Whale*, 539–40.

68 Ritts and Shiga, "Military Cetology."

69 Grimshaw, "Calls from the Deep."

70 Or, at least, baleen whales do not echolocate in the same way. They may use sound to map environmental features using lower frequency sounds than toothed whales' higher and nearer-range calls.

71 Burnett, *Sounding of the Whale*, 547–48, 550–52.

72 Hemilä, Nummela, and Reuter, "Model of the Odontocete Middle Ear."

73 Yamato et al., "Auditory Anatomy."

74 Richardson et al., *Marine Mammals and Noise*, 206, 205. Acoustics research relies on graphic display of scientific information that visualizes noise (Ritts and Shiga, "Military Cetology," 202).

75 Benson, "Endangered Science"; Oreskes, "Science and Public Policy." As the Cold War ended, funding was scaled back, but marine mammals are still in service to the US Navy to this day.

76 Yamato et al., "Auditory Anatomy," 993.

77 United States Code §1362 18A (1972); see Braverman, *Wild Life*, chap. 5.

78 Points of controversy had to do with the display of whales, dolphins, and sea lions in amusement parks; the degree of exploitation permitted in scientific research; and even whether activities like whale-watching and nature photography could constitute harassment (see Benson, "Endangered Science").

79 Richardson et al. 1995: 9, 12–13, 8.

80 Richardson, "Effects of Noise on Aquatic Life," 13.

81 Hawkins, Popper, and Wahlberg, "Introduction: International Conference."

82 Richardson, "Effects of Noise on Aquatic Life." Beaked whales are toothed whales, whose sonic range is higher on the acoustic spectrum than baleen whales.

83 Bijsterveld, "Diabolical Symphony"; Cornell University, "Secrets of Whales' Long-Distance Songs" (emphasis added).

84 In present-day California, smog is actually worse in the Inland Empire than in more "urban" Los Angeles County.

85 Robbins, "Oceans Are Getting Louder"; Ritts "Amplifying Environmental Politics," 1407.

86 Southall et al., "Marine Mammal Noise Exposure Criteria," 274; see Oreskes, "Science and Public Policy," 378.

87 Mills, "Deafening."

88 Richardson et al., *Marine Mammals and Noise*, 30, 426.

89 Burnett, *Sounding of the Whale*, 538.

90 Richardson, "Effects of Noise on Aquatic Life," 15.

91 Southall et al., "Marine Mammal Noise Exposure Criteria," 273.

92 Austin, "Last Chance to Sound Off." Courts weighed in but sometimes in oppos-

ing directions: in 2008, the US Supreme Court struck down limitations on the navy exercises, ruling that national security concerns superseded the safety of sea life in harm's way (Austin, "Last Chance to Sound Off"); a few years later, environmentalists' arguments were more persuasive, when a federal judge in Hawai'i ruled that the navy had vastly underestimated the threat to marine mammals that explosives and sonar testing posed, and sent it back to the drawing board in requesting permit renewal (Perry, "Judge Rules Navy Underestimated Threat").

93 Robbins, "Oceans Are Getting Louder." The former is called cavitation.
94 Ritts, "Amplifying Environmental Politics," 1406–7.
95 NOAA, "Gray Whale Conservation"; De Lara, *Inland Shift.*
96 "Collision Course," *San Diego Union Tribune.*
97 "Collision Course," *San Diego Union Tribune.*
98 City News Service, "Lawsuit Threatened to Protect Whales."
99 "Collision Course," *San Diego Union Tribune.* In the Bay of Fundy, off Nova Scotia, officials moved shipping lanes in 2003 to accommodate whale movement. It worked for a time, but then whales changed their course, probably due to climate change (Moore, *We Are All Whalers*).
100 City News Service, "Lawsuit Threatened to Protect Whales."
101 "Collision Course," *San Diego Union Tribune.*
102 Parsons, "Impacts of Navy Sonar," 5.
103 "Collision Course," *San Diego Union Tribune.*
104 See Mitman, *Reel Nature,* 178–79.
105 Parsons, "Impacts of Navy Sonar," 6, 8, 7.
106 Martin, "Research Highlight: Blue Whales Are Arriving."
107 Parsons, "Impacts of Navy Sonar," 8.
108 Liboiron, *Pollution Is Colonialism,* 59. Liboiron writes of chemical harm, not sonic. Though chemical molecules can linger and acoustic phenomena may dissipate rapidly, the argument fits well enough here nonetheless. For Liboiron, present-day pollution regimes are forms of colonial violence.
109 Liboiron, *Pollution Is Colonialism,* chap. 1; Lerner, *Sacrifice Zones.*
110 Parreñas, *Decolonizing Extinction,* 16.
111 Christiansen et al., "Poor Body Condition."
112 Srinivasan, "What Have We Done to the Whale?" Faroese people and Inuit who eat whale flesh and blubber have been warned to eat less of it, and to be careful breast-feeding their babies; toxins that are stored in fatty tissue like blubber flow readily into breast milk.
113 Parsons, "Impacts of Navy Sonar," 5.
114 Guazzo et al., "Gray Whale Migration Patterns," 196.
115 Xia, "L.A.'s Coast."
116 Xia, "DDT's Toxic Legacy."
117 CBSLA, "'Overwhelming.'"
118 Liboiron, *Pollution Is Colonialism.* I am not drawing a firm line between land and water here, of course; the point is that spatial logics in "permission to pollute" regimes designate some areas as sacrifice zones.
119 Squire, "Companions, Zappers, and Invaders," 1.
120 Ritts and Shiga, "Military Cetology," 197.
121 "Collision Course," *San Diego Union Tribune.*
122 Simon, "Want to Save the Whales?"

123 Ritts, "Amplifying Environmental Politics," 1407.
124 Puente, "Here's Why Dozens of Cargo Ships Are Parked."
125 Curwen, "Officials Knew of Potential for 'Catastrophe.'"
126 Canon, "'It Is There Pretty Much Forever.'"
127 Simon, "Want to Save the Whales?"
128 Incidental takes are also permitted for commercial fishing and other commercial activity, especially those which "will have a negligible impact on such species or stock" (United States Code §1361–1407 [5DiI]).
129 Austin, "Last Chance to Sound Off."
130 Perry, "Judge Rules Navy Underestimated Threat."
131 Puar, *Right to Maim*.
132 One imagines that epigenetic harm from sonic disturbance might operate differently from that caused by chemical exposure, but its occurrence is not out of the realm of possibility. As the whales in the Bay of Fundy showed in 2001, stress hormones are affected by shipping, and, for example, that hormonal state over an adult's life span could potentially affect offspring.
133 Ritts and Shiga, "Military Cetology"; see also Burnett, *Sounding of the Whale*; Oreskes, "Science and Public Policy."
134 My argument is not a call for ignorance but rather that we already likely know what we need to know, and that the problems are more political than technical per se. Ritts suggests that "On Canada's West Coast, there is a consensus that scientific studies will be the basis of reparative work around the human–environmental relations that appear to be driving marine collapse," arguing that scientific knowledge can provide grounds for promoting an understanding that "capitalism is not the best way of organizing social relations with nature in the ocean" ("Amplifying Environmental Politics," 1408, 1420). I am not sure that this analysis is portable to the US context, though I hope Ritts is right and I am wrong.
135 Erbe et al., "Effects of Ship Noise," 1.
136 Ritts states that when compared to the complex and expanding scientific understanding of the biological *impacts* of ocean noise, the *sources* of noise are relatively clear ("Amplifying Environmental Politics," 1406, emphasis added).
137 Robbins, "Oceans Are Getting Louder."
138 Ecological Society of America, "Squid and Octopuses."
139 Robbins, "Oceans Are Getting Louder."
140 *Sonic Sea* trailer.
141 Ritts and Shiga, "Military Cetology," 211; Peters, *Marvelous Clouds*. Zelko adds that the "save the whales" movement may have ironically hindered animal rights more broadly as it made whales' saving contingent on their putatively unique intelligence; the consequences of anthropomorphizing certain animals are "tricky and culturally contingent" ("From Blubber and Baleen," 105–6). He does not make the point, but one could, that animal conservation on the grounds of anthropomorphic "intelligence" is race science of a sort (Dunbar-Hester, "Save the [White] Whales"). See also Belcourt ("Animal Bodies, Colonial Subjects") on how animal welfare activism that commensurates animal suffering with human suffering can easily reproduce settler colonial and white supremacist logics.
142 Wade, "Search for a Sixth Sense," 176.
143 But: the ocean has been a generative site for theorizing alternate sensing relations.

See, e.g., Helmreich, "Anthropologist Underwater"; Lehman, "From Ships to Robots"; Jue, *Wild Blue Media.*

144 Jue, *Wild Blue Media*, 10.

145 Ritts and Shiga, "Military Cetology," 210, 207.

146 Mitman, *Reel Nature*, 178.

147 United Nations, "Universal Declaration of Human Rights"; World People's Conference on Climate Change and the Rights of Mother Earth, 2010.

148 Peters, *Marvelous Clouds*, 85. Though I appreciate Peters's provocation, I do not mean to suggest that dolphins are liberal subjects.

149 Belcourt argues that the politics and boundaries of "animality" should be understood within a politics of space, especially the territorial-acquisition processes of settler colonialism ("Animal Bodies, Colonial Subjects," 3).

150 Belcourt, "Animal Bodies, Colonial Subjects"; Squire, "Companions, Zappers, and Invaders," 1; Pugliese, *Biopolitics.*

151 Thinking about sound as a spatial phenomenon can enable its analysis as a situated means of knowing and being in the world (Ritts and Shiga, "Military Cetology," drawing on musicologist Steven Feld).

152 I do not mean to imply that appealing to "sovereignty" neatly resolves any of the complexities here. Information studies scholar Marisa Duarte's definition of Indigenous sovereignty as "the dynamic relationship between the will of a people to live by the ways of knowing they have cultivated over millennia within a homeland and the legal and political rights they have negotiated with the occupying federal government" is relevant to the present discussion (*Network Sovereignty*, 37). Indigenous sovereignties include access to lifeworlds including mutually or self-determined relations with animals and other life-forms, of course (see Todd, "Fish Pluralities"). Because I locate San Pedro Bay and its inhabitants within structuring dynamics of capitalism and settler colonialism, in this project I find it more fruitful to bring anticolonial Indigenous studies scholarship to bear than (Western) political philosophy about animal recognition. Belcourt argues that much mainstream animal activism (including strands of scholarship) recenters the *settler* as an acting body ("Animal Bodies, Colonial Subjects," 2, emphasis added).

153 Guazzo et al., "Gray Whale Migration Patterns," 195.

154 Some industries have adopted "life cycle assessment" tools (LCAs) for supply-chain governance. Geographer Susanne Freidberg points out that "it is far from clear that LCAs can capture the complexity of products' 'lives' in measures that are simultaneously practical, legible and scientifically credible" ("Calculating Sustainability," 571). The shipping industry's participation in Whale Safe is also in this vein, but as a voluntary measure, it is unenforceable and tepid.

155 Stone, "How Much Is a Whale Worth?"; see also Grimshaw, "Calls from the Deep,"; Paulson, "We Need a New Asset Class.".

156 Wood et al., "Near Real Time Passive Acoustic Monitoring."

157 Ritts and Shiga, "Military Cetology," 201.

158 Pettman writes, "many animals have the capacity for voice, which is not merely an evolutionary expedience to find mates, scare enemies, or communicate food sources but is also a sonic exploration of ontological conditions" (*Sonic Intimacy*, 54).

159 Writing of odor, Morana Alač says, "odors ask us to give up our dominance while

we continue to be involved" ("Beyond Intersubjectivity," 474), but her analysis is generative for thinking about other senses as well. See also Lehman, "From Ships to Robots."

CONCLUSION

1   Nelson, "710 Freeway."
2   Curwen, "L.A. Area Finally Has Its Own 'Postcard' Bridge"; Eaton, "Update: Port of Long Beach"; Lovely, "Port of Long Beach Gets New Bridge." This affected some berths in the Port of Long Beach, which could only accommodate smaller vessels.
3   Curwen, "L.A. Area Finally Has Its Own 'Postcard' Bridge"; Lovely, "Port of Long Beach Gets New Bridge."
4   Tsing, *Friction.*
5   Mody shows that the oil industry was an investor in the microchip ("Spillovers from Oil Firms"). Ensmenger shows how the development of networked computing followed the physical infrastructure of the railroad, which itself relied on and transported fossil fuel ("Environmental History of Computing"). "Shiny" is in scare quotes: computing is very dirty, of course, from mineral mining to data farms' energy consumption to post-use pollution (e-waste).
6   Cowen, *Deadly Life of Logistics*, 38. Rossiter writes, "If infrastructure makes worlds, then software coordinates them" (*Software, Infrastructure, Labor*, xv).
7   Truscello, *Infrastructural Brutalism*, 19; see also Khalili, *Sinews of War and Trade*.
8   Meanwhile the top exports were animal feed, wastepaper, soybeans, scrap metal, and textiles (Port of Los Angeles, "Annual Facts and Figures Card"). Some ships were sent back to Asia bearing mostly empty containers, because the containers were needed for exports more immediately than they would be filled in the United States (Leonard, "Why the Empty Container Math Doesn't Add Up").
9   Tsing, *Friction*, 4.
10 For instance, coal consumption in the twentieth century declined globally relative to other fossil fuels, but still rose in absolute terms (Truscello, *Infrastructural Brutalism*, 17).
11 York, "Why Petroleum Did Not Save the Whales," 4, 5, 6.
12 Burnett, *Sounding of the Whale*; York, "Why Petroleum Did Not Save the Whales," 6–7.
13 York, "Why Petroleum Did Not Save the Whales," 7.
14 US Energy Information Administration, "Profile Analysis."
15 "Kern County Approves Plan," Associated Press. Richer coastal areas are banning drilling (like Culver City on the west side of Los Angeles). Pulido points out that poor communities of color in California are essentially subsidizing cleaner air and water in other places ("Racism and the Anthropocene").
16 Willon and Luna, "Newsom Bans New California Fracking Permits."
17 *Energy efficiency*, not just energy source, is key. Petrochemicals also have many industrial applications beyond fuel, from consumer packaging to pharmaceutical manufacture and much in between. How to live in better relation with petroleum would account for these uses, not only fuel (see Davis, "Imperceptibility and Accumulation"; Todd, "Fish, Kin and Hope").
18 "Plastic pollution and the climate crisis are two inseparable parts of the same

problem, though they aren't treated as such," writes geographer Deirdre McKay ("Fossil Fuel Industry Sees the Future").

19 United States Energy Information Administration, "FAQs"; Volcovici and Kearney, "150 Years of Spills."

20 There are hints of the petroleum infrastructure here being utilized, at a smaller scale, for alternative fuels. A former petroleum pipeline running through North Long Beach was permitted to transport hydrogen, made from biofuel, fabricated in a former petroleum refinery (Echeverry, "City Council OKs Hydrogen Gas"). There is also experimental use of refined kelp for fuel, which could fit into existing petroleum infrastructure for refining and distribution (Maschke, "Kelp Fuel Is Making a Comeback"). Both would contribute to carbon emissions and particulate emissions (the hydrogen in its initial fabrication from biofuel, not in its use as fuel). In other words, these fuel *sources* are potentially renewable, but the devil is in the details in a comparison with petroleum.

21 Communities living near wells suffer asthma and other respiratory ailments at disproportionate levels. One-third of Los Angeles County residents, including me, but disproportionately Black and Latinx people, live within a mile of a well (and some mere feet away) (Johnston and Shamasunder, "Urban Oil Wells").

22 Related was the rise of quantification and economic valuation of nature, such as ecosystem services (Costanza et al. 1997). Originally conceived of as a means to assign value to nature, including that which was not captured within markets, financialization has now moved to "assetize" ever more of nature (see, e.g., Paulson, "We Need a New Asset Class").

23 Bernes, "Logistics, Counterlogistics and the Communist Prospect." Mitchell ties this directly to oil itself, arguing that oil was used to stabilize currency markets and the international monetary system in the postwar period (*Carbon Democracy*, chap. 5).

24 Bernes, "Logistics, Counterlogistics and the Communist Prospect"; see also Cowen, *Deadly Life of Logistics*; De Lara, *Inland Shift*; LiPuma and Lee, "Financial Derivatives."

25 Richardson, "Marine Life Flourishing in San Pedro Bay."

26 See Harris, "Militarism in Environmental Disguise."

27 Woody, "California's Critical Kelp Forests"; USACE representative, interview, May 7, 2021.

28 Industry is currently making voluntary efforts to slow ships in major corridors off California's coast. Slower speeds can benefit whales by giving them a better opportunity to avoid ships. Noise is reduced, but only somewhat: an industry-supplied estimate was four decibels, and given the doubling of ocean noise every decade, the impact of this reduction is not meaningless but likely relatively minor. Emissions are also reduced, but again, it is relative, and compliance is voluntary (*Long Beach Post Partner*, "Sixteen Global Shipping Companies").

29 "Full battle group fleet exercises involving aircraft, surface ships, and submarines are conducted in the sea range *without being affected by the flow of commercial vessels*" (US Department of Homeland Security Navigation Center, "Port Access Route Study," 13–14, emphasis added).

30 As depressing as they are, reports focusing on single-species extinctions have been criticized for being too optimistic.

31 *Los Angeles Times*, "Editorial: Supply Chain Issues."

32 I do not mean to suggest that these effects were experienced equally or universally. Well-off residents in LA live in cooler areas with better air quality due to the presence of trees and parks, and they are more likely to have generators or home battery arrays, and/or second homes to flee to.

33 These are terms used by Los Angeles Mayor Eric Garcetti in 2021 ("Port of Los Angeles Eclipses 10 Million Container Units," Associated Press).

34 Port of Los Angeles, "Annual Facts and Figures Card," emphasis added.

35 Cowen, *Deadly Life of Logistics*, 14–15.

36 Cf. Erie, *Globalizing LA*.

37 *Supply Chain Digest*, "Global Supply Chain News."

38 Many scholars have argued that control over national economies is potentially illusory, as transnational circuits of capital exert great pull, with complex effects (Murphy, *Economization of Life*; Urry, "Complexities of the Global").

39 Bowman, "Shippers Need Alternatives." Vancouver's port was cut off from much of North America when flooding took out railways and roads in November 2021 (Thompson, "Canada's Flood Havoc"). I do not want to overstate fungibility here, as coordinating logistics for movement of goods on the ground is highly complex, and LA has inland distribution infrastructure that makes it better equipped to handle voluminous cargo (De Lara, *Inland Shift*; Danyluk, "Fungible Space").

40 USACE, "Army Corps of Engineers Releases Draft Feasibility Report"; "Halifax Breaks Record," CBC News.

41 But only tailpipe emission. Tires decompose due to friction with road surfaces and leave behind dangerous airborne particulates and toxic runoff (Xia, "Biggest Likely Source of Microplastics"; see Liboiron, *Pollution Is Colonialism*).

42 Sovacool et al., "Imagining Sustainable Energy," 650.

43 "It's marvelous, very 'cool.' . . . It's called 'neoliberal globalization version 6.6.6,' but we prefer to just call it 'the savage' or 'the beast.' Yes, it's an aggressive nickname, but it shows initiative. . . . That's what I learned in my self-help class, 'How to sell a nightmare,'" read a trenchant, surrealist comment from Zapatistas in 2013 (Zapatista Army of National Liberation, "EZLN Communique"). But the problem they identify is the *neoliberal nightmare*, not interconnected peoples within frameworks of socioeconomic and environmental sustainability. See also Steger and Wilson, "Anti-Globalization or Alter-Globalization?"

44 Escobar, *Designs for the Pluriverse*, 227.

45 Hernández et al., "Creatures Collective," 11.

46 Ultra-rich people should absolutely see their consumption curtailed, but everyone else should be able to live comfortably.

47 See Sovacool et al., "Imagining Sustainable Energy," for discussion.

48 Riofrancos, "What Green Costs."

49 Hickel, "Degrowth"; Riofrancos, "What Green Costs."

50 Hickel, "Degrowth"; and see Vgontzas ("Toward Degrowth") for a concrete elaboration of these ideas focusing on the transnational assemblage that is Amazon (the firm).

51 Cowen, "Following the Infrastructures."

52 Ballantine, "River Mouth Speaks."

53 Ballantine, "River Mouth Speaks," 47. See also Mei-Singh, "Routed through Water." I do not mean to flatten either Indigenous sovereignties or ecological relations by suggesting that one site or set of relations is inherently like another.

54 Cowen, "Following the Infrastructures."

55 Cowen, "Following the Infrastructures"; Inwood, Brand, and Quinn ("Racial Capital, Abolition").

56 LaDuke and Cowen, "Beyond Wiindigo Infrastructure," 245, emphasis added.

57 Braverman, *Wild Life.*

58 See Ingold, "Epilogue: Towards a Politics of Dwelling"; TallBear, "An Indigenous Reflection"; Todd, "Indigenizing the Anthropocene"; Todd, "Indigenous Feminist's Take."

59 Hernández et al., "Creatures Collective," 5; Purdy, "Environmentalism's Racist History." Or, as Max Liboiron writes, "Environmentalism does not usually address colonialism and often reproduces it." In this context, Liboiron adds, "Colonial land relations are inherited as common sense, even as good ideas" (*Pollution Is Colonialism*, 11, 12).

60 Anson, "No One Is a Virus"; Price, "Remaking American Environmentalism"; Purdy, "Environmentalism's Racist History."

61 Ruiz, "Federal Regulators' Demand for Pollution Study." Freeway widening is currently on hold due to environmental concerns. The planned expansion of the 710 would have also displaced residents who lived on land claimed to expand the infrastructure, putting them at increased risk of homelessness (Dillon, "710 Freeway Is a Key Link").

62 For more about USACE's role in enforcing in global geopolitical order, see Khalili, "Infrastructural Power of the Military."

63 Justice is "comprised of limits and inherent wants": urgent calls for it only underscore how it represents repeated deferral and denial. Also, in looking to *states* to deliver justice, we may be acquiescing to limits, impossibilities; states' legal orders limit justice to within borders, which are themselves violent artifacts of empire and colony (Tuck and Yang, "What Justice Wants," 5, 8). My invocation of "justice" is more in line with Ron Eglash's conception of generative (bottom-up) justice ("Introduction to Generative Justice").

64 LaDuke and Cowen, "Beyond Wiindigo Infrastructure"; Escobar, *Designs for the Pluriverse.*

65 Crawford, "Pentagon Fuel Use"; see also Belcher et al., "Hidden Carbon Costs."

66 Cowen, *Deadly Life of Logistics*, 227.

67 Escobar, "Whose Knowledge, Whose Nature?"

68 Chua et al., "Introduction: Turbulent Circulation"; Cowen. *Deadly Life of Logistics.*

69 Posner, "See No Evil"; Hockenberry ("Manifest/Manifesto") advocates for supply-chain "reconciliation," using them to make knowledge about where "labor has been exploited, where the earth has been plundered, where waste overruns into rivers, and poison bleeds into the air." LaDuke and Cowen refer to "alimentary infrastructure," infrastructure for life ("Beyond Wiindigo Infrastructure," 245).

70 Truscello calls for "*brisantic politics*, a culture of unmaking capable of slowing the advance of capitalist suicide . . . a wide range of practices dedicated to defeating infrastructural power from an antiauthoritarian perspective" (*Infrastructural Brutalism*, 39, emphasis in original); Chua, "Organizing against Amazon."

71 Estes, *Our History Is the Future*, 248, emphasis in original. Dismantling is world-building, as Jeffrey Insko writes ("Line 5: Dismantling as World-Building").

72 Bosworth and Chua, "Countersovereignty of Critical Infrastructure Security."

73 "Wet'suwet'en Conflict," BBC.

74 LaDuke and Cowen, "Beyond Wiindigo Infrastructure," 255.

75 See Slaton, *Reinforced Concrete*, and Truscello, *Infrastructural Brutalism*, on cement. Cement ingredients are a major commodity in the Los Angeles harbor. Though it is outside the scope of this account, earth-moving is arguably one of the very most important processes of fixing infrastructural modernity, including road-building, cement (used in bridge building, damming, etc.), and dredging.

76 Bernes, "Logistics, Counterlogistics and the Communist Prospect."

77 This was not a true strike, as it was a contractually allowed work stoppage that the ILWU opted to hold in solidarity with BLM. The action was initiated by Keith Shanklin, the first Black union president of ILWU Local 34 in Oakland, who wrote to the ILWU president, "All lives will matter when Black lives matter because an injury to one is an injury to all!" when calling for the action (Kern and Farr, "ILWU Shuts Down West Coast Ports"). In Oakland, the shutdown was accompanied by a massive rally featuring abolitionist scholar and activist Angela Davis, families of people killed by police violence, and radical filmmaker Boots Riley (Severn et al., "'We Don't Want to Just Ask for Things to Get Better'"). Protesters marched from the port to Oakland's City Hall.

78 APM Research Lab, "Color of Coronavirus."

79 As Laura Pulido and Juan De Lara write, "ecological precarity can[not] be overcome without negotiating the entrenched histories and current articulations of racial capitalism" ("Reimagining 'Justice'": 81).

80 Lakoff, "'Supply Chain Must Continue.'" A disproportionate number of workers of color were also classed as "essential" labor, reflecting patterns of racial capitalism that sorted them into poorly paid, hazardous work, essentially marking them as disposable.

81 Port of Los Angeles, "Annual Facts and Figures Card."

82 De Lara "'This Port Is Killing People'"; Alimahomed-Wilson, "Unfree Shipping."

83 Alimahomed-Wilson, "Unfree Shipping," 104. Amazon is a particularly harsh employer: workers suffer repetitive stress injuries; injuries due to heavy lifting; and mental anguish due to the frantic pace of work. Many employees lack health insurance and there is a high rate of turnover.

84 There were around 70,000 unhoused people in Los Angeles County at the time of this writing.

85 Alimahomed-Wilson, "Unfree Shipping," 109–10.

86 The wealth real estate and oil generated has been constituted by racial segregation and racialized dispossession (Cumming, "Black Gold, White Power,"; Davis 1990; De Lara, *Inland Shift*). Cumming points out that LA was founded on settler colonialism and argues that Los Angeles "colonized the underground" when drilling brought oil to the surface and taxed "black and Latino residents' properties, wealth, and health for generations" (89). Thom Davies argues that structural inequality can mutate into *noxious instances of slow violence* ("Slow Violence and Toxic Geographies," emphasis in original).

87 Shalby, Vives, and Campa, "Elementary School Kids Doused."

88 Martin, Myers, and Viseu, "Politics of Care."

89 Mitman, *Reel Nature*, 178.

90 Some "environmentalists" have long been accused of caring more for preservation of "wilderness" and the suffering of animals than of racialized and systemically disadvantaged people (Cronon, "Trouble with Wilderness"; Price, "Remaking American Environmentalism"). John Muir, naturalist and founder of the Sierra Club in 1892, expressed casual racism and ambivalence toward human species-mates, but said of bears, "Poor fellows, they have been poisoned, trapped, and shot at until they have lost confidence in brother man" (quoted in Purdy, "Environmentalism's Racist History"). Speaking of "forest protection" at the expense of "overlapping and contested Native American, Hispano, and public land claims," a Chicano activist called Smokey Bear, emblem of federal control, a "white racist pig" (Kosek, *Understories*, 184).

91 Estes, *Our History Is the Future*; TallBear, "Badass (Indigenous) Women"; Davis, "Imperceptibility and Accumulation."

92 Chua et al., "Introduction: Turbulent Circulation," 623.

93 Pham, "World without Sweatshops."

94 Some troubling answers are being provided by banker and ex-Treasury Secretary Henry Paulson, who has suggested an elaborate financialization of life to create asset flows that favor biodiversity conservation ("We Need a New Asset Class"). See LiPuma and Lee, "Financial Derivatives."

95 Red Nation, *The Red Deal*.

96 See Pulido and De Lara ("Reimagining 'Justice'") for conjoining environmental justice with decolonial border thinking.

97 "Alterlife acknowledges that one cannot simply get out," says Michelle Murphy ("Alterlife," 500).

98 Nading, "Living in a Toxic World."

99 Quivik, "Historical Significance of Tailings."

100 Mitchell, *Carbon Democracy*.

101 This is a reference to the Zapatista slogan/theory, "Un mundo donde quepan muchos mundos" (A world where many worlds fit). It gestures toward solidarities and resistance to the violent universalizing moves that accompany corporate enclosure of natural resources in the pursuit of economic growth. See Escobar, *Designs for the Pluriverse*, 15–16.

102 Tsing, *Friction*, 1. Hockenberry ("Manifest/Manifesto") writes that supply chains "have tied the world into a shape that is both fragmented and fragile, and for every marvel at their end there are countless runs of almost useless, morally broken objects—dead on arrival, and destined for the dump."

103 Escobar, *Designs for the Pluriverse*; LaDuke and Cowen, "Beyond Wiindigo Infrastructure"; Todd, "Fish, Kin and Hope"; see also Enns and Sneyd, "More-Than-Human Infrastructural Violence."

104 Liboiron, *Pollution Is Colonialism*, 132. As Liboiron points out, anticolonial sciences (plural) are an orientation more than a monolithic set of practices.

105 Harding, *Objectivity and Diversity*; Liboiron, *Pollution Is Colonialism*.

106 See Harris, "Militarism in Environmental Disguise"; Martini, "Introduction: Bases, Places, and the Layered Landscapes."

107 Dominant science may leave openings for anticolonial science (Liboiron, *Pollution Is Colonialism*). I am not a scientist, merely a critic.

108 LaDuke and Cowen, "Beyond Wiindigo Infrastructure," 244.

109 Chua et al., "Introduction: Turbulent Circulation," 626; Estes, *Our History Is the Future*, 248. "Logistical solidarity" is sociologist Maggie Davis's term, not yet published.

110 This is an absolutely tongue-in-cheek reference to the "nature is healing" memes that circulated during the COVID-19 pandemic (see Bosworth, "Bad Environmentalism"; Kinefuchi, "'Nature Is Healing'" for critique); LaDuke and Cowen, "Beyond Wiindigo Infrastructure."

ACKNOWLEDGMENTS

1 Prior to colonization, Gabrielino (Kizh, Tongva) people lived on the mainland and Santa Catalina Island (Pimu or Pimugna, occupied at least as early as 7000 BCE). The whole LA basin was called Tovaangar, and a significant site near the port complex was the village and sacred site of Puvungna, in what is now eastern Long Beach. See Jurmain and McCawley, *O, My Ancestor*, for present-day perspectives on Gabrielino-Tongva identity and culture, including the topic of federal recognition; and Castillo, "Blood Came from Their Mouths," for historical detail on Spanish colonization and decimation through disease in the late eighteenth into the nineteenth century.

2 Nader, "Up the Anthropologist."

3 Parreñas, *Decolonizing Extinction*, 185.

Bibliography

Addison, Brian. "Long Beach Lost: The Dramatic Tale of the Disney Theme Park in Downtown." *Long Beach Post*, December 4, 2018. https://lbpost .com/hi-lo/long-beach-lost-port-disney-disneysea.

Adler, Antony. "Deep Horizons: Canada's Underwater Habitat Program and Vertical Dimensions of Marine Sovereignty." *Centaurus* 62 (2020): 763–82.

Alač, Morana. "Beyond Intersubjectivity in Olfactory Psychophysics II: Troubles with the Object." *Social Studies of Science* 50, no. 3 (2020): 474–502.

Alagona, Peter. *After the Grizzly: Endangered Species and the Politics of Place in California*. Berkeley: University of California Press, 2013.

Alameda Corridor Transportation Authority. Annual Report. 2013. http://www .acta.org/revenue_finance/financial_reports/Continuing_Disclosure_Annual _Report_2013.pdf.

Alexander, Ann. "Know Your Oil Bill: Ignorance about CA Crude Is Not Bliss." National Resources Defense Council, February 25, 2020. https://www.nrdc.org/ experts/ann-alexander/know-your-oil-bill-ignorance-about-ca-crude-not-bliss.

Alexander, David. "Bioaccumulation, Bioconcentration, Biomagnification." In *Environmental Geology*, ed. David Alexander. Dordrecht: Springer, 1999.

Alimahomed-Wilson, Jake. "Unfree Shipping: The Racialisation of Logistics Labour." *Work Organisation, Labour & Globalisation* 13, no. 1 (2019): 96–113.

Altrudi, Soledad. "Connecting to Nature through Tech? The Case of the INaturalist App." *Convergence* 27, no. 1 (2021): 124–41.

American Journal of Transportation. "Port of Long Beach Moves a Record 8.1 Million TEUs in 2020." January 15, 2021. https://ajot.com/news/port-of-long -beach-moves-a-record-8.1-million-teus-in-2020.

Anand, Nikhil, Akhil Gupta, and Hannah Appel, eds. *The Promise of Infrastructure*. Durham, NC: Duke University Press, 2018.

Andasan, Jan Victor. "Port Pollution Sickens My Whole Neighborhood. That's Violence." *Los Angeles Times*, October 8, 2021. https://www.latimes.com/opinion/story/2021-10-08/port-pollution-sickens-my-family-video-letter.

Anson, April. "No One Is a Virus: On American Ecofascism." *Environmental History Now*, October 21, 2020. https://envhistnow.com/2020/10/21/no-one-is-the-virus-on-american-ecofascism/.

APM Research Lab. "The Color of Coronavirus: Covid-19 Deaths by Race and Ethnicity in the U.S." March 5, 2021. https://www.apmresearchlab.org/covid/deaths-by-race.

Aquarium of the Pacific. "Aquarium Animal Care." Accessed December 5, 2020. https://www.aquariumofpacific.org/exhibits/animalcarecenter/animal_care.

———. "Molina Animal Care Center." Accessed December 23, 2020. https://www.aquariumofpacific.org/exhibits/animalcarecenter.

———. "Sea Otter Conservation." Accessed December 5, 2020. https://www.aquariumofpacific.org/exhibits/otters/sea_otter_conservation.

———. "Sea Otter Habitat." Accessed March 11, 2022. https://www.aquariumofpacific.org/exhibits/otters/

———. "Southern Sea Otter." Accessed December 5, 2020. https://www.aquariumofpacific.org/exhibits/otters/southern_sea_otter.

Arduino, Giulia, David Carrillo Murillo, and Francesco Parola. "Refrigerated Container versus Bulk: Evidence from the Banana Cold Chain." *Maritime Policy & Management* 42, no. 3 (2015): 228–45.

Arian, David. Port of Los Angeles Oral History, 2007. Accessed October 8, 2020. https://www.youtube.com/watch?v=-3waK_4A2Hw.

Aronoff, Kate. "Obama's Climate Legacy and the Lie of 'Energy Independence.'" *New Republic*, February 19, 2020. https://newrepublic.com/article/156580/obamas-climate-legacy-lie-energy-independence.

Arthur, Ian. "Shipboard Refrigeration and the Beginnings of the Frozen Meat Trade." *Journal of the Royal Australian Historical Society* 92, no. 1 (2006): 63–82.

Associated Press. "The Riskiest Place for a Natural Disaster in the U.S.? You're Living in It, L.A." *Los Angeles Times*, January 2, 2021. https://www.latimes.com/world-nation/story/2021-01-04/watch-out-la-feds-calculate-riskiest-safest-places-in-us.

———. "Kern County Approves Plan to Allow Thousands of New Oil Wells Despite Environmental Objections." March 8, 2021. https://ktla.com/news/california/plan-to-allow-thousands-of-new-oil-wells-faces-vote-in-kern-county/.

———. "Port of Los Angeles Eclipses 10 Million Container Units." *AP News*, June 10, 2021. https://apnews.com/article/los-angeles-health-coronavirus-pandemic-business-7c617e76a3c745c7a474541d1436ef28.

Audubon Society. "Pacific Flyway: Conservation the Length of the Americas." Accessed August 29, 2020. https://www.audubon.org/pacific-flyway.

Austin, Paige. "Last Chance to Sound Off on Navy Drills That Harm Whales." *Patch.com*, Los Alamitos, CA, July 9, 2012. https://patch.com/california/losalamitos/amp/4838528/last-chance-to-sound-off-on-navy-drills-that-harm-whales.

Baker, Linda. "Ditching the Diesel, Keeping the Cool." *Freight Waves*, October 6, 2020. https://www.freightwaves.com/news/ditching-the-diesel-keeping-the-cool.

Ballantine, Amory. "The River Mouth Speaks: Water Quality as Storyteller in Decolonization of the Port of Tacoma." *Water History* 9 (2017): 45–66.

Banerjee, Dwaipayan. "Anthropology's Reckoning with Radical Humanism." *Anthropology Now* 12, no. 3 (2020): 50–55.

Banham, Reyner. *Los Angeles: The Architecture of Four Ecologies*. 1971. Reprint, Berkeley: University of California Press, 2009.

Barboza, Tony. "Port Ships Are Becoming L.A.'s Biggest Polluters: Will California Force a Cleanup?" *Los Angeles Times*, January 3, 2020. https://www.latimes.com/california/story/2020-01-03/port-ships-are-becoming-la-worst-polluters-regulators-plug-in.

———. "Southern California Smog Worsens for Second Straight Year Despite Reduced Emissions." *Los Angeles Times*, November 15, 2017. https://www.latimes.com/local/lanow/la-me-ln-bad-air-days-20171115-story.html.

———. "Wildlife Officials: Abandon Southern California Sea Otter Rules." *Los Angeles Times*, August 19, 2011.

Barsness, Richard W. "Maritime Activity and Port Development in the United States since 1900: A Survey." *Journal of Transport History* ss-2, no. 3 (February 1974): 167–84.

Bauer, Susanne, Nils Güttler, and Martina Schlünder. "Encounters in Borderlands: Borderlining Animals and Technology at Frankfurt Airport." *Environmental Humanities* 11, no. 2 (2019): 247–79.

BBC News. "The Wet'suwet'en Conflict Disrupting Canada's Rail System." February 20, 2020. https://www.bbc.com/news/world-us-canada-51550821.

Becker, Rachel. "Shape Up or Ship Out: California Requires Ships, Trucks to Eliminate Thousands of Tons of Pollution." *CalMatters*, August 27, 2020. https://calmatters.org/environment/2020/08/california-ships-trucks-pollution-ports/.

Belcher, Oliver, Patrick Bigger, Ben Neimark, and Cara Kennelly. "Hidden Carbon Costs of the 'Everywhere War': Logistics, Geopolitical Ecology, and the Carbon Boot-print of the US Military." *Transactions of the Institute of British Geographers* 45, no.1 (2020): 65–80.

Belcourt, Billy-Ray. "Animal Bodies, Colonial Subjects: (Re)Locating Animality in Decolonial Thought." *Societies* 5, no. 1 (2015): 1–11.

Bell, Melissa. "Dawn Dishwashing Detergent Saves Wildlife." *Washington Post*, June 17, 2010. https://www.washingtonpost.com/wp-dyn/content/article/2010/06/15/AR2010061501694.html.

Benjamin, Ruha. *Captivating Technology: Race, Carceral Technoscience, and Liberatory Imagination in Everyday Life*. Durham, NC: Duke University Press, 2019.

———. "Racial Fictions, Biological Facts: Expanding the Sociological Imagination through Speculative Methods." *Catalyst: Feminism, Theory, Technoscience* 2, no. 2 (2016). https://catalystjournal.org/index.php/catalyst/article/view/28798.

Bennett, Jane. *Vibrant Matter: A Political Ecology of Things*. Durham, NC: Duke University Press, 2010.

Benson, Etienne. "Endangered Science: The Regulation of Research by the U.S. Marine Mammal Protection and Endangered Species Acts." *Historical Studies in the Natural Sciences* 42, no. 1 (2012): 30–61.

———. *Surroundings: A History of Environments and Environmentalisms*. Chicago: University of Chicago Press, 2020.

———. *Wired Wilderness: Technologies of Tracking and the Making of Modern Wildlife*. Baltimore: Johns Hopkins University Press, 2010.

Berkner, Alice. "The Genesis of International Bird Rescue." Accessed September 6, 2020. https://www.bird-rescue.org/about/history/founder%27s-story.aspx.

Bernes, Jasper. "Logistics, Counterlogistics and the Communist Prospect." *Endnotes* 3 (September 2013). https://endnotes.org.uk/issues/3/en/jasper-bernes-logistics-counterlogistics-and-the-communist-prospect.

Berti, Adele. "The Impact of Covid-19 on Global Shipping: Part 1, System Shock." *Ship Technology*, April 2, 2020. https://www.ship-technology.com/features/impact-of-covid-19-on-shipping/.

Bijsterveld, Karin. "The Diabolical Symphony of the Mechanical Age: Technology and Symbolism of Sound in European and North American Noise Abatement Campaigns, 1900–40." *Social Studies of Science* 31, no. 1 (February 2001): 37–70.

Bocci, Paolo. "Tangles of Care: Killing Goats to Save Tortoises on the Galápagos Islands." *Cultural Anthropology* 32, no. 3 (2017): 424–49.

Boehm, Mike, and Louis Sahagun. "Recipients of BP Aid Face PR Dilemma." May 19, 2010.

Bosworth, Kai. "The Bad Environmentalism of 'Nature Is Healing' Memes." *Cultural Geographies* (first published April 2021). https://doi.org/10.1177/14744740211012007.

Bosworth, Kai, and Charmaine Chua. "The Countersovereignty of Critical Infrastructure Security: Settler-State Anxiety versus the Pipeline Blockade." *Antipode* (October 2021). https://doi.org/10.1111/anti.12794.

Bowman, Robert. "Shippers Need Alternatives to West Coast Port Congestion." *Supply Chain Brain*, February 22, 2021. https://www.supplychainbrain.com/articles/32679-shippers-need-alternatives-to-west-coast-port-congestion.

Braverman, Irus. *Wild Life: The Institution of Nature*. Stanford, CA: Stanford University Press, 2015.

———. *Zooland: The Institution of Captivity*. Stanford, CA: Stanford University Press, 2012.

Brown, Kate. *Plutopia: Nuclear Families, Atomic Cities, and the Great Soviet and American Plutonium Disasters*. Oxford: Oxford University Press, 2013.

Brunner, Bernd. *The Ocean at Home*. London: Reaktion Books, 2011.

———. "Through a Glass Sadly." *Aeon*, November 30, 2015. https://aeon.co/essays/why-it-s-time-to-put-an-end-to-the-cult-of-the-aquarium.

Bryld, Mette, and Nina Lykke. *Cosmodolphins: Feminist Cultural Studies of Technology, Animals, and the Sacred*. London: Zed, 2000.

Bucheli, Marcelo. "United Fruit Company in Latin America." In *Banana Wars: Power, Production, and History in the Americas*, ed. Steve Striffler and Mark Moberg, 80–100. Chapel Hill, NC: Duke University Press, 2003.

Bucheli, Marcelo, and Ian Read, 2006. "Banana Boats and Baby Food: The Banana in U.S. History." In *From Silver to Cocaine: Latin American Commodity Chains and the Building of the World Economy, 1500–2000*, ed. Steven Topik, Carlos Marichal, and Zephyr Frank, 204–27. Chapel Hill, NC: Duke University Press, 2006.

Burnett, D. Graham. "A Mind in the Water: The Dolphin as Our Beast of Burden." *Orion* (May/June 2010): 38–51.

———. *The Sounding of the Whale: Science and Cetaceans in the Twentieth Century*. Chicago: University of Chicago Press, 2012.

Büscher, Bram. "The Nonhuman Turn: Critical Reflections on Alienation, Entanglement and Nature under Capitalism." *Dialogues in Human Geography* (first published June 2021). https://doi.org/10.1177/20438206211026200.

Büscher, Bram, Sian Sullivan, Katja Neves, Jim Igoe, and Dan Brockington. "Towards a Synthesized Critique of Neoliberal Biodiversity Conservation." *Capitalism Nature Socialism* 23, no. 2 (2012): 4–30.

California Energy Commission. "California Oil Refinery History." Updated June 10, 2020. https://www.energy.ca.gov/data-reports/energy-almanac/californias-petroleum-market/californias-oil-refineries/california-oil.

———. "California's Oil Refineries." Accessed September 6, 2020. https://www.energy.ca.gov/data-reports/energy-almanac/californias-petroleum-market/californias-oil-refineries.

Camphuysen, C. J., and M. Heubeck. "Marine Oil Pollution and Beached Bird Surveys: The Development of a Sensitive Monitoring Instrument." *Environmental Pollution* 112, no. 3 (2001): 443–61.

Canon, Gabrielle. "'It Is There Pretty Much Forever': Huntington Beach Oil Spill May Permanently Affect Birds." *Guardian*, October 6, 2021. https://www.theguardian.com/us-news/2021/oct/06/huntington-beach-oil-spill-may-permanently-endanger-birds.

Cardozo, Bradley. "'Wetlands Protectors' vs. Big Oil in Southern California: Oil Drilling, Wetlands Restoration, Indigenous Sovereignty, and the Struggle for the Future of the Los Cerritos/Puvungna Wetlands in Long Beach, CA." Working paper, University of California-LA LABYRINTH Research Group, October 2021. https://labyrinth.garden/papers/Wetlands-Protectors-WorkingPaper-Draft-Oct2021.pdf.

Carpenter, Susan. "Toyota, Kenworth and Shell Partner on Port of L.A. Fuel-Cell Project." Trucks.com, September 17, 2018. https://www.trucks.com/2018/09/17/toyota-kenworth-shell-partner-port-la-fuel-cell-project/.

Carrington, Damian. "Climate Crisis Pushing Great White Sharks into New Waters." *Guardian*, February 9, 2021. https://www.theguardian.com/environment/2021/feb/09/climate-crisis-pushing-great-white-sharks-into-new-waters.

———. "Migratory River Fish Populations Plunge 76% In Past 50 Years." *Guardian*, July 27, 2020. https://www.theguardian.com/environment/2020/jul/27/migratory-river-fish-populations-plunge-76-in-past-50-years.

Carse, Ashley. *Beyond the Big Ditch: Politics, Ecology, and Infrastructure at the Panama Canal*. Cambridge, MA: MIT Press, 2014.

———. "Keyword: Infrastructure: How a Humble French Engineering Term Shaped the Modern World." In *Infrastructures and Social Complexity*, ed. Penelope Harvey, Casper Jensen, and Atsuro Morita, 27–39. London: Routledge, 2016.

———. *The Dredge: Logistics Is an Environmental Project*. Princeton, NJ: Princeton University Press, forthcoming.

Carse, Ashley, and Joshua Lewis. "New Horizons for Dredging Research: The Ecology and Politics of Harbor Deepening in the Southeastern United States." *WIREs Water* 7, no. 6 (2020): 1–16.

Carse, Ashley, Townsend Middleton, Jason Cons, Jatin Dua, Gabriela Valdivia, and Elizabeth Cullen Dunn. "Chokepoints: Anthropologies of the Constricted Contemporary." *Ethnos* (first published May 2020). https://doi.org/10.1080/00141844.2019.1696862.

Carter, Harry. "Oil and California's Seabirds: An Overview." *Marine Ornithology* 31 (2003): 1–7.

Casteneda, Vera. "Sea Lion Found with Gunshot Wounds in Newport Beach Is Euthanized." *Los Angeles Times*, January 7, 2020. https://www.latimes.com/

socal/daily-pilot/news/story/2020-01-07/sea-lion-found-with-gunshot
-wounds-in-newport-beach-is-euthanized.

Castillo, Edward. "Blood Came from Their Mouths: Tongva and Chumash
Responses to the Pandemic of 1801." *American Indian Culture and Research
Journal* 23, no. 3 (1999): 47–61.

Catalina Water Company. Homepage. Accessed December 22, 2020. https://
www.catalinawater.com/index.html.

Cattelino, Jessica. "The Cultural Politics of Water in the Everglades and Beyond:
Transcript of the Lewis Henry Morgan Lecture Given on October 14, 2015."
HAU: Journal of Ethnographic Theory 5, no. 3 (Winter 2015): 235–50.

CBC News. "Halifax Breaks Record after Welcoming Massive Container Ship."
May 18, 2021. https://www.cbc.ca/news/canada/nova-scotia/marco-polo
-halifax-breaks-record-biggest-cargo-ship-1.6030678.

CBS Los Angeles. "'Overwhelming': Scientists Confirm Massive DDT Dumping Ground on Ocean Floor between Long Beach, Catalina Island." April 12,
2021. https://losangeles.cbslocal.com/2021/04/12/overwhelming-scientists
-confirm-massive-ddt-dumping-ground-ocean-floor-between-long-beach
-catalina-island/.

Center for Land Use Interpretation. "Refrigerated Nation: The Landscape of
Perishable Food in America." Winter 2014. https://clui.org/newsletter/
winter-2014/refrigerated-nation.

Chris, Cynthia. *Watching Wildlife*. Minneapolis: University of Minnesota Press,
2006.

Christiansen, F., F. Rodríguez-González, S. Martínez-Aguilar, J. Urbán, S.
Swartz, H. Warick, F. Vivier, and L. Bejder. "Poor Body Condition Associ-
ated with an Unusual Mortality Event in Gray Whales." *Marine Ecology
Progress Series*, 658 (2021) 237–52.

Chua, Charmaine. "Organizing against Amazon Requires Strategizing across
Global Supply Chains." *Jacobin* (April 13, 2021). https://www.jacobinmag
.com/2021/04/amazon-global-supply-chains-organizing-unionize-logistics.

Chua, Charmaine, Martin Danyluk, Deborah Cowen, and Laleh Khalili. "Introduction: Turbulent Circulation: Building a Critical Engagement with Logistics." *Environment and Planning D: Society and Space* 36, no. 4 (2018): 617–29.

Churm, Steven. "Tanker Spills Crude Oil Off Huntington Beach." *Los Angeles
Times*, February 8, 1990.

City News Service. "Lawsuit Threatened to Protect Whales in L.A. Shipping
Lanes." March 2, 2020. https://fox5sandiego.com/news/california-news/
lawsuit-threatened-to-protect-whales-in-l-a-shipping-lanes/.

City of Long Beach. "Energy Resources: Subsidence." Accessed January
26, 2021. http://www.longbeach.gov/energyresources/about-us/oil/
subsidence/.

Clark, Douglas. "Officials Tout New Port of Long Beach Bridge." *Transportation Today*, October 6, 2020. https://transportationtodaynews.com/news/19893 -officials-tout-new-port-of-long-beach-bridge/.

Coffey, Tim. "Dole's Productivity Sweet Since Moving to San Diego Port." *Daily Transcript*, July 17, 2003.

Colby, Jason. *The Business of Empire: United Fruit, Race, and U.S. Expansion in Central America*. Ithaca, NY: Cornell University Press, 2011.

Cole, Peter. "The Tip of the Spear: How Longshore Workers in the San Francisco Bay Area Survived the Containerization Revolution." *Employee Responsibilities and Rights Journal* 25 (2013): 201–16.

Collier, Stephen, and Andrew Lakoff. "Vital Systems Security: Reflexive Biopolitics and the Government of Emergency." *Theory, Culture & Society* 32, no. 2 (2015): 19–51.

Collins, Leigh. "Hydrogen 'Can Power Virtually All Container Ships Crossing the Pacific.'" *Recharge*, March 4, 2020. https://www.rechargenews.com/ transition/hydrogen-can-power-virtually-all-container-ships-crossing-the -pacific/2-1-767073.

Cooke, Jason. "Energy Landscape: Los Angeles Harbor and the Establishment of Oil-Based Capitalism in Southern California, 1871–1930." *Planning Perspectives* 32, no. 1 (2017): 67–86.

Cooper, Melinda. *Life as Surplus: Biotechnology and Capitalism in the Neoliberal Era*. Seattle: University of Washington Press, 2008.

Cornell University. "Secrets of Whales' Long-Distance Songs Are Being Unveiled." *ScienceDaily*, March 2, 2005. www.sciencedaily.com/releases/2005/ 02/050223140605.htm.

Costanza, R., R. d'Arge, R. de Groot, S. Faber, M. Grasso, B. Hannon, K. Limburg. "The Value of the World's Ecosystem Services and Natural Capital." *Nature* 387 (1997): 253–60.

Cowen, Deborah. *The Deadly Life of Logistics: Mapping Violence in Global Trade*. Minneapolis: University of Minnesota Press, 2014.

———. "Following the Infrastructures of Empire: Notes on Cities, Settler Colonialism, and Method." *Urban Geography* 41, no. 4 (2020): 469–86.

Crandell, John. "The L.A. River's 'Natural' History: Until 1825, the Los Angeles Basin Was Vastly Different from the Current Desert. What Was the Area's Environment in the Distant Past?" *Los Angeles Times*, August 14, 1994. https:// www.latimes.com/archives/la-xpm-1994-08-14-me-27083-story.html.

Crawford, Neta. "Pentagon Fuel Use, Climate Change, and the Costs of War." Working Paper, Costs of War Series, Watson Institute for International and Public Affairs, Brown University. June 12, 2019. https://watson.brown .edu/costsofwar/files/cow/imce/papers/2019/Pentagon%20Fuel%20Use, %20Climate%20Change%20and%20the%20Costs%20of%20War%20Final.pdf.

Creative States. "What If We Could Translate Other Species' Language to Co-create Our World?" Accessed January 24, 2021. https://creative-states.org/explore/what-if-we-could-translate-other-species-languages-to-co-create-our-future-world/.

Cronon, William. *Nature's Metropolis: Chicago and the Great West, 1848–1893*. New York: Norton, 1991.

———. "The Trouble with Wilderness, Or, Getting Back to the Wrong Nature." *Environmental History* 1, no. 1 (1996): 7–28.

Crouch, Stacey, Carol Paquette, and David Vilas. "Relocation of a Large Black-Crowned Night Heron Colony in Southern California." *Waterbirds: The International Journal of Waterbird Biology* 25, no. 4 (2002): 474–78.

Cumming, Daniel. "Black Gold, White Power: Mapping Oil, Real Estate, and Racial Segregation in the Los Angeles Basin, 1900–1939." *Engaging Science, Technology, and Society* 4 (2018): 85–110.

Cunningham, George, and Carmela Cunningham. *Port Town: How the People of Long Beach Built, Defended and Profited from Their Harbor*. Long Beach, CA: Port of Long Beach, 2016.

Curwen, Thomas. "L.A. Area Finally Has Its Own 'Postcard' Bridge—a $1.4-Billion Landmark in Long Beach." *Los Angeles Times*, October 2, 2020. https://www.latimes.com/california/story/2020-10-02/long-beach-gerald-desmond-bridge.

———. "Officials Knew of Potential for 'Catastrophe' when O.C. Oil Platforms Approved in 1970s." *Los Angeles Times*, October 14, 2021. https://www.latimes.com/california/story/2021-10-14/early-concerns-about-o-c-oil-platforms-were-drowned-out-by-the-1970s-energy-crisis.

Daggett, Cara. "Petro-Masculinity: Fossil Fuels and Authoritarian Desire." *Millennium* 47, no. 1 (2018): 25–44.

Danyluk, Martin. "Fungible Space: Competition and Volatility in the Global Logistics Network." *International Journal of Urban and Regional Research* 43 (2019): 94–111.

David, Emilia. "Philippines Not Yet a Viable Source for Bananas for US." *Invisible Hand*, April 10, 2014. http://bizeconreporting.journalism.cuny.edu/2014/04/10/philippines-not-yet-a-viable-source-for-bananas-for-us/.

Davies, Thom. "Slow Violence and Toxic Geographies: 'Out of Sight' to Whom?" *Environment and Planning C: Politics and Space* 40, no. 2 (2022): 409–27.

Davis, Heather. "Imperceptibility and Accumulation: Political Strategies of Plastic." *Camera Obscura* 31, no. 2 (2016): 187–93.

Davis, Janae, Alex Moulton, Levi Van Sant, and Brian Williams. "Anthropocene, Capitalocene, . . . Plantationocene?: A Manifesto for Ecological Justice in an Age of Global Crises." *Geography Compass* 13 (2019): e12438.

Davis, Mike. *City of Quartz: Excavating the Future in Los Angeles*. London: Verso, 1990.

Dean, Sam. "Is the Ports Logjam Really Getting Better? The Numbers Don't Tell the Whole Story." *Los Angeles* Times, December 3, 2021. https://www.latimes .com/business/story/2021-12-03/officials-say-the-ports-logjam-is-easing-but -numbers-dont-tell-the-whole-story.

Dedina, Serge. *Saving the Gray Whale: People, Politics, and Conservation in Baja California*. Tucson: University of Arizona Press, 2000.

Degnarain, Nishan. "Global Toxic Ship Fuel Controversy Revealed by Mauritius Oil Spill: Key Takeaways." *Forbes*, December 21, 2020. https://www.forbes .com/sites/nishandegnarain/2020/12/21/global-toxic-ship-fuel-scandal -revealed-by-mauritius-oil-spill-a-special-report/.

De Lara, Juan. *Inland Shift: Race, Space, and Capital in Southern California*. Berkeley: University of California Press, 2018.

———. "'This Port Is Killing People': Sustainability without Justice in the Neo-Keynesian Green City." *Annals of the American Association of Geographers* 108, no. 2 (2018): 538–48.

Detrow, Scott, and Franco Ordoñez. "White House Convenes Summit to Address Supply Shortage Crippling Auto Plants." National Public Radio, April 12, 2021. https://www.npr.org/2021/04/12/986266208/white-house -convenes-summit-to-address-supply-shortage-crippling-auto-plants.

De Voss, Donald. "A Comparative Analysis of Organizational and Functional Aspects of the Los Angeles and Long Beach Port Administrations." Master's thesis, University of Southern California, 1949.

Didion, Joan. "Trouble in Lakewood." *New Yorker*, July 19, 1993.

Dillon, Liam. "710 Freeway Is a Key Link in the U.S. Economy, but Pollution and Evictions Doom Its Expansion." *Los Angeles Times*, May 22, 2021. https:// www.latimes.com/california/story/2021-05-22/710-freeway-expansion-stalls.

Dillon, Lindsey. "Civilizing Swamps in California: Formations of Race, Nature, and Property in the Nineteenth Century U.S. West." *Environment and Planning D: Society and Space* 40, no. 2 (2022): 258–75.

Duane, Daniel. "The Long, Strange Tale of California's Surf Nazis." *New York Times*, September 28, 2019.

Duarte, Marisa Elena. *Network Sovereignty: Building the Internet across Indian Country*. Seattle: University of Washington Press, 2017.

Duclos, Vincent, and Tomás Sánchez Criado. "Care in Trouble: Ecologies of Support from Below and Beyond." *Medical Anthropology Quarterly* 34, no. 2 (2019): 153–73.

Dunbar-Hester, Christina. "'Average, Annual'? Temporalizing Habitat Restoration in San Pedro Bay." Temporal Belongings: The Material Life of Time Conference, University of Edinburgh, Edinburgh, Scotland, March 2021.

————. "Save the (White) Whales." *Resonance: The Journal of Sound and Culture*, forthcoming.

Eaton, Allison Jean. "Update: Port of Long Beach, Caltrans Select Bidders for Bridge Project." *Long Beach Post*, March 7, 2011. https://lbpost.com/news/update-port-of-long-beach-caltrans-select-bidders-for-bridge-project.

Ebird.com. "Dominguez Gap Wetlands." Accessed May 27, 2021. https://ebird.org/hotspot/L4792086.

Echeverry, Sebastian. "City Council OKs Hydrogen Gas to Flow through Converted Oil Pipeline in North Long Beach." *Long Beach Post*, May 1, 2021. https://lbpost.com/news/hydrogen-gas-pipeline-north-long-beach.

Ecological Society of America. "Squid and Octopuses Experience Massive Acoustic Trauma from Noise Pollution in the Oceans." *ScienceDaily*, April 11, 2011.

Edelstein, Stephen. "Hyundai Will Test 500-Mile Hydrogen-Cell Semis in California." *Green Car Reports*, July 27, 2021. https://www.greencarreports.com/news/1133014_hyundai-will-test-500-mile-hydrogen-fuel-cell-semis-in-california.

Edwards, Paul. "Infrastructure and Modernity: Force, Time, and Social Organization in the History of Sociotechnical Systems." In *Modernity and Technology*, ed. Thomas Misa, Philip Bray, and Andrew Feenberg, 185–226. Cambridge, MA: MIT Press, 2004.

Eglash, Ron. "An Introduction to Generative Justice." *Teknokultura* 13, no. 2 (2016): 369–404.

Embrey, Monica. "Los Angeles County Forms Just-Transition Taskforce to Clean Up Old Oil Wells." Sierra Club, September 29, 2020. https://www.sierraclub.org/articles/2020/09/los-angeles-county-forms-just-transition-taskforce-clean-old-oil-wells.

Enns, Charis, and Adam Sneyd. "More-Than-Human Infrastructural Violence and Infrastructural Justice: A Case Study of the Chad–Cameroon Pipeline Project." *Annals of the American Association of Geographers* 111, no. 2 (2021): 481–97.

Ensmenger, Nathan. "The Environmental History of Computing." *Technology and Culture* 59, no. 4, suppl. (2018): S7–S33.

Erbe, Christine, Sarah A. Marley, Renée P. Schoeman, Joshua N. Smith, Leah E. Trigg, and Clare Beth Embling. "The Effects of Ship Noise on Marine Mammals—A Review." *Frontiers in Marine Science* (first published October 2019). https://doi.org/10.3389/fmars.2019.00606.

Erie, Steven. *Globalizing LA: Trade, Infrastructure, and Regional Development.* Stanford, CA: Stanford University Press, 2004.

Escobar, Arturo. "After Nature: Steps to an Antiessentialist Political Ecology." *Current Anthropology* 40, no. 1 (1999): 1–30.

————. *Designs for the Pluriverse: Radical Interdependence, Autonomy, and the Making of Worlds*. Durham, NC: Duke University Press, 2018.

————. "Whose Knowledge, Whose Nature? Biodiversity, Conservation, and the Political Ecology of Social Movements." *Journal of Political Ecology* 5, no. 1 (1998): 53–82.

Estes, J. A. "Concerns about Rehabilitation of Oiled Wildlife." *Conservation Biology* 12, no. 5 (1998): 1156–57.

Estes, James, Brian Hatfield, Katherine Ralls, and Jack Ames. "Causes of Mortality in California Sea Otters during Periods of Population Growth and Decline." *Marine Mammal Science* 19 (2003): 198–216.

Estes, Nick. *Our History Is the Future: Standing Rock Versus the Dakota Access Pipeline, and the Long Tradition of Indigenous Resistance*. London: Verso, 2019.

Evans, William E. "A Short History of the Navy's Marine Mammal Program." *Aquatic Mammals* 34, no. 3 (2008): 368–80.

Ewing, Jack. "World's Largest Long-Haul Truckmaker Sees Hydrogen-Fueled Future." *New York Times*, May 23, 2021. https://www.nytimes.com/2021/05/23/business/hydrogen-trucks-semis.html.

Filipino Reporter. "PH Bananas Available in U.S. Finally." September 20, 2013.

Fiske, Amelia. "Naked in the Face of Contamination: Thinking Models and Metaphors of Toxicity Together." *Catalyst: Feminism, Theory, Technoscience* 6, no. 1 (2020): 1–30. https://catalystjournal.org/index.php/catalyst/article/view/32093/26026.

Forbes. "How Hydrogen Trucks Are Shaping the Future of the Port of Los Angeles." October 29, 2020. https://www.forbes.com/video/6205379326001/how-hydrogen-trucks-are-shaping-the-future-of-the-port-of-los-angeles/.

Freidberg, Susanne. "Calculating Sustainability in Supply Chain Capitalism." *Economy and Society* 42, no. 4 (2013): 571–96.

————. *Fresh: A Perishable History*. Cambridge, MA: Harvard University Press, 2009.

Gerasimchuk, Ivetta, Andrea M. Bassi, Carlos Dominguez Ordonez, Alexander Doukas, Laura Merrill, and Shelagh Whitley. "Zombie Energy: Climate Benefits of Ending Subsidies to Fossil Fuel Production." International Institute for Sustainable Development Working Paper, February 2017. https://www.iisd.org/system/files/publications/zombie-energy-climate-benefits-ending-subsidies-fossil-fuel-production.pdf.

Gibson, James. *Otter Skins, Boston Ships, and China Goods: The Maritime Fur Trade of the Northwest Coast, 1785–1841*. Montreal: McGill-Queen's University Press, 1992.

Gilmore, Ruth Wilson. *Golden Gulag: Prisons, Surplus, Crisis, and Opposition in Globalizing California*. Berkeley: University of California Press, 2007.

Giraud, Eva Haifa. "Animal Studies." *The Year's Work in Critical and Cultural Theory* 2021. https://doi.org/10.1093/ywcct/mbaboo8.

Grimshaw, Sophy. "Calls from the Deep: Do We Need to Save the Whales All Over Again?" *Guardian*, December 31, 2020. https://www.theguardian.com/environment/2020/dec/31/calls-from-the-deep-do-we-need-to-save-the-whales-all-over-again.

Guazzo, Regina, Alisa Schulman-Janiger, Michael H. Smith, Jay Barlow, Gerald D'Spain, Dennis Rimington, and John A. Hildebrand. "Gray Whale Migration Patterns through the Southern California Bight from Multi-year Visual and Acoustic Monitoring." *Marine Ecology Progress Series* 625 (2019): 181–203.

Gumbs, Alexis P. *Undrowned: Black Feminist Lessons from Marine Mammals.* Chico, CA: AK Press, 2020.

Güttler, Nils. "'Hungry for Knowledge': Towards a Meso-History of the Environmental Sciences." *Berichte zur Wissenschaftsgeschichte* 42 (2019): 235–58.

Hacking, Norman. "Fine Long Beach Port Built with Oil Profits." *The Province*, May 13, 1966.

Halvorson, Bengt. "Toyota Will Make Hydrogen Fuel-Cell Modules in the US Starting in 2023." *Green Car Reports*, August 26, 2021. https://www.greencarreports.com/news/1133367_toyota-will-make-hydrogen-fuel-cell-modules-in-the-us-starting-in-2023.

Haraway, Donna. *Staying with the Trouble: Making Kin in the Chthulucene.* Durham, NC: Duke University Press, 2016.

Harding, Sandra. *Objectivity and Diversity: Another Logic of Scientific Research.* Chicago: University of Chicago Press, 2016.

Harris, Peter. "Militarism in Environmental Disguise: The Greenwashing of an Overseas Military Base." *International Political Sociology* 9 (2015): 19–36.

Hartford Courant. "Pugnacious Porpoise to Aid Sealab Scientists." August 9, 1965.

Harvey, David. "Globalization and the 'Spatial Fix.'" *Geographische Revue* 2 (2001): 23–30.

Hawkins, Anthony, Arthur Popper, and Magnus Wahlberg. "Introduction: International Conference on the Effects of Noise on Aquatic Life." *Bioacoustics: The International Journal of Animal Sound and Its Recording* 17, no. 1–3 (2008): 1–3.

Hein, Carola. "Between Oil and Water: The Logistical Petroleumscape." In *The Petropolis of Tomorrow*, ed. Neeraj Bhatia and Mary Casper, 436–47. New York: Actar Publishers and Architecture at Rice, 2013.

Hellwarth, Ben. *SEALAB: America's Forgotten Quest to Live and Work on the Ocean Floor.* New York: Simon & Schuster, 2012.

Helmreich, Stefan. *Alien Ocean: Anthropological Voyages in Microbial Seas.* Berkeley: University of California Press, 2009.

———. "An Anthropologist Underwater: Immersive Soundscapes, Submarine Cyborgs, and Transductive Ethnography." *American Ethnologist* 34, no. 4 (2007): 621–41.

———. "Species of Biocapital." *Science as Culture* 17, no. 4 (2008): 463–78.

Hemilä, Simo, Sirpa Nummela, and Tom Reuter. "A Model of the Odontocete Middle Ear." *Hearing Research* 133, no. 1–2 (1999): 82–97.

Hendlin, Yogi Hale. "From *Terra Nullius* to *Terra Communis.*" *Environmental Philosophy* 11, no. 2 (2014): 141–74.

Henkel, Laird, and Michael Ziccardi. "Life and Death: How Should We Respond to Oiled Wildlife?" *Journal of Fish and Wildlife Management* 9, no. 1 (2018): 296–301.

Henson, Pamela M. "American Zoos: A Shifting Balance between Recreation and Conservation." In *The Ark and Beyond: The Evolution of Zoo and Aquarium Conservation*, ed. Ben Minteer, Jane Maienschein, and James P. Collins, 65–76. Chicago, University of Chicago Press: 2018.

Hernández, K. J., June M. Rubis, Noah Theriault, Zoe Todd, Audra Mitchell, Bawaka Country, Laklak Burarrwanga, Ritjilili Ganambarr, Merrkiyawuy Ganambarr-Stubbs, Banbapuy Ganambarr, Djawundil Maymuru, Sandie Suchet-Pearson, Kate Lloyd, and Sarah Wright. "The Creatures Collective: Manifestings." *Environment and Planning E: Nature and Space* 4, no. 3 (2021): 838–63.

Herr, Alexandria. "An Oil Well Right Next to Your House? The California Senate Says That's OK." Grist.com, August 19, 2020. https://grist.org/politics/an-oil-well-right-next-to-your-house-the-california-senate-says-thats-ok/.

Hersher, Rebecca. "The Dawn of Low-Carbon Shipping." National Public Radio, July 16, 2019. https://www.npr.org/2019/07/16/716693006/the-dawn-of-low-carbon-shipping.

Hickel, Jason. "Degrowth: A Theory of Radical Abundance." *Real-World Economics Review* 87 (2019): 54–68.

Hockenberry, Matthew. "Manifest/Manifesto: Toward Supply Chain Reconciliation." *Supply Studies*, September 29, 2021. https://supplystudies.com/2021/09/29/manifest-manifesto-toward-supply-chain-reconciliation/.

Hsu, Ben. "Study Shows Hydrogen Made from Natural Gas Dirtier Than Burning the Natural Gas Directly." *Microsoft News*, August 12, 2021. https://www.msn.com/en-us/autos/news/study-shows-hydrogen-made-from-natural-gas-dirtier-than-burning-the-natural-gas-directly/ar-AANfUaN.

Huber, Matt. "Oil for Life: The Bureau of Mines and the Biopolitics of the Petroleum Market." In *Subterranean Estates: Life Worlds of Oil and Gas*, ed. Hannah Appel, Arthur Mason, and Michael Watts, 31–44. Ithaca, NY: Cornell University Press, 2015.

Hughes, Thomas. *Human-Built World: How to Think about Technology and Culture*. Chicago: University of Chicago Press, 2005.

———. "Technological Momentum." In *Does Technology Drive History?*, ed. Merritt Roe Smith and Leo Marx, 101–13. Cambridge, MA: MIT Press, 1994.

Hultman, Martin. "The Making of an Environmental Hero: A History of Ecomodern Masculinity, Fuel Cells and Arnold Schwarzenegger." *Environmental Humanities* 2 (2013): 79–99.

INCITE! *The Revolution Will Not Be Funded: Beyond the Non-Profit Industrial Complex*. Chapel Hill, NC: Duke University Press, 2017.

Ingold, Tim. "Epilogue: Towards a Politics of Dwelling." *Conservation and Society* 3, no. 2 (2005): 501–8.

Insko, Jeffrey. "Line 5: Dismantling as World-Building." *Energy Humanities*, June 15, 2021. https://www.energyhumanities.ca/news/line-5-dismantling-as-world-building.

International Bird Rescue. "Heroic Efforts Couldn't Save Wayward Nazca Booby." September 23, 2020. https://www.birdrescue.org/heroic-efforts-couldnt-save-wayward-nazca-booby/.

———. Live "PeliCam," Los Angeles Center. Accessed September 8, 2020. https://www.bird-rescue.org/birdcams/live-los-angeles-center.aspx.

———. "Timeline." Accessed September 6, 2020. https://www.bird-rescue.org/about/history/timeline.aspx.

International Whaling Commission. "Commercial Whaling." Accessed February 8, 2021. https://iwc.int/commercial.

Inwood, Joshua, Anna Livia Brand, and Elise Quinn. "Racial Capital, Abolition, and a Geographic Argument for Reparations." *Antipode* 53, no. 4 (2021): 1083–1103.

Jackson, Zakiyyah. *Becoming Human: Matter and Meaning in an Antiblack World*. New York: New York University Press, 2020.

Jameson, Marnell. "She's One Happy Pup: A Young Otter Name [*sic*] Summer Once Faced Certain Death, but Today Is Safe, Warm and Getting a Good, if Soggy, Education." *Los Angeles Times*, June 17, 1999.

Jessup, David, and Jonna Mazet. "Rehabilitation of Oiled Wildlife: Why Do It?" *Oil Spill Management Conference Proceedings* (1999): 573–75.

Johnson, Eric. "Long Beach, Calif., Gets a Boost as Oil Prices Soar." *Press Telegram*, October 31, 2004.

Johnson, Nathanael. "What's Driving California's Emissions? You Guessed It: Cars." *Grist*, October 8, 2019. https://grist.org/article/whats-driving-californias-emissions-you-guessed-it-cars/.

Johnston, Jill, and Bhavna Shamasunder. "Urban Oil Wells Linked to Asthma and Other Health Problems in Los Angeles." *The Conversation*, June 2, 2021.

https://theconversation.com/urban-oil-wells-linked-to-asthma-and-other
-health-problems-in-los-angeles-160162.

Jørgensen, Dolly. "Mixing Oil and Water: Naturalizing Offshore Oil Platforms in American Aquariums." In *Oil Culture*, ed. Ross Barrett and Daniel Worden, 267–88. Minneapolis: University of Minnesota Press, 2014.

Jue, Melody. *Wild Blue Media: Thinking through Seawater.* Chapel Hill, NC: Duke University Press, 2020.

Jurmain, Claudia, and William McCawley. *O, My Ancestor: Recognition and Renewal for the Gabrielino-Tongva People of the Los Angeles Area.* Berkeley, CA: Heyday Books, 2009.

Karnes, Thomas. *Tropical Enterprise: The Standard Fruit and Steamship Company in Latin America.* Baton Rouge: Louisiana State University Press, 1978.

Karp, Myles. "The Banana Is One Step Closer to Disappearing." *National Geographic*, August 12, 2019. https://www.nationalgeographic.com/ environment/2019/08/banana-fungus-latin-america-threatening-future/.

Keating, Cecilia. "Shell Steers Course toward Net-zero Shipping, with Hydrogen on the Horizon." *Green Biz*, October 1, 2020. https://www.greenbiz.com/ article/shell-steers-course-toward-net-zero-shipping-hydrogen-horizon.

Kelley, Alexandra. "Trump Administration Proposes Rollbacks in Protections for Migratory Birds." *The Hill*, February 3, 2020. https://thehill .com/changing-america/sustainability/environment/481200-the-trump -administration-looks-to-reduce.

Kern, Michelle, and Alex Farr. "ILWU Shuts Down West Coast Ports to Honor Juneteenth." *People's World*, June 22, 2020. https://peoplesworld.org/article/ ilwu-shuts-down-west-coast-ports-to-honor-juneteenth/.

Khalili, Laleh. "The Infrastructural Power of the Military: The Geoeconomic Role of the US Army Corps of Engineers in the Arabian Peninsula." *European Journal of International Relations* 24, no. 4 (2018): 911–33.

———. *Sinews of War and Trade: Shipping and Capitalism in the Arabian Peninsula.* London: Verso, 2020.

Kinefuchi, Etsuko. "'Nature Is Healing': Environmental Infodemic and the Pitfall of Dualism." *Journal of Environmental Media* 1S1 (2020): 3.1–3.8(1).

Kingsley, Barbara. "Aquarium of the Pacific Turns 20 Today, Hopes to Make a Splash When Pacific Visions Opens in 2019." *Daily Breeze*, June 15, 2018.

Kirksey, Eben. *Emergent Ecologies.* Chapel Hill, NC: Duke University Press, 2015.

Knatz, Geraldine. "A Century of Marine Science at the Port of Los Angeles." Presentation to Altasea.org, Los Angeles, CA (remote due to COVID-19), June 17, 2020.

———. "The Marine Biological Laboratory at Terminal Island, Los Angeles

Harbor." *Bulletin, Southern California Academy of Sciences* 115, no. 2 (2016): 84–97.

———. *Port of Los Angeles: Conflict, Commerce, and the Fight for Control.* Los Angeles: Angel City Press/Huntington-USC Institute on California and the West, 2019.

Kolbert, Elizabeth. *The Sixth Extinction: An Unnatural History.* New York: Picador, 2014.

Kopetman, Roxana. "Spruce Goose to Be Moved to Oregon." *Los Angeles Times,* July 10, 1992.

Kosek, Jake. *Understories: The Political Life of Forests in Northern New Mexico.* Durham, NC: Duke University Press, 2006.

Kranking, Kathy. "Floating through Life." National Wildlife Federation, February 2015. https://www.nwf.org/~/media/PDFs/Kids/Ranger%20Rick/Spreads/Sea%20Otters%20Feb%202015.pdf.

Krauss, Clifford. "'Is Exxon a Survivor?' The Oil Giant Is at a Crossroads." *New York Times,* December 10, 2020. https://www.nytimes.com/2020/12/10/business/energy-environment/exxon-mobil-pandemic-energy-transition.html.

Kurashige, Scott. *The Shifting Grounds of Race: Black and Japanese Americans in the Making of Multiethnic Los Angeles.* Princeton, NJ: Princeton University Press, 2008.

LaDuke, Winona and Deborah Cowen. "Beyond Wiindigo Infrastructure." *South Atlantic Quarterly* 119, no. 2 (2020): 243–68.

Lakoff, Andrew. "The Indicator Species: Tracking Ecosystem Collapse in Arid California." *Public Culture* 28, no. 2 (2016): 237–59.

———. "'The Supply Chain Must Continue': Becoming Essential in the Pandemic Emergency." Social Science Research Council, *Items,* November 5, 2020. https://items.ssrc.org/covid-19-and-the-social-sciences/disaster-studies/the-supply-chain-must-continue-becoming-essential-in-the-pandemic-emergency/.

Lehman, Jessica. "From Ships to Robots: The Social Relations of Sensing the World Ocean." *Social Studies of Science* 48, 1 (2018): 57–79.

LeMenager, Stephanie. *Living Oil: Petroleum Culture in the American Century.* Oxford: Oxford University Press, 2014.

Leonard, Matt. "Why the Empty Container Math Doesn't Add Up in US Exporters' Favor." *Supply Chain Dive,* February 3, 2021. https://www.supplychaindive.com/news/empty-container-ports-ocean-supply-chain-explained/593493/.

Lerner, Steve. *Sacrifice Zones: The Front Lines of Toxic Chemical Exposure in the United States.* Cambridge, MA: MIT Press, 2010.

Levinson, Marc. *The Box: How the Shipping Container Made the World Smaller and the World Economy Bigger*. Princeton, NJ: Princeton University Press, 2006.

Liboiron, Max. *Pollution Is Colonialism*. Durham, NC: Duke University Press, 2021.

Liboiron, Max, Manuel Tironi, and Nerea Calvillo. "Toxic Politics: Acting in a Permanently Polluted World." *Social Studies of Science* 48, no. 3 (June 2018): 331–49.

Linn, Gene. "Ports Add Reefer Facilities." *Journal of Commerce* (June 19, 2000): 33.

LiPuma, Edward, and Benjamin Lee. "Financial Derivatives and the Rise of Circulation." *Economy and Society* 34, no. 3 (2005): 404–27.

Littlejohn, Donna. "Military Launches Study to Close All or Part of San Pedro's Navy Fuel Storage Property on North Gaffey." *Daily Breeze*, February 27, 2015 (updated September 6, 2017). https://www.dailybreeze.com/2015/02/27/military-launches-study-to-close-all-or-part-of-san-pedros-navy-fuel-storage-property-on-north-gaffey/.

———. "Port of LA Has Best Month in 114 Years as Trucks and Rails Struggle to Keep Pace." *Daily Breeze*, November 18, 2020. https://www.dailybreeze.com/2020/11/18/port-of-la-breaks-another-cargo-record-but-challenges-have-emerged/.

Long Beach Post Partner. "Sixteen Global Shipping Companies Slowed Cargo Ships off California Coast to Protect Blue Whales and Blue Skies." June 1, 2021. https://lbpost.com/ads/sixteen-global-shipping-companies-slowed-cargo-ships-off-california-coast-to-protect-blue-whales-and-blue-skies.

Lorimer, Jamie. "Multinatural Geographies for the Anthropocene." *Progress in Human Geography* 36, no. 5 (2012): 593–612.

———. "Nonhuman Charisma." *Environment and Planning D: Society and Space* 25, no. 5 (2007): 911–32.

Los Angeles Conservancy. "Star Kist Tuna Cannery Main Plant." Accessed May 31, 2021. https://www.laconservancy.org/locations/star-kist-tuna-cannery-main-plant.

Los Angeles County Economic Development Corporation. "Exports and Goods Movement." Accessed January 17, 2021. https://laedc.org/wtc/choose lacounty/infrastructure-goods-movement/.

Los Angeles County Public Works. "Los Angeles County Flood Control District Opens Historic LA River Wetlands Project." May 8, 2008. http://dpw.lacounty.gov/wmd/documents/DominguezGap_article.cfm.

Los Angeles Times. "Editorial: Supply Chain Issues Affect Almost Everything, but Surge in Port Pollution Threatens Our Lungs." November 22, 2021.

https://www.latimes.com/opinion/story/2021-11-22/supply-chain-issues
-port-pollution.

———. "Porpoise Fails Sealab Tryout as Postman." September 17, 1965.

———. "Porpoise Makes Good, Delivers Sealab Mail." September 17, 1965.

Lovely, Lori. "Port of Long Beach Gets New Bridge."
ConstructionEquipmentGuide.com, October 31, 2013. https://www
.constructionequipmentguide.com/port-of-long-beach-gets-new-bridge/
21467.

Luske, Boki. "Comprehensive Carbon Footprint Assessment Dole Bananas." Soil
& More International B.V. Report, March 2010. http://dolecrs.com/uploads/
2012/06/Soil-More-Carbon-Footprint-Assessment.pdf.

Lynch, Michael. "Ontography: Investigating the Production of Things, Deflating
Ontology." *Social Studies of Science* 43, no. 3 (June 2013): 444–62.

Marine Mammal Commission. "Southern Sea Otter." Accessed March 11, 2022.
https://www.mmc.gov/priority-topics/species-of-concern/southern-sea
-otter/

Marine Technology Society. "Transactions of the Joint Symposium: Man's
Extension into the Sea." Washington, DC, January 11–12, 1966.

Marrero, Meghan, and Stuart Thornton. "The Gray Whale: Past, Present, and
Future." *National Geographic*, June 28, 2019. https://www.nationalgeographic
.org/article/gray-whale-past-present-and-future/.

Martin, Aryn, Natasha Myers, and Ana Viseu. "The Politics of Care in Technoscience." *Social Studies of Science* 45, no. 5 (2015): 625–41.

Martin, Chase. "Research Highlight: Blue Whales Are Arriving in Southern
California Earlier and Earlier." Scripps Institution of Oceanography, June 19,
2020. https://scripps.ucsd.edu/news/research-highlight-blue-whales-are
-arriving-southern-california- earlier-and-earlier.

Martini, Edwin. "Introduction: Bases, Places, and the Layered Landscapes of
American Empire." In *Proving Grounds: Militarized Landscapes, Weapons
Testing, and the Environmental Impact of U.S. Bases*, ed. Edwin Martini, 3–18.
Seattle: University of Washington Press, 2015.

Marzec, Robert. *Militarizing the Environment: Climate Change and the Security
State*. Minneapolis: University of Minnesota Press, 2016.

Maschke, Alena. "Kelp Fuel Is Making a Comeback 50 Years after It Was First
Proposed Thanks to New Technology." *Long Beach Post*, May 23, 2021.
https://lbpost.com/news/kelp-fuel-biofuel-cultivation-technology-oil.

Mayer, Karl A., M. Tim Tinker, Teri E. Nicholson, Michael J. Murray, Andrew B.
Johnson, Michelle M. Staedler, Jessica A. Fujii, and Kyle S. Van Houtan. "Sur-
rogate Rearing a Keystone Species to Enhance Population and Ecosystem
Restoration." *Oryx* 55, no. 4 (2021): 535–45.

MBC Applied Environmental Sciences and Merkel and Associates. "2013–2014 Biological Surveys of Long Beach and Los Angeles Harbors." 2014.

Mbembe, Achille. *Necropolitics*. Durham, NC: Duke University Press, 2019.

McCarthy, Elena, and Flora Lichtman. "The Origin and Evolution of Ocean Noise Regulation under the U.S. Marine Mammal Protection Act." *Ocean & Coastal Law Journal* 13, no. 1 (2007): 1–46.

McCrary, M. D., D. E. Panzer, and M. O. Pierson. "Oil and Gas Operations Offshore California: Status, Risks, and Safety." *Marine Ornithology* 31 (2003): 43–49.

McKay, Deirdre. "Fossil Fuel Industry Sees the Future in Hard-to-Recycle Plastic." *The Conversation*, October 10, 2019. https://theconversation.com/fossil -fuel-industry-sees-the-future-in-hard-to-recycle-plastic-123631.

McNeil, J. R. *Something New under the Sun: An Environmental History of the Twentieth-Century World*. New York: Norton, 2001.

McPherson, Meredith, Dennis Finger, Henry Houskeeper, Tom Bell, Mark Carr, Laura Rogers-Bennett, and Raphael Kudela. "Large-Scale Shift in the Structure of a Kelp Forest Ecosystem Co-occurs with an Epizootic and Marine Heatwave." *Communications Biology* 4, no. 1 (2021): 298.

McVeigh, Karen. "Silence Is Golden for Whales as Lockdown Reduces Ocean Noise." *Guardian*, April 27, 2020, https://www.theguardian.com/ environment/2020/apr/27/silence-is-golden-for-whales-as-lockdown -reduces-ocean-noise-coronavirus.

Meierotto, Lisa. "A Disciplined Space: The Co-evolution of Conservation and Militarization on the US-Mexico Border." *Anthropological Quarterly* 87, no. 3 (2014): 637–64.

Mei-Singh, Laurel. "Routed through Water: Decolonial Ecologies on the Wai'anae Coast of Hawai'i." *Funambulist* 35, May 1, 2021. https://the funambulist.net/magazine/decolonial-ecologies/routed-through-water -decolonial-ecologies-on-the-waianae-coast-of-hawaii.

Mills, Mara. "Deafening: Noise and the Engineering of Communication in the Telephone System." *Grey Room* 43 (Spring 2011): 118–43.

Mitchell, Audra, and Aadita Chaudhury. "Worlding beyond 'the' 'End' of 'the World': White Apocalyptic Visions and BIPOC Futurisms." *International Relations* 34, no. 3 (2020): 309–32.

Mitchell, Timothy. *Carbon Democracy: Political Power in the Age of Oil*. London: Verso, 2013.

Mitman, Gregg. *Reel Nature: America's Romance with Wildlife on Film*. Seattle: University of Washington Press, 2009.

Mody, Cyrus. "Spillovers from Oil Firms to U.S. Computing and Semiconductor Manufacturing: Smudging State–Industry Distinctions and Retelling Conventional Narratives." *Enterprise & Society* (first published February 2022). https://doi.org/10.1017/eso.2022.6.

Mongelluzzo, Bill. "LA-LB Proves Ability to Handle Mega-ships, but Landside Pressures Remain." *Journal of Commerce*, June 23, 2020. https://www.joc .com/port-news/terminal-operators/la-lb-proves-ability-handle-mega-ships -landside-pressures-remain_20200623.html.

———. "Sweet Deal: Dole Moves to San Diego." *Journal of Commerce*, May 14, 2001. https://www.joc.com/maritime-news/sweet-deal-dole-moves-san -diego_20010514.html.

Moore, Michael. *We Are All Whalers: The Plight of the Whales and Our Responsibility*. Chicago: University of Chicago Press, 2021.

Morris, Asia. "Long Beach Aquarium Mourns the Loss of Brook the Sea Otter." *Long Beach Post*, January 30, 2019. https://lbpost.com/hi-lo/long-beach -aquarium-mourns-the-loss-of-brook-the-sea-otter.

Muka, Samantha. "Conservation Constellations: Aquariums in Aquatic Conservation Networks." In *The Ark and Beyond: The Evolution of Zoo and Aquarium Conservation*, ed. Ben Minteer, Jane Maienschein, and James P. Collins, 90–103. Chicago: University of Chicago Press, 2018.

Murphy, Michelle. "Alterlife and Decolonial Chemical Relations." *Cultural Anthropology* 32, no. 4 (2017): 494–503.

———. *The Economization of Life*. Chapel Hill, NC: Duke University Press, 2017.

———. "Reproduction." In *Marxism and Feminism*, ed. Shahrzad Mojab. London: Zed Books, 2015.

Murray, Sarah. *Moveable Feasts: From Ancient Rome to the 21st Century, the Incredible Journeys of the Food We Eat*. New York: St. Martin's Press, 2007.

Nader, Laura. "Up the Anthropologist: Perspectives Gained from Studying Up." In *Reinventing Anthropology*, ed. Dell Hymes, 285–311. New York: Pantheon Books, 1972.

Nading, Alex. "Living in a Toxic World." *Annual Review of Anthropology* 49 (2020): 209–24.

Nagle, Molly, Justin Gomez, and Libby Cathey. "Biden Floors Electric Ford Truck in Test Drive as He Pushes Infrastructure Plan." *ABC News*, May 18, 2021. https://abcnews.go.com/Politics/biden-floors-electric-ford-truck-test -drive-pushes/story?id=77764009.

National Oceanic and Atmospheric Administration (NOAA). "Gray Whale Conservation and Management." Accessed July 3, 2021. https://www.fisheries .noaa.gov/species/gray-whale#conservation-management.

Neimanis, Astrida. "'The Chemists' War' in Sydney's Seas: Water, Time, and Everyday Militarisms." *Environment and Planning E: Nature and Space* 4, no. 2 (2021): 337–53.

Nelson, Laura. "710 Freeway Is a 'Diesel Death Zone' to Neighbors—Can Vital Commerce Route Be Fixed?" *Los Angeles Times*, March 1, 2018. https://www .latimes.com/local/lanow/la-me-ln-710-freeway-expansion-20180301-story .html.

Netburn, Deborah. "A Retired Teacher Found Some Seahorses off Long Beach. Then He Built a Secret World for Them." *Los Angeles Times*, July 9, 2019. https://www.latimes.com/science/la-sci-col1-seahorse-pacific-california -20190709-htmlstory.html.

Newman, S. H., M. H. Ziccardi, A. B. Berkner, J. Holcomb, C. Clumpner, and J. A. K. Mazet. "A Historical Account of Oiled Wildlife Care in California." *Marine Ornithology* 31 (2003): 59–64.

Nicholson, Teri E., Karl A. Mayer, Michelle M. Staedler, and Andrew B. Johnson. "Effects of Rearing Methods on Survival of Released Free-Ranging Juvenile Southern Sea Otters." *Biological Conservation* 138 (2007): 313–20.

Nixon, Rob. *Slow Violence and the Environmentalism of the Poor*. Cambridge, MA: Harvard University Press, 2011.

Normandin, Sebastian, and Charles T. Wolfe. "Vitalism and the Scientific Image: An Introduction." In *Vitalism and the Scientific Image in Post-Enlightenment Life Science, 1800–2010*, ed. Sebastian Normandin and Charles T. Wolfe, vol. 2 of *History, Philosophy and Theory of the Life Sciences*. Dordrecht: Springer, 2013.

Norton, Bryan. "Zoos and Sustainability: Can Zoos Go beyond Ethical Individualism to Protect Resilient Systems?" In *The Ark and Beyond: The Evolution of Zoo and Aquarium Conservation*, ed. Ben Minteer, Jane Maienschein, and James P. Collins, 239–51. Chicago: University of Chicago Press, 2018.

Ogden, Adele. *The California Sea Otter Trade, 1784–1848*. Berkeley: University of California Press, 1941.

Onaga, Lisa. "Bombyx and Bugs in Meiji Japan: Toward a Multispecies History?" *Scholar & Feminist Online* 11, no. 3 (2013). https://sfonline.barnard.edu/life -un-ltd-feminism-bioscience-race/bombyx-and-bugs-in-meiji-japan-toward -a-multispecies-history/.

Oreskes, Naomi. "Science and Public Policy: What's Proof Got to Do with It?" *Environmental Science & Policy* 7 (2004): 369–83.

Paddleford, Clementine. "On United Fruit Boat: Food Editor Describes Voyage to Banana Land." *New York Herald Tribune*, May 5, 1954, 20.

Pandya, Mihir. "After Automation: The Fight to Narrate the Afterlives of Labor." Unpublished manuscript, 2021.

Paredes, Alyssa. "Chemical Cocktails Defy Pathogens and Regulatory Paradigms." *Feral Atlas*. Accessed November 6, 2020. https://feralatlas.supdigital .org/poster/chemical-cocktails-defy-pathogens-and-regulatory-paradigms.

Parreñas, Juno. *Decolonizing Extinction: The Work of Care in Orangutan Rehabilitation*. Chapel Hill, NC: Duke University Press, 2018.

Parreñas, Rhacel. "The Reproductive Labour of Migrant Workers." *Global Networks* 12 (2012): 269–75.

Parsons, E. C. M. "Impacts of Navy Sonar on Whales and Dolphins: Now Beyond a Smoking Gun?" *Frontiers in Marine Science* 4 (2017): 295.

Pasek, Anne. "Carbon Vitalism: Life and the Body in Climate Denial." *Environmental Humanities* 13, no. 1 (2021): 1–20.

Pauli, D. C., and G. P. Clapper, eds. "Project Sealab Report: An Experimental 45-day Undersea Saturation Dive at 205 Feet [by] Sealab II Project Group." ONR Report ACR 124. Washington, DC: United States Office of Naval Research, 1967.

Paulson, Henry. "We Need a New Asset Class of Healthy Soils and Pollinators." *Financial Times*, September 8, 2020. https://www.ft.com/content/f04fc37b-f5ba-4a17-b964-ebd7ee3e8f1f.

Paxson, Heather, and Stefan Helmreich. "The Perils and Promises of Microbial Abundance: Novel Natures and Model Ecosystems, from Artisanal Cheese to Alien Seas." *Social Studies of Science* 44, no. 2 (2014): 165–93.

Perry, Tony. "Judge Rules Navy Underestimated Threat to Marine Mammals from Sonar." *Los Angeles Times*, April 1, 2015. https://www.latimes.com/local/lanow/la-me-ln-judge-marine-mammals-20150401-story.html.

Peters, John Durham. *The Marvelous Clouds*. Chicago: University of Chicago Press, 2015.

Petro Industry News. "What Is Petcoke? And What Is It Used For?" February 6, 2015. https://www.petro-online.com/news/fuel-for-thought/13/breaking-news/what-is-petcoke-and-what-is-it-used-for/33235.

Pettman, Dominic. *Sonic Intimacy: Voice, Species, Technics (Or, How to Listen to the World)*. Stanford, CA: Stanford University Press, 2017.

Pham, Minh-Ha. "A World without Sweatshops: Abolition Not Reform." Social Science Ressearch Network, June 15, 2021. https://papers.ssrn.com/sol3/papers.cfm?abstract_id=3860253.

Phillips, Gervase. "Pigeons in the Trenches: Animals, Communications Technologies and the British Expeditionary Force, 1914–1918." *British Journal for Military History* 4, no. 3 (2018): 60–80.

Pierrepont, Julia III. "Roundup: Southern California Port Authorities Look to Protect Their Essential Workers with COVID-19 Vaccines." *Xinhuanet*, January 27, 2021. http://www.xinhuanet.com/english/2021-01/27/c_139699889.htm.

Pinho, Faith. "Bird Rescue Operation in Long Beach Seeks to Save Elegant Terns." *Los Angeles Times*, July 16, 2021. https://www.latimes.com/california/

story/2021-07-16/major-bird-rescue-in-long-beach-seeks-to-save-elegant
-terns.

Port of Long Beach. Annual Report. 1976.

———. Annual Report. 1999.

———. Annual Report. 2004.

———. Annual Report. 2009.

———. "Electric Grid Demand and Shore Power." September 4, 2020. https://
polb.com/port-info/news-and-press/power-grid-demand-and-shore-power
-09-04-2020/.

———. Harbor Highlights. Fall 1962.

———. Harbor Highlights. Fall 1979.

———. Harbor Highlights. Spring 1979.

———. Harbor Highlights Annual Report. 1964.

———. Harbor Highlights Annual Report. 1966.

———. Harbor Highlights Annual Report. 1967.

———. Harbor Highlights Annual Report. 1969.

———. Harbor Highlights Annual Report. 1970.

———. Harbor Highlights Report. 1971.

———. The Action Port. September 1979.

———. Harbor Highlights. Spring 1982.

———. Interport Annual Report. 1987.

———. Interport Annual Report. 1990.

———. Interport Annual Report. 1998.

———. Interport Annual Report. 2005.

———. Interport Annual Report. 2006.

———. "Port Exempts Natural Gas Vehicles from Clean Truck Fund Rate."
May 24, 2021. https://polb.com/port-info/news-and-press/port-exempts
-natural-gas-vehicles-from-clean-truck-fund-rate-05-24-2021/.

Port of Los Angeles. "Annual Facts and Figures Card." 2021. https://www
.portoflosangeles.org/business/statistics/facts-and-figures.

———. "Berth 147." Accessed October 8, 2020. http://www.laporthistory.org/
level3/berth_147.html.

———. "The California Petroleum Company: The Trend, 2." Accessed October 16, 2020. http://www.laporthistory.org/level4/Berth171/berth171_trend2
.html.

———. "Container Statistics." Accessed December 3, 2021. https://www.port
oflosangeles.org/business/statistics/container-statistics.

———. "Harbor Habitat: Our Biological Treasures." 2013.

———. "Tonnage Data (1971–2019)." June 30, 2019. https://www
.portoflosangeles.org/business/statistics/tonnage-statistics.

———. "The United Fruit Company: The People, 1." Accessed October 8, 2020. http://www.laporthistory.org/level4/Berth147/berth147_people.html.

———. "The United Fruit Company: The People, 2." accessed October 8, 2020. http://www.laporthistory.org/level4/Berth147/berth147_people2.html.

———. "The United Fruit Company: The Product, 1." Accessed October 8, 2020. http://www.laporthistory.org/level4/Berth147/berth147_product .html.

———. "The United Fruit Company: The Product, 2." Accessed October 8, 2020. http://www.laporthistory.org/level4/Berth147/berth147_product2 .html.

———. "The United Fruit Company: The Trend, 2." Accessed October 8, 2020. http://www.laporthistory.org/level4/Berth147/berth147_trend2.html.

Port of New York and New Jersey. "Port of New York and New Jersey Ends 2020 with Record-Highs in Volume." February 16, 2021. https://www.portbreaking waves.com/port-of-new-york-and-new-jersey-ends-2020-with-record-highs -in-volume/.

Porter, Theodore. *Trust in Numbers: The Pursuit of Objectivity in Science and Public Life*. Princeton, NJ: Princeton University Press, 1995.

Posner, Miriam. "See No Evil." *Logic*, April 1, 2018. https://logicmag.io/scale/ see-no-evil/.

Pratt, Joseph. "Maritime Fuel Cell Generator Project." Sandia National Laboratories, June 9, 2016. https://www.hydrogen.energy.gov/pdfs/review16/ mto13_pratt_2016_0.pdf.

Price, Jenny. "Remaking American Environmentalism: On the Banks of the L.A. River." *Environmental History* 13, no. 3 (2008): 536–55.

Princeton University Office of Engineering Communications. "For Hydrogen Fuel Cells, Mundane Materials Might Be Almost as Good as Pricey Platinum." June 17, 2019. https://www.princeton.edu/news/2019/06/17/ hydrogen-fuel-cells-mundane-materials-might-be-almost-good-pricey -platinum.

Pringle, Thomas Patrick. "The Tech Ecosystem and the Colony." *Environmental Media Lab*, May 12, 2021. https://environmentalmedialab.com/heliotrope/ the-tech-ecosystem-and-the-colony.

Pritchard, Sara. *Confluence: The Nature of Technology and the Remaking of the Rhône*. Cambridge, MA: Harvard University Press, 2011.

Pritchard, Sara, and Thomas Zeller. "The Nature of Industrialization." In *The Illusory Boundary: Environment and Technology in History*, ed. Martin Reuss and Stephen H. Cutcliffe. Charlottesville: University of Virginia Press, 2010.

PR Newswire. "Long Beach, CA, Aquarium Revenue Bonds 'BBB' by Fitch." October 23, 1995.

Puar, Jasbir. *The Right to Maim*. Chapel Hill, NC: Duke University Press, 2017.

Puente, Kelly. "Here's Why Dozens of Cargo Ships Are Parked for Days off Long Beach's Coast." *Long Beach Post*, January 15, 2021. https://lbpost.com/news/heres-why-dozens-of-cargo-ships-are-parked-for-days-off-long-beachs-coast.

Pugliese, Joseph. *Biopolitics of the More-Than-Human: Forensic Ecologies of Violence*. Durham, NC: Duke University Press, 2020.

Puig de la Bellacasa, Maria. "Matters of Care in Technoscience: Assembling Neglected Things." *Social Studies of Science* 41, no. 1 (2011): 85–106.

Pulido, Laura. "Racism and the Anthropocene." In *Future Remains: A Cabinet of Curiosities for the Anthropocene*, ed. Gregg Mitman, Marco Armiero, and Robert S. Emmett, 116–28. Chicago: University of Chicago Press, 2018.

Pulido, Laura, and Juan De Lara. "Reimagining 'Justice' in Environmental Justice: Radical Ecologies, Decolonial Thought, and the Black Radical Tradition." *Environment and Planning E: Nature and Space* 1, no. 1–2 (March 2018): 76–98.

Purdy, Jedediah. "Environmentalism's Racist History." *New Yorker*, August 13, 2015. https://www.newyorker.com/news/news-desk/environmentalisms-racist-history.

Pynn, Larry. "What's the True Scientific Value of Scientific Whaling?" *Hakai*, October 27, 2016. https://www.hakaimagazine.com/news/whats-true-scientific-value-scientific-whaling/.

Quivik, Fredric. "The Historical Significance of Tailings and Slag: Industrial Waste as Cultural Resource." *Journal of the Society for Industrial Archeology* 33, no. 2 (2007): 35–52.

Raby, Megan. *American Tropics: The Caribbean Roots of Biodiversity Science*. Chapel Hill: University of North Carolina Press, 2017.

Rajak, Dinah. "Waiting for a Deus Ex Machina: 'Sustainable Extractives' in a 2°C World." *Critique of Anthropology* 40, no. 4 (December 2020): 471–89.

Rapier, Robert. "California's Oil Hypocrisy Presents a National Security Risk." *Forbes*, June 21, 2019. https://www.forbes.com/sites/rrapier/2019/06/21/californias-oil-hypocrisy-presents-a-national-security-risk/.

Rathbun, Galen B., Brian B. Hatfield, and Thomas G. Murphey. "Status of Translocated Sea Otters at San Nicolas Island, California." *Southwestern Naturalist* 45, no. 3 (2000): 322–28.

Ravalli, Richard. "The Near Extinction and Reemergence of the Pacific Sea Otter, 1850–1938." *Pacific Northwest Quarterly* 100, no. 4 (2009): 181–91.

Ravalli, Richard. *Sea Otters: A History*. Lincoln: University of Nebraska Press, 2018.

Ray, G. Carleton, and Frank Potter. "The Making of the Marine Mammal Protection Act of 1972." *Aquatic Mammals* 37, no. 4 (2011): 522–52.

Red Nation. *The Red Deal: Indigenous Action to Save Our Earth.* Brooklyn, NY: Common Notions, 2021.

Reed, Mack. "Top Banana: Tons of Fruit Are Unloaded Weekly at Port." *Los Angeles Times,* October 10, 1991.

Reed-Smith, Jan, and Shawn Larson. "Otters in Captivity." In *Animal Welfare,* vol. 17, *Marine Mammal Welfare,* ed. Andy Butterworth, 573–84. Cham: Springer, 2017.

Reich, Robert. *Just Giving: Why Philanthropy Is Failing Democracy and How It Can Do Better.* Princeton, NJ: Princeton University Press, 2018.

Reinert, Hugo. "The Care of Migrants." *Environmental Humanities* 3 (2013): 1–24.

Reish, D. J., D. F. Soule, and J. D. Soule. "The Benthic Biological Conditions of Los Angeles—Long Beach Harbors: Results of 28 Years of Investigations and Monitoring." *Helgoländer Meeresunters* 34 (1980): 193–205.

Reyes, Emily. "Navy's Plans to Revive a San Pedro Fueling Facility Worry Some Residents." *Los Angeles Times,* May 16, 2019. https://www.latimes.com/local/lanow/la-me-ln-san-pedro-fueling-facility-20190516-story.html.

Richardson, Brandon. "Marine Life Flourishing in San Pedro Bay Ports' Harbors." *Long Beach Business Journal,* June 18, 2021. https://lbbusinessjournal.com/marine-life-flourishing-in-san-pedro-bay-ports-harbors.

Richardson, Brian. "Council Members Livid over Temporary Shipping Container Overflow storage." *Long Beach Post,* October 22, 2020. https://lbpost.com/news/councilmembers-livid-over-temporary-shipping-container-overflow-storage.

Richardson, W. John. "Effects of Noise on Aquatic Life: Much Known, Much Unknown." *Bioacoustics: The International Journal of Animal Sound and Its Recording* 17, no. 1–3 (2008): 13–16.

Richardson, W. John, Charles R. Greene, Charles Malme, and Denis Thomson, eds. *Marine Mammals and Noise.* San Diego: Academic Press, 1995.

Riofrancos, Thea. *Resource Radicals: From Petro-Nationalism to Post-Extractivism in Ecuador.* Chapel Hill, NC: Duke University Press, 2020.

———. "What Green Costs." *Logic,* December 7, 2019. https://logicmag.io/nature/what-green-costs/.

Ritchie, Hannah. "Do Rich Countries Import Deforestation from Overseas?" Our World in Data, University of Oxford, March 1, 2020. https://ourworldindata.org/exporting-deforestation.

Ritts, Max. "Amplifying Environmental Politics: Ocean Noise." *Antipode* 49, no. 5 (2017): 1406–26.

Ritts, Max, and John Shiga. "Military Cetology." *Environmental Humanities* 8, no. 2 (2016): 196–214.

Robbins, Jim. "Oceans Are Getting Louder, Posing Potential Threats to Marine

Life." *New York Times*, January 22, 2019. https://www.nytimes.com/2019/01/22/science/oceans-whales-noise-offshore-drilling.html.

Roberts, David. "California Has a Climate Problem, and Its Name Is Cars." *Vox*, August 22, 2017. https://www.vox.com/energy-and-environment/2017/8/22/16177820/california-transportation.

Rock, Julia. "Fossil Fuel Companies Profited, Now We Owe Billions." *Daily Poster*, October 1, 2020. https://www.dailyposter.com/p/fossil-fuel-companies-profited-now.

Root, Al. "This Is Why Oil Turned Negative, and Why It Will Be at $20 on Tuesday." *Barron's*, April 20, 2020. https://www.barrons.com/articles/oil-turned-negative-may-contract-june-commodities-markets-storage-delivery-51587411176.

Rossiter, Ned. *Software, Infrastructure, Labor: A Media Theory of Logistical Nightmares*. New York: Routledge, 2016.

Ruiz, Jason. "Federal Regulators' Demand for Pollution Study Could Derail 710 Widening Project." *Long Beach Post*, May 10, 2021. https://lbpost.com/news/federal-regulators-demand-for-pollution-study-could-derail-710-widening-project.

Rust, Susanne. "How the US Betrayed the Marshall Islands, Kindling the Next Nuclear Disaster." *Los Angeles Times*, November 10, 2019. https://www.latimes.com/projects/marshall-islands-nuclear-testing-sea-level-rise/.

Rutz, Christian, Matthias-Claudio Loretto, and Amanda E. Bates. "COVID-19 Lockdown Allows Researchers to Quantify the Effects of Human Activity on Wildlife." *Nature Ecology & Evolution* 4 (2020): 1156–59.

Sabin, Paul. "Beaches versus Oil in Greater Los Angeles." In *Land of Sunshine: An Environmental History of Metropolitan Los Angeles*, ed. William Deverell and Greg Hise, 95–114. Pittsburgh, PA: University of Pittsburgh Press, 2005.

Saez, Lauren, Dan Lawson, and Monica DeAngelis. "Large Whale Entanglements off the U.S. West Coast, from 1982–2017." National Oceanic and Atmospheric Administration (NOAA) Technical Memorandum NMFS-OPR-63A. March 2021.

San Diego Union Tribune. "Collision Course: Whales and Ships in SoCal." January 14, 2012. https://www.sandiegouniontribune.com/news/environment/sdut-collision-course-whales-and-ships-socal-2012jan14-htmlstory.html.

Sanchez, Jesus. "The Un-Banana Boat: Technology Transforms the Shipping of Fruit, Eliminating Waste—and Jobs." *Los Angeles Times*, April 10, 1989. https://www.latimes.com/archives/la-xpm-1989-04-10-fi-1720-story.html.

Schoell, Mark. "The Marine Mammal Protection Act and Its Role in the Decline of the San Diego Fishing Industry." *Journal of San Diego History* 45, no. 1 (1999): 33–52.

Science Applications International Corporation. "Final 2008 Biological Surveys of Los Angeles and Long Beach Harbors." April 2010.

Scott, Anna. "Homelessness in Los Angeles County Rises Sharply." *All Things Considered*, National Public Radio, June 12, 2020. https://www.npr.org/2020/06/12/875888864/homelessness-in-los-angeles-county-rises-sharply.

Scoville, Caleb. "Hydraulic Society and a 'Stupid Little Fish': Toward a Historical Ontology of Endangerment." *Theory and Society* 48 (2019):1–37.

SeaTrees. "Palos Verdes, California Giant Kelp Forest Regeneration." Accessed July 5, 2021. https://sea-trees.org/pages/palos-verdes-kelp.

Segura, Joe. "Long Beach Aquarium's Beloved Otter Dies." *Daily Bulletin*, September 15, 2010. https://www.dailybulletin.com/2010/09/15/long-beach-aquariums-beloved-otter-dies/.

Sekula, Allan, and Noël Burch. "Notes on *The Forgotten Space*." July 2010. http://www.theforgottenspace.net/static/notes.html.

Severn, Carly, Matthew Green, Beth LaBerge, and Vanessa Rancaño. "'We Don't Want to Just Ask for Things to Get Better': Thousands March in Oakland for Juneteenth." KQED, June 19, 2020. https://www.kqed.org/news/11825274/updates-bay-area-honors-juneteenth-on-the-streets.

Shalby, Colleen, Ruben Vives, and Andrew Campa. "Elementary School Kids Doused as Jet Dumps Fuel before LAX Emergency Landing." *Los Angeles Times*, January 14, 2020. https://www.latimes.com/california/story/2020-01-14/plane-dumps-fuel-on-students-on-school-playground-en-route-to-lax-officials-say.

Shawn, Terry. "DLA Energy's Pacific Pivot Begins in the Americas." Defense Logistics Agency, June 24, 2015. https://www.dla.mil/Energy/About/News/Article/617985/dla-energys-pacific-pivot-begins-in-the-americas/.

Shiga, John. "Sonar: Empire, Media and the Politics of Underwater Sound." *Canadian Journal of Communication* 38, no. 3 (2013): 357–78.

Showley, Roger. "Port Extends Dole Lease to 2036 at Marine Terminal." *San Diego Union Tribune*, August 14, 2012. https://www.sandiegouniontribune.com/business/growth-development/sdut-port-extends-dole-lease-2036-marine-terminal-2012aug14-htmlstory.html.

Shuit, Douglas. "Running the Show in Long Beach." *Los Angeles Times*, February 21, 1997.

Shulman, Peter. *Coal and Empire: The Birth of Energy Security in Industrial America*. Baltimore: Johns Hopkins University Press, 2015.

Simon, Matt. "Want to Save the Whales? Eavesdrop on Their Calls." *Wired*, September 17, 2020. https://www.wired.com/story/want-to-save-the-whales-eavesdrop-on-their-calls/.

Simons, Nolan, and Anatoly Zhuplev for the Port of Los Angeles. "Comparative Analysis of International Business Practices & Solutions for Competitiveness,

Independent Study MGMT 4699." April 30, 2014. http://www.lachamber
.com/clientuploads/Global_Programs/WTW/2014/PortLA_report
_May2014.pdf.

Slaton, Amy. *Reinforced Concrete and the Modernization of American Building,
1900–1930*. Baltimore: Johns Hopkins University Press, 2001.

Soluri, John. *Banana Cultures: Agriculture, Consumption, and Environmental
Change in Honduras and the United States*. Austin: University of Texas Press,
2005.

Sonic Sea. Trailer. 2016. Accessed February 27, 2021. https://www.youtube.com/
watch?v=T-jabL64UZE.

Southall, B., A. Bowles, W. Ellison, J. Finneran, R. Gentry, C. Greene Jr.,
D. Kastak, D. Ketten, J. Miller, P. Nachtigall, W. Richardson, J. Thomas, and
P. Tyack. "Marine Mammal Noise Exposure Criteria: Initial Scientific Rec-
ommendations." *Aquatic Mammals* 33, no. 4 (2008): 273–75.

South Coast Air Quality Management District. "Clean Port." Accessed October
27, 2020. https://www.aqmd.gov/nav/about/initiatives/clean-port.

Sovacool, Benjamin, Noam Bergman, Debbie Hopkins, Kirsten Jenkins, Sabine
Hielscher, Andreas Goldthau, and Brent Brossman. "Imagining Sustainable
Energy and Mobility Transitions: Valence, Temporality, and Radicalism in 38
Visions of a Low-Carbon Future." *Social Studies of Science* 50, no. 4 (2020):
642–79.

Squire, Rachael. "Companions, Zappers, and Invaders: The Animal Geopolitics
of Sealab I, II, and III (1964–1969)." *Political Geography* 82 (2020): 102224.

———. "Immersive Terrain: The US Navy, Sealab and Cold War Undersea Geopolitics." *Area* 48, no. 3 (2016): 332–38.

Srinivasan, Amia. "What Have We Done to the Whale?" *New Yorker*, August 17,
2020. https://www.newyorker.com/magazine/2020/08/24/what-have-we
-done-to-the-whale.

Star, Susan Leigh. "The Ethnography of Infrastructure." *American Behavioral
Scientist* 43 (1999): 377–91.

Steger, Manfred, and Erin Wilson. "Anti-Globalization or Alter-Globalization?
Mapping the Political Ideology of the Global Justice Movement." *International Studies Quarterly* 56, no. 3 (2012): 439–54.

Stephens, Tim. "The Collapse of Northern California Kelp Forests Will Be Hard
to Reverse." *University of California-Santa Cruz News Center*, March 5, 2021.
https://news.ucsc.edu/2021/03/kelp-forests-norcal.html.

Sterngold, James. "Long Beach, in Los Angeles' Shadow, Strives for a Spotlight."
New York Times, July 27, 2000, A14.

Stolzenbach, Kevin, Thomas Johnson, Chris Stransky, John Rudolph, Bill
Isham, Keith Merkel, Brandon Stidum, Claire Gonzales, Victoria Wood,
Kat Prickett, Rachel Mcpherson, Cristian Centeno, and Justin Luedy. "2018

Biological Surveys of the Los Angeles and Long Beach Harbors." Prepared for Port of Los Angeles and Port of Long Beach. April 2021.

Stone, Madeline. "How Much Is a Whale Worth?" *National Geographic*, September 24, 2019. https://www.nationalgeographic.com/environment/2019/09/how-much-is-a-whale-worth/.

Sunder Rajan, Kaushik. *Biocapital: The Constitution of Postgenomic Life*. Durham, NC: Duke University Press, 2006.

Supply Chain Digest. "Global Supply Chain News: Growing Congestion Has Ports of Los Angeles and Long Beach Pondering 24 x 7 Operations." April 27, 2021. http://www.scdigest.com/ontarget/21-04-27_Ports_LA_Long_Beach_Consider_24x7.php.

TallBear, Kim. "Badass (Indigenous) Women Caretake Relations: #NoDAPL, #IdleNoMore, #BlackLivesMatter." Society for Cultural Anthropology Forum, December 22, 2016. https://culanth.org/fieldsights/badass-indigenous-women-caretake-relations-no-dapl-idle-no-more-black-lives-matter.

———. "An Indigenous Reflection on Working beyond the Human/Not Human." *GLQ: A Journal of Lesbian and Gay Studies* 21, no. 2–3 (2015): 230–35.

———. "Why Interspecies Thinking Needs Indigenous Standpoints." *Fieldsights*, November 18, 2011. https://culanth.org/fieldsights/why-interspecies-thinking-needs-indigenous-standpoints.

Tamkin, Emily. "Is It Imperialist to 'Green' the Military?" *New Republic*, November 27, 2019. https://newrepublic.com/article/155855/imperialist-green-military.

Tejani, James. "Dredging the Future: The Destruction of Coastal Estuaries and the Creation of Metropolitan Los Angeles, 1858–1913." *Southern California Quarterly* 96, no. 1 (2014): 5–39.

———. "Harbor Lines: Connecting the Histories of Borderlands and Pacific Imperialism in the Making of the Port of Los Angeles, 1858–1908." *Western Historical Quarterly* 45, no. 2 (2014): 125–46.

Thackrey, Donald. "Porpoise Shows Man How to Live under Sea." *Minneapolis Star*, April 6, 1967.

Thomas, Kimberley Anh. "Enduring Infrastructure." In *A Research Agenda for Geographies of Slow Violence: Making Social and Environmental Injustice Visible*, ed. Shannon O'Lear, 107–22. Cheltenham: Edward Elgar, 2021.

Thompson, Vikki. "Canada's Flood Havoc after Summer Heatwave Shows How Climate Disasters Combine to Do Extra Damage." *The Conversation*, November 19, 2021. https://theconversation.com/canadas-flood-havoc-after-summer-heatwave-shows-how-climate-disasters-combine-to-do-extra-damage-172187.

Todd, Zoe. "Fish, Kin and Hope: Tending to Water Violations in amiskwaciwâskahikan and Treaty Six Territory." *Afterall: A Journal of Art, Context and Enquiry* 43 (Spring/Summer 2017): 102–7.

———. "Fish Pluralities: Human-animal Relations and Sites of Engagement in Paulatuuq, Arctic Canada." *Cultures inuit, gouvernance et cosmopolitiques/ Inuit cultures, governance and cosmopolitics* 38, no. 1–2 (2014): 217–38.

———. "From Fish Lives to Fish Law: Learning to See Indigenous Legal Orders in Canada." *Somatosphere*, February 1, 2016. http://somatosphere.net/2016/ from-fish-lives-to-fish-law-learning-to-see-indigenous-legal-orders-in-canada .html/.

———. "Indigenizing the Anthropocene." In *Art in the Anthropocene: Encounters among Aesthetics, Politics, Environments and Epistemologies*, ed. Heather Davis and Etienne Turpin, 241–54. London: Open Humanities Press, 2015.

———. "An Indigenous Feminist's Take on the Ontological Turn: 'Ontology' Is Just Another Word for Colonialism." *Journal of Historical Sociology* 29, No. 1 (2016): 4–22.

Toscano, Alberto. "The Mirror of Circulation." *Society and Space*, July 30, 2018. http://societyandspace.org/2018/07/30/the-mirror-of-circulation-allan -sekula-and-the-logistical-image/.

Toussaint, Marie. "Ecocide: Towards International Recognition." *Green European Journal*, December 21, 2020. https://www.greeneuropeanjournal.eu/ ecocide-towards-international-recognition/.

Truscello, Michael. *Infrastructural Brutalism: Art and the Necropolitics of Infrastructure*. Cambridge, MA: MIT Press, 2020.

Tsing, Anna. *Friction: An Ethnography of Global Connection*. Princeton, NJ: Princeton University Press, 2005.

———. *The Mushroom at the End of the World*. Princeton, NJ: Princeton University Press, 2015.

———. "On Nonscalability: The Living World Is Not Amenable to Precision-Nested Scales." *Common Knowledge* 18, no. 3 (2012): 505–24.

———. "Supply Chains and the Human Condition." *Rethinking Marxism* 21, no. 2 (2009): 148–76.

Tuana, Nancy. "Viscous Porosity: Witnessing Katrina." In *Material Feminisms*, ed. S. Alaimo, S. Hekman, and M. Hames-Garcia, 188–213. Bloomington: Indiana University Press, 2008.

Tuck, Eve, and K. Wayne Yang. "What Justice Wants." *Critical Ethnic Studies* 2, no. 2 (2016): 1–15.

Twilley, Nicola. "Spaces of Banana Control." *Edible Geography*, November 29, 2011. https://www.ediblegeography.com/spaces-of-banana-control/.

United Fruit Historical Society. "Chronology." Accessed July 3, 2021. http:// www.unitedfruit.org/chron.htm.

United Nations. "Universal Declaration of Human Rights." December 10, 1948. https://www.un.org/en/universal-declaration-human-rights/.

United Press International. "Lassie in the Sea? Could Be." *The Province*, June 30, 1966.

United States Army Corps of Engineers. "Army Corps of Engineers Releases Draft Feasibility Report for New York & New Jersey Harbor Deepening and Channel Improvements." November 10, 2020. https://www.usace.army.mil/Media/News-Releases/News-Release-Article-View/Article/2411778/army-corps-of-engineers-releases-draft-feasibility-report-for-new-york-new-jers/.

United States Army Corps of Engineers, Los Angeles District. "Appendix D: Habitat Evaluation and Model Documentation, East San Pedro Bay Ecosystem Restoration Study." Long Beach, California, November 2019.

———. "East San Pedro Ecosystem Restoration Study Integrated Feasibility Report and Environmental Impact Statement/Environmental Impact Report." Long Beach, California, November 2019.

United States Code. Title 16, Chapter 31 §1361–1362. Marine Mammal Protection Act. 1972 (later amendments).

United States Department of Homeland Security Navigation Center. "Port Access Route Study Approaches to Los Angeles—Long Beach and in the Santa Barbara Channel, Docket #USCG-2009–0765." September 2011.

United States Energy Information Administration. "Despite the U.S. Becoming a Net Petroleum Exporter, Most Regions Are Still Net Importers." February 6, 2020. https://www.eia.gov/todayinenergy/detail.php?id=42735.

———. "FAQs: When Was the Last Refinery Built in the United States?" January 1, 2020. https://www.eia.gov/tools/faqs/faq.php?id=29.

———. "Profile Analysis." Accessed March 15, 2022. https://www.eia.gov/state/analysis.php?sid=CA.

United States Environmental Protection Agency. "Current Nonattainment Counties for All Criteria Pollutants." May 31, 2021. https://www3.epa.gov/airquality/greenbook/ancl.html.

United States Navy. *All Hands: The Bureau of Naval Personnel Career Publication.* October 1968, no. 621.

———. "The Dolphins That Joined the Navy" (film). 1964.

———. "Draft Environmental Assessment: Renewed Fueling Operations at Defense Fuel Support Point, San Pedro, California." April 2019.

United States of America Department of Defense, Office of the Under Secretary of Defense for Acquisition and Sustainment. "Report on Effects of a Changing Climate to the Department of Defense." January 2019.

United States of America Fish and Wildlife Service Coastal Program. "Urban Restoration." February 28, 2019. https://www.fws.gov/coastal/highlights/UrbanRestoration.html.

————. "Least Tern." Updated November 29, 2017. https://www.fws.gov/refuge/Ten_Thousand_Islands/wildlife_and_habitat/least_tern.html.

Urry, John. "The Complexities of the Global." *Theory, Culture & Society* 22, no. 5 (2005): 235–54.

Van de Graaf, Thijs, and Benjamin Sovacool. *Global Energy Politics.* Cambridge: Polity, 2020.

Van Dooren, Thom. *Flight Ways: Life and Loss at the Edge of Extinction.* New York: Columbia University Press, 2014.

Vgontzas, Nantina. "Toward Degrowth: Worker Power, Surveillance Abolition, and Climate Justice at Amazon." *New Global Studies* 16, no. 1 (2022): 49–67.

Vidal, Fernando, and Nélia Dias, eds. *Endangerment, Biodiversity and Culture.* London: Routledge, 2016.

Vock, Daniel. "Can America's Biggest Ports Go Green?" *Governing: The Future of States and Localities,* May 20, 2019. https://www.governing.com/topics/transportation-infrastructure/gov-california-ports-emissions-air-pollution.html.

Volcovici, Valerie, and Laila Kearney. "150 Years of Spills: Philadelphia Refinery Cleanup Reveals Toxic Legacy of Fossil Fuels." *Insurance Journal,* February 16, 2021. https://www.insurancejournal.com/news/national/2021/02/16/601447.htm.

Wade, Nicholas. "The Search for a Sixth Sense: The Cases for Vestibular, Muscle, and Temperature Senses." *Journal of the History of the Neurosciences* 12, no. 2 (2003): 175–202.

Wang, Dan. "Meet Dole, the World's Full-Stack Banana Company." *Flexport Blog,* December 18, 2015. https://www.flexport.com/blog/why-dole-owns-container-ships/.

Wang, Tao. "Managing China's Petcoke Problem." Carnegie-Tsinghua Center for Global Policy. May 31, 2015. https://carnegietsinghua.org/2015/05/31/managing-china-s-petcoke-problem-pub-60023.

Watts, Vanessa. "Indigenous Place-Thought and Agency amongst Humans and Non-humans (First Woman and Sky Woman Go on a European World Tour!)." *Decolonization: Indigeneity, Education & Society* 2, no. 1 (2013): 20–34.

Weber, Bruce. "Life." In *Stanford Encyclopedia of Philosophy,* Summer 2018 edition, ed. Edward N. Zalta. https://plato.stanford.edu/archives/sum2018/entries/life/.

Weheliye, Alexander. *Habeas Viscus: Racializing Assemblages, Biopolitics, and Black Feminist Theories of the Human.* Durham, NC: Duke University Press, 2014.

Weiss, Kenneth. "U.S. Scraps 'Otter-Free Zone' in Southern California Waters." *Los Angeles Times,* December 19, 2012.

Weston, Kath. "Lifeblood, Liquidity, and Cash Transfusions." *Journal of the Royal Anthropological Institute* 19 (2013): S24–S41.

Whyte, Kyle Powys. "Is It Colonial Déjà Vu? Indigenous Peoples and Climate Injustice." In *Humanities for the Environment: Integrating Knowledges, Forging New Constellations of Practice*, ed. Joni Adamson, Michael Davis, and Hsinya Huang, 88–104. London: Routledge/Earthscan, 2017.

Wiese, Francis. "Sinking Rates of Dead Birds: Improving Estimates of Seabird Mortality Due to Oiling." *Marine Ornithology* 31 (2003): 65–70.

Wigglesworth, Alex. "A Generation of Seabirds Was Wiped out by a Drone in O.C.: Scientists Fear for Their Future." *Los Angeles Times*, June 7, 2021. https://www.latimes.com/california/story/2021-06-07/thousands-of-eggs-abandoned-after-drone-crash-at-orange-county-nature-reserve.

Willon, Phil, and Taryn Luna. "Newsom Bans New California Fracking Permits Starting in 2024." *Los Angeles Times*, April 23, 2021. https://www.latimes.com/california/story/2021-04-23/gavin-newsom-executive-limit-fracking-california.

Wilson, Janet, and Lylla Younes. "Oil Companies Are Profiting from Illegal Spills. And California Lets Them." *Desert Sun/Propublica*, September 18, 2020. https://www.propublica.org/article/oil-companies-are-profiting-from-illegal-spills-and-california-lets-them.

Wisckol, Martin. "Oil Wells in Bolsa Chica Reserve Could Jeopardize Wetlands." *Orange County Register*, October 15, 2021. https://www.ocregister.com/2021/10/15/oil-wells-in-bolsa-chica-reserve-could-jeopardize-wetlands/.

Wood, Megan, Mark Baumgartner, Morgan Visali, and Ana Širović. "Near Real Time Passive Acoustic Monitoring in the Santa Barbara Channel." *Journal of the Acoustical Society of America* 148, no. 4 (2020): 2773.

Woodward, Rachel. "Military Landscapes: Agendas and Approaches for Future Research." *Progress in Human Geography* 38, no. 1 (2014): 40–61.

Woody, Todd. "California's Critical Kelp Forests Are Disappearing in a Warming World. Can They Be Saved?" *National Geographic*, April 30, 2020. https://www.nationalgeographic.com/science/2020/04/california-critical-kelp-forests-disappearing-warming-world-can-they-be-saved/.

World People's Conference on Climate Change and the Rights of Mother Earth. "Universal Declaration of Rights of Mother Earth." Cochabamba, Bolivia, April 22, 2010. https://www.garn.org/universal-declaration/.

World Wildlife Federation. "A Warning Sign from Our Planet: Nature Needs Life Support." 10/30/2018. https://www.wwf.org.uk/updates/living-planet-report-2018.

Wright, Sylvia. "World-Class Oiled-Bird Rescue Center Opens in L.A." University of California, Davis, March 21, 2001. https://www.ucdavis.edu/news/world-class-oiled-bird-rescue-center-opens-la/.

Wynter, Sylvia. "Unsettling the Coloniality of Being/Power/Truth/Freedom: Towards the Human, after Man, Its Overrepresentation—An Argument." *CR: The New Centennial Review* 3, no. 3 (2003): 257–337.

Xia, Rosanna. "The Biggest Likely Source of Microplastics in California Coastal Waters? Our Car Tires." *Los Angeles Times*, October 2, 2019. https://www.latimes.com/environment/story/2019–10–02/california-microplastics-ocean-study.

———. "DDT's Toxic Legacy Can Harm Granddaughters of Women Exposed, Study Shows." *Los Angeles Times*, April 14, 2021. https://www.latimes.com/environment/story/2021-04-14/toxic-legacy-of-ddt-can-harm-grand daughters-of-women-exposed.

———. "L.A.'s Coast Was Once a DDT Dumping Ground." *Los Angeles Times*, October 25, 2020. https://www.latimes.com/projects/la-coast-ddt-dumping-ground/.

Yamato, Maya, Darlene Ketten, Julie Arruda, Scott Cramer, and Kathleen Moore. "The Auditory Anatomy of the Minke Whale (*Balaenoptera acuto-rostrata*): A Potential Fatty Sound Reception Pathway in a Baleen Whale." *Anatomical Record* 295 (2012): 991–98.

York, Richard. "Why Petroleum Did Not Save the Whales." *Socius: Sociological Research for a Dynamic World* 3 (2017): 1–13.

Young, Christian. "Zoos and Aquariums." *A Companion to the History of American Science*, ed. Georgina M. Montgomery and Mark A. Largent, 553–65. Malden, MA: John Wiley & Sons, 2016.

Zapatista Army of National Liberation (EZLN). "EZLN Communique: Them and Us II. The Machine in Almost 2 Pages." January 24, 2013. https://schoolsforchiapas.org/wp-content/uploads/2014/06/EZLN-communique-Them-and-Us-II.-The-Machine-in-Almost-2-Pages.pdf.

Zelko, Frank. "From Blubber and Baleen to Buddha of the Deep: The Rise of the Metaphysical Whale." *Society & Animals* 20 (2012): 91–108.

Index

Page numbers in italics refer to figures.